THE AutoCAD Database Book

Accessing and Managing CAD Drawing Information

Frederic H. Jones
Lloyd Martin

Ventana Press
Chapel Hill, North Carolina

Library of Congress Catalog No.: 87-081332
ISBN: 0-940087-04-9

Book design by David M. Kidd, Oakland, CA
Concept and cover design by Suzanne Anderson-Carey, Berkeley, CA
Cover illustration by Marc W. Ericksen, San Francisco, CA
Technical Editor: Greg Malkin
Typesetting by Lloyd Martin & Shanna Compton on Ventura Publisher

First Edition, Second Printing
Printed in the United States of America

Ventana Press, Inc.
P.O. Box 2468
Chapel Hill, NC 27515
919/490-0062

Limits of Liability and Disclaimer of Warranty

Trademark Acknowledgements

About the Authors

Frederic H. Jones is C.E.O of éclat Intelligent Systems, Inc., producers of ei:MicroSpec™ and ei:VersaSpec™, two integrated CAD expert design systems. He is the author of four books on architecture, design and CAD.

Lloyd Martin is the president of Creative Technologies, Inc., a firm involved in the development of systems applications software based on AutoCAD. He is currently involved in developing an expert design system, based on AutoLISP, for facilities design.

Both of the Authors can be reached at:
éclat Intelligent Systems, Inc.
2414 Merced Avenue
San Leandro, CA 94577
(415) 483-2030

Acknowledgements

The authors and publisher wish to express appreciation to Greg Malkin, who provided many valuable suggestions during the production of this book.

We also express our gratitude to the following individuals who assisted in the writing and production of this book:

Shanna Compton	Lynn Echnoz
John Sergneri	Lindy Martin
Judith K. Jones	Rob Holmes
J. B. Compton	Thomas T. Compton

Contents

Chapter One: Getting Started

Chapter Two: Data Basics

Chapter Three: Attributes

Chapter Four: A Bill of Materials Program

Chapter Five: AutoLISP Programming

Chapter Six: Drawing Database and AutoLISP

Chapter Seven: Understanding the Drawing Database

Chapter Eight: Modifying the Drawing Database

Chapter Nine: Understanding and Using DXF Files

chapter 1   GETTING STARTED

CAD's IMPORTANT OTHER HALF

If you've been using AutoCAD® for any length of time, you've probably experienced great leaps in productivity over traditional "board & pencil" techniques—that's why you (or your company) bought all that equipment and software in the first place!

Drawings can quickly be revised and updated, repetitive graphic images can be accessed from symbol libraries, elements from one drawing can be easily transferred to another. In short, drafting with CAD allows you more time for creative tasks.

But what about CAD's important other half—the database? One of the great things about CAD is that while you make your drawings, your computer can be quietly creating databases full of information which save you even more time.

For example, a civil engineer can automatically link map data to road intersections. A mechanical engineer can track the VAV boxes for the HVAC system. An architect drawing a 15-story building can simultaneously keep track of how much conduit is needed.

For nearly every design project, there's an associated need to access and manipulate the information contained in your drawings. A properly managed database can result in enormous time-savings and free creative juices.

With the help of *The AutoCAD Database Book*, any user in any discipline can learn important techniques for saving hours of project time every week.

WHAT'S INSIDE

The AutoCAD Database Book addresses both the principles and practice of database use, design and programming for the CAD environment. You'll learn how to create and revise attributes, create data extraction files, and use blocks and symbols in database management. You'll learn basic techniques of data conversion and transfer between CAD systems. And you'll be exposed to many useful database utilities in AutoLISP™, BASIC and dBASE®.

Because AutoCAD is actually a database, nearly any AutoCAD-related subject could be considered appropriate for *The AutoCAD Database Book*. The next eight chapters are concerned with extracting visible and invisible information from a drawing, putting this information into a readable format, then translating it to a different environment (such as a word processor, spreadsheet or database manager) to generate bills of materials, reports, charts, material take-offs and other useful information. Parametric programming and other topics indirectly related to CAD database management fall outside the scope of this book.

After reading the book, you should be able to create your own non-graphic database link for a bill of materials and similar applications. You also will become more familiar with methods of manipulating **DXF** files to modify drawings and check data.

The programs and procedures can be typed in and used as presented, or form the foundation of more complex custom implementations that you create. To save typing time, an optional diskette is available that contains the programs and routines featured throughout the book.

HOW THE ALPHANUMERIC DATABASE FITS IN

The three primary elements of contract document development for engineers and architects consume varying percentages of the project's resources. In fact, in many design offices, the non-graphic database is more central than CAD itself!

In the typical project, 30 percent of the designer's resources are spent on drawings, 50 percent on the selection and specification of products and materials, and 20 percent on managing logistics, generating reports and scheduling.

In other words, keeping track of materials, ordering and specifying, counting, figuring and record-keeping often consume more than twice as much time as does the actual drawing! Although the ratio varies by discipline and project, it's clear that many designers and managers need to be free of all that paperwork, and non-graphic database management offers that break!

INCREASED PRODUCTIVITY

CAD has been widely credited with enhancing production, making revisions easier and decreasing errors and omissions. Clearly, a computer-aided drafting program can cut back on mistakes because it cannot forget to record changes the designer makes. And it's easier and faster to make changes on a computer screen—then have the machine implement the revisions—than to change all those paper drawings manually.

However, even with those advantages, a CAD program alone doesn't address the area of specification and administration of materials. While the drawing and drafting area of the project have been streamlined, the overwhelming amount of paperwork—coupled with documenting time, money and materials—still presents the same old grind.

You can realize a significant design advantage when you integrate drafting/design and data management. Written specifications, job-costing and project management can be developed simultaneously and automatically as products and materials are inserted into the design drawing.

Furthermore, the earliest design can become the skeleton of the following stage (and so on) without redrawing. Typically, a designer may have to estimate costs based on square footage and building type, a very generalized procedure. Good information management makes it possible to develop early cost estimates based on actual design quantities. The generic door, window, electrical outlet or service pump type can be easily replaced by specific products as they're selected and the estimate becomes progressively more accurate.

Productivity increases realized with CAD alone rarely exceed two or three times manual output. Effective management of CAD database information can result in big productivity leaps and eliminate tedious and time-consuming project tasks.

ENHANCED QUALITY

Productivity increases alone aren't the only justification for using alphanumeric design systems for your document production. The arduous and error-prone job of developing project specifications can be greatly relieved, allowing the designer or project manager to focus on the exciting and creative part of a design project—developing the actual design—while streamlining the management process.

The use of electronic catalogs and project scheduling software to select and track products and contractors are just two ways to save time and avoid headaches. Many more design alternatives become possible, more time for checking and evaluating delivery and pricing strategies is allowed, and a greater percentage of the project time can be allotted to client development. Imagine actually being able to practice design like you dreamed of in school!

NEW SERVICES TO OFFER

Ever-increasing competition in the business of design, engineering and architecture, combined with dwindling profits, makes it important to find new services to offer your clients. Those services can become both profit centers and ways to get an edge on the rest of the pack.

Engineering cost studies and product evaluations become feasible with good database management. A renewed emphasis on the design process is possible when the cost of contract documents can be proportionally decreased.

More advanced database management and document systems can allow you to offer facilities management services that continue beyond the installation phase. Many firms are maintaining product inventory and helping clients reallocate resources. This can give you an inside edge on future business and bring in additional revenues.

The possibilities are nearly limitless—and all make good business sense.

HOW TO USE THIS BOOK

The AutoCAD Database Book is a learning tool for CAD users interested in extending their knowledge and increasing the power and versatility of their graphic CAD programs. The book also serves as a reference for CAD users, managers and consultants who need to know how CAD can be extended into the full range of production applications in a design or engineering office.

The AutoCAD Database Book shows you several distinct techniques for working with CAD database information. Skim Chapters 1-3 and introductory pages of Chapters 4-9 to become acquainted with those techniques and decide what's best for your projects and applications.

The book should be used in close conjunction with your computer. We suggest you actually key the tutorial sections and sample programs—that's the quickest way to learn techniques for CAD database management and utility programming. The first chapters are tutorialized to get you started; programs in later chapters are well-explained and documented.

Though the longer programs in Chapters 6-9 are more advanced, they offer you a unique opportunity to understand how AutoCAD's database works, and how AutoLISP, dBASE, BASIC and other languages can greatly enhance CAD information management.

For those who would rather "plug in and go," the programs will work either by keying them in from the book or loading them from the optional diskette.

Finally, Appendix A and B provide valuable reference material not currently available elsewhere for working with **DXF**, and attribute exchange and manipulation files.

HOW WELL SHOULD YOU KNOW AUTOCAD AND PROGRAMMING?

We assume you have a basic knowledge of MS/PC DOS and AutoCAD or your CAD system. However, we explain the specific topics, commands and techniques related to data handling and extraction. If you haven't read your *AutoCAD Reference Manual* recently, you should at least skim it before beginning the exercises in this book. Keep the manual handy for reference as you use this book and extend or design your own CAD database programs.

Although programming knowledge isn't necessary to use this book, the more you know, the better. You can key in the programs or buy the companion diskette and use the programs discussed without ever reading the programming section of the book.

The AutoCAD Database Book will also be useful to readers working with a consultant or programmer to develop a database system. The book will help you understand how to develop program specifications, and give you a good working knowledge of the many techniques involved with CAD database management.

SOFTWARE AND HARDWARE REQUIREMENTS

The AutoCAD Database Book can be used with any version of AutoCAD later than 2.18. Source code for all the AutoLISP routines are included on the companion diskette. dBASE II Version 2.x is required to run the dBASE code throughout. A compiled version of the bill of materials program, which will run without dBASE II, is included on the companion diskette. The dBASE II code can be converted to dBASE III if you wish. A dBASE III version also is included on the diskette.

A GWBASIC or BASICA interpreter is required to run the BASIC programs in the book. Generally, those programs are included with an IBM or compatible PC. If you don't have either of those, any compatible BASIC interpreter will suffice.

In most cases, the programs can be compiled for easier use. The source code for the programs is included on the diskette along with compiled versions of the programs.

No hardware is required other than that required to run AutoCAD or your CAD system.

CONVENTIONS AND NOTATIONS

To be sure we're all speaking the same language, the items below serve as a guide to the naming and notational conventions used consistently throughout the book. These rules must be followed carefully.

1. 0's and O's; 1's and I's—These are noticeably different in the text and cannot be used interchangeably. O's must be typed as letters, and 0's as numerical values. The same is true of 1's and I's. Your routines won't work if these aren't entered correctly.

2. <ENTER> and <RETURN>—The **<ENTER>** key is used interchangeably with **<RETURN>** or Carriage Return or **[CR]**. Throughout this book, **<RETURN>** will be used.

During an AutoCAD drawing session, a space bar can be substituted for **<RETURN>** when entering a command or an option. Until **<RETURN>** is hit, you can change what's on your screen (CRT) by using the back space key, ‹-, and retyping the command.

3. Type:—Whenever you see this word in the page margins, type exactly what's shown in the proper case, including brackets, parentheses, forward and backward slashes, colons, semicolons, commas, spaces, etc. After Type:, explanations, reminders and other information will sometimes appear in parentheses. Don't type those notes.

4. Response:—Following Response: you'll see the computer's response as it appears on the screen. This may be a close approximation because of differences in your version of software, brand of computer and how your files have been created.

5. FILENAME.EXT—Several generalized names for files and directories are used throughout the book. You're expected to supply your actual filename and extension or directory required. For example, ACAD refers to the directory where you save AutoCAD files. Your actual name may be different. Remember that AutoCAD automatically places a .DWG extension on your drawing files. A .DWG extension is assumed if it's in the AutoCAD program.

6. Directories—You always should be in the same subdirectory as the current step in the exercises.

7. CTRL-X—Where X can be any other key, CTRL-X indicates that the CTRL (Control) key should be held down while you tap the designated letter key. Control <CTRL> keys used throughout this book include:

CTRL-S and CTRL NumLock—Freeze the display and the scrolling of a directory or other information.

CTRL-C—Cancels or aborts an action, such as a directory.

CTRL-Q—Toggles the printer on and off, valuable for printing directories and README files.

8. Command:—This is the AutoCAD Command: prompt, which indicates you should be in AutoCAD to take the next step.

   Many other helpful rules and tips are prominently featured throughout the book.

YOU'RE ON YOUR WAY...

...to explore a largely untapped area of AutoCAD's power. You'll begin working with CAD database information in the next few pages. You'll be challenged to find creative solutions to suit your particular needs. And you'll learn just how important the non-graphic part of CAD can be in your daily work. Let's get started!

DATA BASICS

IN THIS CHAPTER

This chapter introduces you to the basic concepts of databases, how AutoCAD stores information and structures its data, and how that information can be accessed and used to make your job easier. This chapter just hits the high points and leaves the finer details to later chapters.

Some users may be surprised to learn that AutoCAD isn't just a drafting program but is also a database manager. Most of you have heard of database managers, such as dBASE II, RBASE and others. Perhaps you've also heard of The Oracle or Dialog databases. But AutoCAD a database manager?

In fact, AutoCAD users can manage data in three ways. The first is with graphic information managed with the AutoCAD editor itself—this is the drafting function. The second is with AutoLISP, a programming language within AutoCAD that allows you to write programs that will manage and manipulate the graphic and non-graphic data in ways that are impossible to do with AutoCAD alone. The third way is to actually extract the desired data from the drawing file and organize it outside of AutoCAD with external data management programs, such as dBASE or Lotus 1-2-3. We'll be covering these last two techniques in greater detail throughout this book.

Our first task is to understand graphic and non-graphic databases and what they do. What are the differences and how can they help us?

WHAT IS A DATABASE?

A database is a collection of information about a related subject organized to make it readily accessible by the user. The Source, for instance, is a public database about various financial and academic topics. A mailing list is also a database.

A database *manager*, on the other hand, is a computer program that allows you to create, organize and access all the data contained in the database. dBASE, for example, can be used to create, organize and access a database such as a mailing list.

AutoCAD is also a database manager. It can be used to create, organize and access graphic data—this is called drafting. What is more important, and perhaps less obvious, is the way that AutoCAD can manage the non-graphic information about a drawing. Not only can AutoCAD keep track of the pictures of your project but it can also keep track of the alphanumeric data associated with those pictures as well. Anything you can draw with AutoCAD, whether it be a mechanical assembly or a toaster or a building, can be tracked both as drawings and as specifications within the AutoCAD database.

Designed to support a specific purpose, a database must be organized in such a way that it will contain the necessary information to achieve that purpose.

A mailing list, for example, can be used to send announcements to all the people on the list. To do that, the database must be structured so it contains enough of a description about each individual so that the announcement reaches them.

A very simple mailing list database might look like this:

```
# <NAME>       <ADDRESS>      <CITY>      <ST><ZIP>
1 JONES, JOHN 1234 MAIN ST   PALO ALTO  CA 94291
2 SMITH, MARY 4567 FRONT ST SANTA CRUZ CA 95060
```

This database is called a *file*, which consists of all the records that might be related by specific criteria. In this simple example, the criteria is a mailing list of people living in California.

Each line in the file shown above is called a *record*, which contains the name and address of each individual in the file, and is indexed by a unique record number.

Each *record* in this mailing list file contains five pieces of information, each of which is contained in a *field*. The fields in this example are **NAME**, **ADDRESS**, **CITY**, **STATE** and **ZIP**.

A field is simply a location within a record. In the above example, you know that you'll always find a **NAME** in the first 12 columns of each record.

A drawing database is structured exactly the same way as any other database. Its purpose is to describe a drawing in a non-graphic way. A drawing database file consists of records of alphanumeric descriptions of *drawing primitives* (AutoCAD calls these *drawing entities*).

A drawing primitive is a basic shape or form used in a drawing, such as a **LINE**, **ARC**, **CIRCLE**, **POINT** and **TEXT**. When you draw a line in AutoCAD, you're actually calling up a primitive called **LINE** and defining its starting and ending points. AutoCAD then places a description of that primitive in its database, and a graphic representation of that database record is displayed on the screen.

Let's look at an example of a simplified drawing database:

```
# <NAME >        <START>        <END>         <LAYER >
1 LINE           0,0            0,2           0
2 LINE           0,2            2,2           0
3 LINE           2,2            0,2           0
4 LINE           0,2            0,0           0
5 CIRCLE         1,1            1             6
```

This database describes a square, 2" per side with a circle of 1" radius inscribed in the square with all the drawing primitives (**LINE** and **CIRCLE**) residing on Layer **0**, except for the circle, which resides on Layer **6**.

Notice how similar the above hypothetical database looks to the mailing list example described earlier. The only difference between this sample and AutoCAD's drawing database is that the latter contains more fields. Let's quickly compare them.

NON-GRAPHIC DATABASE

```
# <NAME>        <ADDRESS>       <CITY>      <ST><ZIP>
1 JONES, JOHN 1234 MAIN ST  PALO ALTO  CA 94291
2 SMITH, MARY 4567 FRONT ST SANTA CRUZ CA 95060
```

HYPOTHETICAL GRAPHIC DATABASE

```
# <NAME >       <START>         <END>       <LAYER >
1 LINE          0,0             0,2         0
2 LINE          0,2             2,2         0
```

Now, you can begin to see the similarity between the two types of databases.

At this point, the only difference between the hypothetical graphic database and the AutoCAD drawing database example on page 15 is the names for the fields. **#** is **-1**; **NAME** is **0**; **START** is **10**; **END** is **11**; and **LAYER** is **8**. AutoCAD's field names are numbers* because it's faster and more efficient to access the information by number than by name.

LOOKING AT THE DRAWING DATABASE

When working with AutoCAD, you're automatically adding, changing and deleting information in the database. This is the first type of CAD data management.

---

* These are called Group Codes.

The second type, mentioned earlier in this chapter involves AutoLISP. Below you can see what an actual AutoCAD drawing database looks like (and also get a taste of AutoLISP).

Enter AutoCAD's drawing editor and draw one line from **1,4** to **6,6**. Press the **F1** key to put the screen into the text mode. At the **Command** prompt:

Type: `(setq a (entget (entlast))) <RETURN>`

AutoCAD should return with a list that looks like this:

Response: `((-1 . <Entity name : 60000014>) (0 . "LINE")`
`(8 . "0") (10 1.000000 4.000000) (11 6.000000`
`6.000000))`

`(-1 . <Entity name: 60000014>)`

That's the **ENTITY NAME** and is the unique index number for the entity. The AutoLISP function, **entlast**, retrieved this number from the drawing database.

`(0 . "LINE")`

That's the **ENTITY TYPE**, in this case a line.

`(8 . "0")`

That's the name of the **LAYER** on which the entity was drawn, in this case Layer "**0**."

`(10 1.000000 4.000000)`

Those are the absolute **X Y** coordinates of the starting point of the line.

`(11 6.000000 6.000000)`

Those are the absolute **X Y** coordinates of the ending point of the line.

The length of the database record will vary depending on the type of entity described.

Appendices A and B of this book describe all the Group Codes (or field names) assigned to different entity types.

Next, we'll look at a special entity called an *Attribute*.

WHAT ARE ATTRIBUTES?

The *Attribute* is a drawing entity designed to hold textual data and to link that data to graphic objects within the drawing database. Each time you insert one of these graphic objects (called a *block*) into a drawing, if that block has an attribute attached to it, you will be prompted by that attribute to add textual information to that block. This information will remain with that block forever. Later on, you can extract the data contained in these attributes and use that information to keep track of the objects in your drawing. Let's take a look at how attributes work.

The best way to demonstrate how attributes work is by an example. Let's say you just got the contract to supply the entire Pentagon with new chairs. That's a lot of chairs. Since you were the low bidder, you have to make sure you don't order too many chairs or you'll lose money. You also learn that each chair is assigned a specific location within the building. Then you find out that there are 12 different kinds of chairs because the generals have to have better chairs than the colonels and so on down the line.

Easy, you say—just have twelve different chair symbols, insert the appropriate symbol in the proper location and then count all the different chair symbols. But we're talking thousands of chairs here.* What if you miscount? What would happen if a general had to sit in a private's chair? Would you be held responsible for upsetting the balance of world power? Never fear, because here is where attributes will save your day.

---

* Actually we're just talking thousands of chair *symbols*.

The solution to your dilemma is to add attributes to your chair symbols. If your chair symbols had attributes for chair type and location, it would be a simple matter to extract all this information from your drawing once the symbols have been inserted. Then you would have a list that would contain the exact quantity for each chair type and the location for each chair—and you wouldn't have to count a single chair.

This is just one example of how you can manipulate the information behind the drawing to accomplish a number of important tasks. Here are a few more.

You can make a block or symbol automatically generate manufacturer's parts numbers and prices. A subdivision map can display descriptions and addresses of each house shown. Electronics schematics can contain the values and ratings of resistors and ICs.

AutoCAD database functions have the ability to make the alphanumeric data in attributes visible or non-visible, to extract complete lists of parts with quantities, and to calculate the cost of a design automatically as the drawing is created. Attributes are the "building-blocks" of dynamic alphanumeric information made into or linked to a graphic block. They also can be free-standing entities not linked to graphic elements.

ATTRIBUTE BLOCKS

You can create "talking" symbols for your drawings with attributes. When a graphic block that has an attribute linked to it is selected and inserted into an AutoCAD drawing, the block "talks" by prompting the user for associated information.

You can make the block "ask" for the name of the person assigned to a desk when a desk block is added to a furniture layout. The value of an electronic part can be added when that part is selected for a circuit diagram. The manufacturer's catalog number and associated colors and prices can be requested when adding products to an interior design drawing.

Any or all of the text information linked to a block can be made visible or be hidden from view. Both the visible and non-visible information, however, is available to the computer for detailed reports and bills of materials.

Blocks of information can be created independently of graphic information. A *tag* can be created that links information on wall-paper, carpet, paint or other products, materials or services related to the drawing but not appropriately represented by a drawing symbol. That can be done completely non-graphically or can be linked to bubbles, arrows or tags for location identification.

By adding attributes to existing blocks, you can make a "nested" block out of a text attribute block and a graphic block. The new combined block will have the characteristics of both. This means that attributes can be added to graphic information initially or at any time required.

Each instance of a block is unique, but contains the same structure of information. For example, a **CHAIR** symbol can prompt for the catalog number each time, or even automatically supply a default one. As each one is selected and inserted, a different color fabric can be chosen. That feature, called "Instance Attributes," is extremely powerful for data management. (The above techniques are covered in great detail in Chapter 3.)

DEFINING AND STORING ATTRIBUTE STRUCTURES

What information do you want to store? When you add attribute definitions to drawing blocks, you're really creating a database within the drawing itself. As we mentioned, your attribute database can be linked to a more sophisticated and extensive database outside the drawing. That outside database can allow the storage of more detailed information about items referred to in the drawing, so don't feel compelled to store every possible bit of information in the drawing itself.

(In Chapter 4, you'll learn how to both link and design external database management programs that work with AutoCAD.)

OUTPUT TO REPORTS

Your AutoCAD drawing and its associated database are only useful when you can print or plot reports from them. For graphic data, that can be done by using the **PLOT** command. When you want non-graphic data to be printed or sent to external database manager programs, you can use the **ATTEXT** command to create reports or transfer files to access, print or use that data.

SUMMARY

In this chapter, you've been introduced to graphic and non-graphic databases and the three basic ways they are used in and with AutoCAD and other CAD applications. In Chapter 3, you'll focus on attributes, and how to use them to generate bills of materials and other reports.

chapter 3 ATTRIBUTES

IN THIS CHAPTER

In this chapter, you'll learn the basic attribute commands and how to use them to create intelligent symbols. Next, you'll insert these "talking symbols" into a drawing and find out how to extract the data contained in these symbols. Finally, you'll see how this extracted data can be used to produce a simple bill of materials.

THE ATTRIBUTE COMMANDS

Four attribute commands allow you to create, edit, extract and format attribute text:

- **ATTDEF** is the **ATT**ribute **DEF**ining command. This is the basic AutoCAD Command you'll use when you define attributes. There are many options within this Command for formatting the way your attribute text will look. You can also specify the prompts for data that will come up when you use the attribute.

- **ATTDISP** is the **ATT**ribute **DISP**lay command. ATTDISP can be used in your drawing to make the normally visible attributes invisible or to make the normally invisible attributes visible. You'll use ATTDISP if you want to see all of the attributes in your drawing.

- **ATTEXT** is the **ATT**ribute **EXT**raction command. You'll use ATTEXT when you want to extract all of the information from the attributes in your drawing to use for creating reports about your drawing.

- **ATTEDIT** is the **ATT**ribute **EDIT** command used to change the values of existing attributes in your drawing. This editing function is similar to the CHANGE Command for non-intelligent text.

Let's work with a simple example to see how these commands work. Get into AutoCAD and draw a 2" square, with the lower left corner at **3,3**. Now, inscribe a 2" circle inside the square. Let's say the drawing is a chair.

Now you are going to take this "dumb" chair drawing, add some attributes to it and save it as a block—the next time you see this "chair" it will talk to you.

CREATING ATTRIBUTES WITH ATTDEF

ATTRIBUTE FORMATS

The first thing you have to do is to decide how you want your attributes to look when you insert your chair symbol into a drawing. As you recall from Chapter 2, attributes are primarily carriers of textual data—so all the formatting possibilities that exist for ordinary text in your drawings are available for use with attributes as well.

You can have attributes displayed in any text style that you have available—at any size you desire. Attribute text can be formatted to be flush left, flush right, centered or aligned. You can even specify that you want your attribute text to be invisible so it won't clutter up your drawing. It all depends on how you want your finished symbol to look.

For the sake of this example, you will be adding three attributes to your chair drawing; A *visible* attribute, a *constant* attribute (which will also be visible) and an *invisible* attribute. This way, you'll have a chance to work with each different type of attribute.

Here are the three different attributes that you'll be working with for your chair symbol:

```
ATTRIBUTE TAG DISPLAY      CONSTANT
TYPE          Invisible    yes
NAME          Visible      no
LOCATION      Visible      no
```

The text for your attributes will be 3/8" high and centered.

When you finish creating your attributes, your "chair" should look like the one in Figure 1.

The first attribute that you'll be creating will be the *constant* attribute.

THE CONSTANT ATTRIBUTE

There are basically two types of attributes—*variable* attributes and *constant* attributes. Every time you insert a block with a variable attribute in it, you'll be prompted by that attribute to type in a value. A constant attribute, on the other hand, always carries the value that was assigned to it when it was created with the ATTDEF command.* So let's create the first attribute.

At AutoCAD's **Command** prompt:

Type: ATTDEF <RETURN>

Response: Attribute modes Invisible:N Constant:N
        Verify:N
Enter (ICV) to change, RETURN when done:

This is the Main ATTDEF prompt. Upon selecting the **ATTDEF** command, your first prompt is **"Attribute modes."** The system wants to know how you want the attribute field being created to appear. The **Invisible** option defaults to **No** and controls whether the text appears on the screen and in your graphic plot.

---

* You won't be prompted for a value when you insert a constant attribute.

Figure 1: The Chair symbol with attribute tags and as it is inserted into a drawing.

The **Constant** option which defaults to **No** is a non-editable value. This can be used for item titles and other non-changeable information. If you wish to be able to edit the field information, don't answer **Yes**.

Verify allows you to edit the changeable attribute data before inserting it into the drawing. If this option is chosen, you can verify your answers to the prompts and respond to AutoCAD's **O.K.** query before accepting the entry in your database.

You can select **Yes** or **No** for any combination of the modes you want. AutoCAD also allows you to change your mind about the mode of any field at a later time by typing **I**, **C**, or **V** and then **<RETURN>** before entering data into the field.

Because you want this first attribute to be constant:

Type: C <RETURN>

Response: Attribute modes Invisible:N Constant:Y
         Verify:N
Enter (ICV) to change, RETURN when done:

Notice that the letter after the word **Constant** is now a **Y**. This indicates that AutoCAD accepted your last response and changed the attribute mode to **Constant**. You will now see that the letter after the word **Invisible** is an **N**. This means that an attribute created at this point would be *Not* Invisible. Since this first attribute is supposed to be Invisible, you must:

Type: I<RETURN>

Response: Attribute modes Invisible:Y Constant:Y
            Verify:N
         Enter (ICV) to change, RETURN when done:

The letter after **Invisible** is now **Y**.
    Now that the attribute mode is the way you want it, you'll be creating an **Invisible Constant** attribute. Next:

Type: <RETURN>

Response: Attribute tag:

Now, you can type in the attribute tag for this attribute:[*]

Type: TYPE <RETURN>

AutoCAD then prompts:

Response: Attribute value

    Let's make this chair symbol represent the type of chair that will be ordered for the generals[**].

Type: GENERAL <RETURN>

    Now AutoCAD will prompt for the type of text formatting that you want to use on this attribute.

---

[*]   This attribute tag can be a string of characters or numbers, but it *must not* contain blanks. All characters are changed automatically to upper case. The tag becomes the identifying code for every occurrence of this attribute in your drawing.

[**]   We're going to continue using the chairs in the Pentagon example from Chapter 2.

Response: `Start point or Align/Center/Fit/Mid-`
`dle/Right/Style:`

Because you want to **Center** this attribute in the chair symbol:

Type: `C <RETURN>`

Response: `Center point:`

AutoCAD is prompting for the **Center** point for the attribute:

Pick: a point with your pointing device on the screen at about the middle of the top line of your chair.

Response: `Height <0.2000>:`

Now you can enter the **Height** of the attribute text, in this case **3/8** or **.375** inches:

Type: `.375<RETURN>`

Finally you will be prompted for the **Rotation angle** for this attribute:

Response: `Rotation angle <0>:`

Type: `<RETURN>`

Response: The word TYPE should appear centered just above your chair symbol. This is the first attribute tag for your chair symbol.

Now let's create the next two attributes for your chair.

VARIABLE ATTRIBUTES

The other two attributes to be added to your chair drawing will be *variable* attributes. When you insert a block into a drawing that has a variable attribute attached, you'll be prompted to type in a value from the keyboard and that instance of that attribute will contain whatever variable you typed. Where does this prompt come from?

Tell AutoCAD how you want it to prompt you when inserting the block with the linked attribute when you create the attribute. If you press **<RETURN>** without entering any text, AutoCAD automatically uses the attribute tag as the prompt. So let's see how that works.

If you haven't used an AutoCAD Command since you created your last attribute, all you have to do is[*]:

Type: `<RETURN>`

And AutoCAD will already be set up to create your next attribute one line down from your last one with the same text size and formatting:

Response: `Attribute modes Invisible:Y Constant:Y`
             `Verify:N`
    `Enter (ICV) to change, RETURN when done:`

The next attribute will be a visible (Not Invisible) variable (Not Constant) attribute, so first:

Type: `I<RETURN>`

Response: `Attribute modes Invisible:N Constant:Y`
             `Verify:N`
    `Enter (ICV) to change, RETURN when done:`

---

[*] If you have used other AutoCAD Commands since creating the last attribute, then the ATTDEF Command dialog will prompt you through the text formatting and the text insertion point again. If this happens, you will just have to pick a new starting point for your next line of text by eye.

To change the attribute mode to **Visible,** and then:

Type: C<RETURN>

Response: Attribute modes Invisible:N Constant:N
            Verify:N
Enter (ICV) to change, RETURN when done:

Now you have the mode you want:

Type: <RETURN>

Response: Attribute tag:

AutoCAD prompts for the attribute tag. The next tag for this chair is LOCATION:

Type: LOCATION<RETURN>

Response: Attribute prompt:

This is where you add the Attribute prompt. AutoCAD allows you to create your own prompts or instruction for entering data in the field you create. For example, a prompt for entering a chair location might be: **"Enter chair location now..."** or **"Please enter a room number for this item."** This is optional if the attribute tag is sufficient for you to know what response to give or data to enter.

If you want to just use the attribute tag (in this case, the prompt would be LOCATION:) then simply:

Type: <RETURN>

If, on the other hand, you would like the prompt to be less cryptic, then make up your own:

Type: Location for this chair<RETURN>

Finally, **"Default attribute value,"** allows the entry of the text or number which will automatically be entered if you type nothing and just press **<RETURN>.** This value can be nothing or anything at all. For example, the default value of **Quantity** could be **1**, the default value of **Chair** could be **Executive, swivel**.

Response: `Default attribute value:`

Type: `<RETURN>`

For no default value.
The word LOCATION will now appear centered directly under the word TYPE on your chair drawing.
Creating the third and final attribute for this chair is done exactly the same way as the last one, but we'll walk you through it anyway (without comments):

Type: `<RETURN>`

Response: `Attribute modes Invisible:N Constant:N`
`        Verify:N`
`Enter (ICV) to change, RETURN when done:`

Type: `<RETURN>`

Response: `Attribute tag:`

Type: `NAME<RETURN>`

Response: `Attribute prompt:`

Type: `Name of occupant<RETURN>`

Response: `Default attribute value:`

Type: `<RETURN>`

Response: The third attribute tag NAME appears underneath the previous one.

LINKING ATTRIBUTES TO A BLOCK

Now that you've created an attribute, you can simply save it along with the block drawing it relates to, with AutoCAD's **BLOCK** command.

Be sure to save your block to disk file with **WBLOCK** if you plan to use it again in another drawing.

If you're using attributes by themselves to tag parts of your drawing (rather than as part of a graphic symbol), you can save just the attributes as a block with the **BLOCK** command.

Type: BLOCK <RETURN>

Response: Block name (or ?)

Type: CHAIR-G<RETURN>

The "-G" is to differeniate the general's chair from the private's chair.

Response: Insertion base point:

Pick: The desired point on your drawing you want to have for the insertion point of your symbol.

Response: Select objects:

At this point, you can select the objects you want to include as part of your symbol (including attributes and other entities) by using any or all of the AutoCAD entity selection methods, including **Window**, **Crossing**, **Last** and **Pick**.

After you've picked all the desired objects on the screen, press **<RETURN>** and the chosen objects will disappear, indicating that your block has been saved. If you wish to keep the objects you defined your block with on the screen,

Type: OOPS <RETURN>

Response: All of the objects that disappeared when you created the block will return to your screen.

After you've saved your symbol block, you can insert it anywhere in your drawing with AutoCAD's **INSERT** command. Once you've picked the insertion point for your symbol and have entered the **SCALE** and **ROTATION** angle, you'll be prompted for the attribute values for that block.

Type: INSERT <RETURN>

Response: Block Name (or ?):

Type: CHAIR-G <RETURN>

Response: Insertion point:

Pick: the desired insertion point.

Response: X scale factor<1>/Corner/XYZ:

Type: 1 <RETURN>

Or any other appropiate scale factor.

Response: Y scale factor (default=X):

Type: <RETURN>

Or another scale factor if it is different from the **X** scale.

Response: Rotation angle <0>:

Type: 90<RETURN>

The attribute prompts will now appear on the **Command** line.

Response: Name of Occupant:

Type: Mustard <RETURN>

Response: `Location for this chair:`

Type: `100 <RETURN>`

Response: and the chair symbol will appear at the spot you indicated with the words **Mustard** and **100** on the symbol.

At this point, you'll notice that the attribute prompts will be returned to you in the reverse order in which they were created. This is because AutoCAD stores all the data for the block definitions in reverse order. If it's important that the attribute prompts for a block appear in a particular order, then you must write the attribute definitions in the opposite order that you want them to appear.

Project: Now that you've created your first block with attributes and have played around with it a bit, here's a little project for you. Make a chair symbol for privates. Draw a square like you did for the generals' chair only leave out the circle.

Now create the same three attributes that you used for the first chair but use the value PRIVATE for the constant attribute tag TYPE. Finally, save this chair symbol under the name CHAIR-P. You will be using both of these chair symbols in an example at the end of this chapter.

TIP: Here's a method we've developed for quickly creating a large number of blocks with attributes. This tip will work only if all the symbols have the same attributes.

Let's say that you need to create a library of fifty different furniture symbols with attributes.

First, start an AutoCAD drawing, and draw all fifty pieces of furniture in that drawing.

Using **ATTDEF**, **DEF**ine a series of **ATT**ributes for this furniture in the order you wish to see the prompts.

Create and save a block that consists of only the attributes you've just produced. For example, let's call this block **ATT**.

INSERT the block **ATT** into all the furniture symbols using the following form:

Type: `INSERT <RETURN>`

Response: `Block name (or ?):`

   Type: `*ATT<RETURN>`

     After the usual **INSERT** prompts appear, the **ATT** block will be inserted into the drawing, exploded into its component parts.

     Save each of the furniture drawings with the **BLOCK** command.

     Save each of the blocks to your hard disk with the **WBLOCK** command.

     Now when you **INSERT** one of those furniture symbols, the attribute prompts will appear in the order in which they were first written when you created the block called **ATT**.

USING THE ATTDISP COMMAND

     The **ATTDISP** command turns the attribute block on and off to view. When the attributes aren't activated, it speeds up **REDRAW** and presents a more pristine view of the drawing data. When you wish to view or plot the text data, merely activate them.

     The default setting for attributes is visible unless Invisible is turned on. Entering **N** selects the normal mode. Entering **ON** makes all visible and **OFF** makes all invisible. Changing any display mode automatically regenerates the drawing unless **REGENAUTO** isn't activated.

   Type: `ATTDISP <RETURN>`

Response: `Normal/On/Off <Normal>:`

   Type: `OFF <RETURN>`

Notice the results of changing the parameters.

   Type: `ATTDISP <RETURN>`

Response: `Normal/On/Off <Off>:`

Type: ON <RETURN>

Now we're back where we started.

EDITING AN ATTRIBUTE WITH ATTEDIT

Often you'll discover that the values of a particular attribute have changed and the data entered must be changed to reflect the new condition. The **ATTEDIT** command allows you to edit the values. The first thing to do if you wish to edit an attribute is to select an object for editing using **Object/Window/Last.** Select one of your Chair symbols. Then call the **ATTEDIT** command.

Type: ATTEDIT <RETURN>

Response: Edit attributes one by one? <Y>

If you enter **Y,** you can edit attributes individually. This mode will only edit attributes currently visible on the screen. Any of the properties of the attribute being edited, including placement and values, can be changed.

Selecting **N** allows you to do global editing. That is, you can change all instances of a value within a given attribute tag. For example, say you have 500 chair symbols in a drawing, and one of the attribute tags is for MANUFAC-TURER. At the last minute, you find that you can get a better deal with a different chair manufacturer. You could use the ATTEDIT Command to change the name of the manufac-turer for all of the chair symbols.

SINGLE CHANGES

When editing attributes individually, you may select the attributes by **tag, value** or **blocks**. The first prompt is:

Select attributes:

Selection may occur by Pointing, Windowing or Last. Defaults may be selected by entering **<RETURN>.** Selected attributes are marked by an **X** and you are prompted:

Response: `Value/Position/Height/Angle/Style/Layer`
`/Color/Next :`

Original definitions aren't included in the prompts. For example, if the text were **A**ligned, the **H**eight wouldn't be included in the prompt.

If you select **V**alue, you may change the attribute's value. You are prompted:

Response: `Change or Replace?`

Type: `C <RETURN>`

Response: `String to change:`

Enter name of the string you wish to change.

Type: `Executive, Swivel`

Response: `New string:`

Type: `Secretarial, Swivel`

Type: `R <RETURN>`

Response: New attribute value:

Selecting **<RETURN>** automatically enters blanks.

If **POSITION** is selected, you're asked for a new Starting, Center or End point. If Height, Angle, Type or Layer are selected, they may be appropriately edited. **Color** allows the selection of any color number from **1** to **255** or standard color names such as **White**. Special colors such as **BYLAYER** or **BYBLOCK** also can be entered.

GLOBAL CHANGES

When globally editing, AutoCAD prompts:

Response: `Global edit of Attribute values.`

Response: `Edit only attributes visible on screen? <Y>`

Selecting **N** changes AutoCAD to text mode and prompts:

Response: `Drawing must be regenerated afterwards.`

Changes made in the drawing will only be affected after the drawing is regenerated. If you're editing visible attributes, you're prompted:

Response: `Select attributes:`

Attributes can be selected by **P**ointing, **W**indowing or **L**ast. Entering **<RETURN>** edits all attributes.* An **X** is drawn at the starting point of all selected attributes and you're prompted:

Response: `String to change:`
`New string:`

If you're editing visible and invisible attributes, there are no **X** marks for the screen in text mode. For example:

Response: `String to change:CHAIR-TYPE`
`New string:TABLE-TYPE`

Tip: Refer to the **CHANGE** command in your *AutoCAD Reference Manual* for more ways to edit attribute values and parameters.

USING THE ATTEXT COMMAND

Attribute data extraction and reporting are done by invoking the **ATTEXT** command, which stands for **ATT**ribute **EXT**ract. At AutoCAD's **Command** prompt,

Type: `ATTEXT <RETURN>`

---

*   **CTRL-C** terminates the command if you wish to stop.

Response: CDF, SDF, or DXF attribute extract
(or Entities)?

If **CDF** is selected, AutoCAD produces a standard **C**omma **D**elimited **F**ormat file. That file contains, at most, one record for each block reference in the drawing file. Each field of each record is separated by a comma, with character fields enclosed in quotes. dBASE II can read these files directly using the **APPEND FROM .... DELIMITED** command. There will be more discussion of **CDF** in Chapter 4

If **SDF** is selected, a **S**pace **D**elimited **F**ile is created, which is the most standard file and is basically a columnar list of information. dBASE II reads this file using the **AP-PEND FROM ... SDF** command. Here, one record is written for each block reference. Fields are affixed so your program knows where one stops and the other starts. Again, there will be more discussion of **SDF** in Chapter 4

If **DXF** is selected, AutoCAD creates a subset of the **DXF** file with only **Block References**, **Attribute** and **End of Sequence** entities. If **Entities** is selected, you'll be prompted to select the objects whose attributes you want to extract. You then must select **CDF**, **SDF** or **DXF** for the format of the file you wish to create. More on this in Chapter 9.

DEFINING ATTRIBUTE AND DATABASE STRUCTURES

When you add attribute information to a block, you're actually creating an alphanumeric database within the drawing database. This database within a database can act as link between the graphic information contained in the drawing and a more sophisticated and extensive database outside the drawing.

The outside database allows the storage of more detailed information about items referred to in the drawing. For example, a block for a chair may have only two attributes linked to it (such as TYPE and LOCATION). These two attributes are all that are necessary to identify any chair symbol as a unique item.* All these attribute values can be extracted and used as an index to a much larger outside database. This database could contain much more detailed information about each unique chair symbol than it would be practical to do within the AutoCAD drawing database.

Even though there doesn't seem to be a theoretical limit to the number of attributes that can be linked to an individual block, there does seem to be a *practical* limit. You've probably noticed that the larger and more detailed that your drawings get, the more sluggishly your computer seems to operate. This is because when you increase the size of your drawing database, AutoCAD has more records to search through before it can find a specified record—with really large drawings, this can slow things down to a crawl (where you can take a lunch break on a REGEN)!

Attributes take up record space. If you create a block with 10 attributes linked to it and just insert that block once, you have added 12 records to the drawing database.** If you insert this block into your drawing only 10 times, that adds 120 records to your drawing file.

The consequence of this information inflation is a huge and slow drawing. A better strategy would be to track only identification and quantity data in your drawing and link that information to more detailed data in Lotus 1-2-3 or other external database managers. So don't feel compelled to store every possible bit of information you might ever wish to know about a symbol in your drawing.

---

* For example, there would only be one chair TYPE *general* in LOCATION *100*.

** Each record takes up approximately the same amount of storage space whether it is an attribute or a complex block.

At this point, the first question you must ask is, what data do you want to track? When you select the data to store, make a list of needed information. Be thorough and don't worry about what will be in the drawing and what will be external to it. It's easier to add data structure in the beginning than to go back and edit a large drawing database.

Once you've made your list, check off all the things you need to see on the drawing itself, or what would be appropriate to decide during the drawing process.

It's often easier to tag a chair symbol with a code like **CH1** and a generic description like **Executive Chair**. Later, you can go to the manufacturer's catalog and select the details of color, finish, casters, etc. It's easier than loading your desk with catalogs and cluttering the database with excess baggage during the drawing or designing process. It's better to store this kind of information externally.

On the other hand, when you're inserting a door into a wall, it might be both appropriate and desirable to force the designer to choose whether the door is fire-rated. That not only creates a more accurate door schedule but also assures that all the details related to building codes are thoroughly considered and not overlooked during the specification process.

While it's wise to store much of your data in an external database, don't be shy about using the drawing. Be realistic about the impact of large amounts of internal data on **REDRAW** time, and how your drawing rhythm might be impeded by having to stop and answer multiple questions on inserting each attribute linked block.

Once your list is compiled and analyzed as to what's appropriate for both the drawing and for the external database, make a separate list for each type of data. Next, determine the amount of space needed on each data "line" and what each line is to be called.

DEFINING THE DATABASE FIELD

It's important to review the terms *field* and *record*, which were first introduced to you in Chapter 2. Each group or line of data information, such as manufacturer number and price, is called a *field*, and each block of data, including one or more fields linked to an attribute block, is called a *record*.

AutoCAD and other database systems require you to indicate the maximum amount of information you intend to store in a field so the program can identify and retrieve it in the future. The database also requires you to give each field an ID code so it understands what it's looking at later.

Estimate the maximum number of characters each field should contain and assign each a brief **ID** code. For example, **MFGNO, 30 CHARACTERS**, might represent the manufacturer's catalog number and would allow a maximum of 30 characters.

In addition to giving each field a size and **ID** code, you also will be required to determine whether the field is to contain alphabetical or mathematical data. If it's to contain values upon which a mathematical such as pricing operation must be performed, then the field is a **Numeric**. If it's text or non-mathematical (numbers requiring no calculation), then **Character** is appropriate.

A field can be Visible or Non-visible on an AutoCAD drawing. If you need to see the information all the time, or for block **ID** purposes, designate the field Visible; otherwise, select Non-visible. Too much text data on a drawing becomes cluttered and difficult to handle, so work sparingly on the visible data.

Much of the information and advice given here about formatting your AutoCAD internal database will be directly applicable to the external databases you create later. If you plan to use both, plan them early so that they're compatible and efficient. Thinking ahead as much as possible eliminates tedious, time-consuming and often tricky database structural conversions.

PROCESS

- Make your data list.
- Know how the information is to be used. Will it best be inserted at drawing time or later?
- Define your field sizes and types
- Assign ID codes.
- What data needs to be visible and what non-visible.

ATTRIBUTE TEMPLATE FILES

Before we go back and create an extract file we must create a *template* file, which contains the desired structure for your attribute extract file. It tells the **ATTEXT** command which attribute tags to look for, and in what order to place the information contained in those attributes. Below is a simple template file that tells **ATTEXT** to extract any values associated with attribute tags **ROOMNO** and **EMPNAME** in any blocks named **ROOMTAG**:

```
BL:NAME  C008000   (Block name, 8 Chars)*
ROOMNO   C005000   (Room Number, 5 Chars)
EMPNAME  C020000   (Employee Name, 20 Chars)
```

The database file produced by using this template file should look like this:

```
ROOMTAG 100 John Smith
ROOMTAG 102 Bill Johnson
ROOMTAG 105 Mary Hartman
```

---

* Do not add the text in parentheses to your template file; these are just comments.

Let's try it.   Exit AutoCAD and create a template file named **CHAIRS.TXT** with your text editor that looks like this[*]:

```
BL:NAME      C008000
TYPE         C012000
LOCATION     C008000
NAME         C020000
```

Save the file and make sure it is on the same directory as your AutoCAD drawings.   Restart AutoCAD and load your **CHAIR** drawing[**].

If you haven't already done so, get out your Pentagon plans and insert both of your chair symbols (CHAIR-G and CHAIR-P) into your drawing, using different values when you are prompted for name and location. Insert these symbols at least twice for each chair type.

You are now ready to continue creating your extract file.

Type: ATTEXT

Response: CDF, SDF or DXF Attribute extract (or Entities)? <C>

Type: S<RETURN>

Response: Template file <default>

Type: CHAIRS<RETURN>

Then:

Response: Extract file name <default>

---

[*] Or if you have set up your ACAD.PGP file as suggested in Appendix D you can just type EDIT at the AutoCAD Command line to enter your favorite text editor.

[**] Or simply exit the text editor.

Pressing **<RETURN>** selects the default setting, which is usually the name of the current drawing file, for the name of your data extract file—or you could type in a name of your own choosing. If you enter **CON**, the output is sent to the screen; typing **PRN** at this prompt will send it directly to a printer.

Response: (An output file that looks something like this.)

Here is what we got when we tried this example:

```
CHAIR-G GENERAL      100      MACARTHUR
CHAIR-P PRIVATE      234      CHAPLIN
CHAIR-G GENERAL      345      MUSTARD
CHAIR-G GENERAL      201      CLARK
CHAIR-P PRIVATE      394      HAWKINS
CHAIR-G GENERAL      239      RIDDLEY
```

BILL OF MATERIALS

A bill of materials can easily be created by sending an **SDF** file associated with an appropriate template file to your disk. That file can be quite sufficient for a basic materials list. Of course, a more sophisticated report or database can be created by linking an AutoCAD **SDF** or **CDF** file with a database manager like dBASE II or III. We'll show you how that's done in Chapter 4.

SUMMARY

The basic commands and techniques learned here are some of the most important in the AutoCAD program. They make it easy for you to add intelligence to your drawing and to share that information with a host of other programs.

As you'll learn in later chapters, it's possible to make more sophisticated links to the outside and extract more detailed information using **DXF** and AutoLISP. However, the basic attribute commands you learned in this chapter are the meat and potatoes for most users.

chapter 4 CREATING A BILL OF MATERIALS PROGRAM

IN THIS CHAPTER

In the last chapter, you learned how to create attribute blocks and export attribute information from AutoCAD to other programs. In this chapter you'll go on to create a simple dBASE program to manage and print bills of materials based on information extracted from your AutoCAD drawing, using the **ATTEXT** command discussed in the previous chapter.

A bill of materials is basically a list of specifications found in a drawing or project, organized in a useful way. When such specifications are carried inside the drawing as attributes, your drawing file will quickly become cumbersome, and your computer's performance sluggish.

A better way to manage such information is to assign a minimum number of attributes to desired drawing symbols (See Chapter 3), then create your list on an outside database manager or spreadsheet, linked to the attributes in your drawing.

The bill of materials program found in this chapter is comparable to some that might cost you hundreds of dollars. It's a relatively simple program, but based on a sophisticated concept. If you don't want to type in all the code, an optional diskette contains dBASE II and dBASE III versions of this program. For those who don't wish to use dBASE, this diskette also includes a compiled version.

The program is heavily commented throughout, so that you can revise it to suit your application, or create your own bill of materials program based on techniques outlined in this Chapter.

AUTOCAD BILL OF MATERIALS DATA

Let's create the AutoCAD attribute data structure you'll use in the Bill Of Materials (BOM) program. Refer to Chapter 3 for a refresher course in creating attribute fields and extract files to use with your database program.

Enter AutoCAD and begin a drawing called **TEST**. Then create a sample block of a **Chair**. For our purposes, it can be a 2" square with a 1" circle in the middle, as in Chapter 3.

When you assign attributes to blocks in AutoCAD, remember to predefine the attributes using the **ATTDEF** command with the following setup:

1. The attributes should be invisible except for the **ITEM-NO**. You may make others visible if you prefer.

2. Attribute tags and prompts should be:

```
TAGS:          PROMPTS:
STATUS:        STATUS (I or A)
ITEMNO:        ITEM NUMBER
QTY:           QUANTITY (default value of 1)
IORA:          ITEM OR ASSEMBLY (default of I)
CLASS:         CLASS (default of A)
CTGRYNO:       CATEGORY
MISC:          MISCELLANEOUS
```

Any other fields you add won't be reported to the BOM program. When you've defined the block attributes, **INSERT** several blocks into the drawing and give a variety of answers to the prompts. Finally, you must extract the data once with the **ATTEXT** command, using the **CDF** file option, and a second time using the **SDF** option. The **CDF** file should be named **TEST.CDF** and the **SDF** file, **TEST.SDF**. Use the following template file in both cases:

BOMACAD.TXT

```
STATUS       C001000
ITEMNO       C010000
QTY          N009002
CTGRYNO      C010000
MISC         C040000
IORA         C001000
CLASS        C002000
```

The files you just created will be used in the next section as samples.

WHY USE dBASE?

dBASE II and its big brother, dBASE III, are database management programs published by Ashton-Tate, Inc. Because of their power, flexibility and popularity, those programs have become the database standards for personal computers.

Like AutoCAD, those programs contain a built-in language styled after the general purpose language, Pascal. What most differentiates dBASE from other database management programs is the ease with which database files and reports can be created. With Pascal or BASIC, many more pages of code must be written to do those chores. In fact, dBASE makes it so much easier to create custom database programs that it's become vital to any CAD user wanting to manage complex information with a minimum of effort.

Here and throughout, dBASE II has been chosen over dBASE III because it's more universal, and the code written for it can be easily and simply converted to work on dBASE III.

The purpose of this book isn't to teach you dBASE, but rather to give you enough information to use it to create a small custom program. More experienced users will learn the essential CAD interfaces from which they can build more complex systems.

dBASE, like BASIC and AutoLISP, can be run from AutoCAD's **Command** line. In the case of dBASE, it runs from the "dot" prompt. That's the way the input line is identified when dBASE is started. You can easily create, edit, query and format files directly from the dot prompt. Many times that will be the preferable method of using dBASE.

Let's take a minute to load dBASE and create a mini-demonstration bill of materials with the dot prompt. First, get into the directory in which you've loaded dBASE. Then:

Type: DBASE<RETURN>

Response: Will be a small period at the upper left hand edge of the screen. This is the "dot" prompt.

The first step in any dBASE program is to create the database file. With a structured file and basic dBASE, you can manage a sophisticated bill of materials database without any other programming. Let's create our own file now.

CREATING A DATABASE FILE

At the dBASE dot prompt:

Type: CREATE<RETURN>

Response: Enter File Name:

Type: ITEMDB<RETURN>

Response: Enter Record Structure As Follows:
        Field Name,Type,Width,Decimal Places
        001

Type: STATUS,C,001<RETURN>

Response: 002

Type: ITEMNO,C,010<RETURN>

Response: 003

   Type: QTY,N,009,002<RETURN>

Response: 004

   Type: CTGRYNO,C,010<RETURN>

Response: 005

   Type: DESC,C,030<RETURN>

Response: 006

   Type: IORA,C,001<RETURN>

Response: 007

   Type: CLASS,C,002<RETURN>

Response: 008

   Type: MISC1,C,040<RETURN>

Response: 009

   Type: MISC2,C,040<RETURN>

Response: 010

   Type: MISC3,C,040<RETURN>

Response: 011

   Type: MISC4,C,040<RETURN>

Response: 012

Type: `MISC5,C,040<RETURN>`

Response: `013`

Type: `COST,N,009,002<RETURN>`

Response: `014`

Type: `<RETURN>`

Response: `INPUT DATA NOW?`

Type: `N <RETURN>`

Response: `.`

IMPORTING DATA FROM AutoCAD TO dBASE

The next step in using data from AutoCAD is to import the data output—the **CDF** or **SDF** file—you created with AutoCAD's **ATTEXT** command above. That's done by using the **APPEND** command in dBASE. At the dBASE dot prompt:

Type: `USE ITEMDB<RETURN>`

Response: `???`

Type: `APPEND FROM TEST.CDF DELIMITED<RETURN>`

Response: `Three (Or number of records added.)`

If you're using an **SDF** file:

Type: `APPEND FROM TEST.TXT SDF<RETURN>`

Response: `Three (Or number of records added.)`

EDITING YOUR NEW dBASE FILE

When you've added the AutoCAD data to your dBASE file, you then may edit it in several ways, including **EDIT** and **BROWSE**. The most common is **EDIT**, if you know the record you want to edit, or **BROWSE** if you want to start at the beginning of the file and scroll through it at will. Let's use **BROWSE** to view and change existing data.

At the dBASE dot prompt:

Type: USE ITEMDB<RETURN>

Type: BROWSE<RETURN>

Response: (You're given a columnar list of the data file to view or edit.)

CURSOR MOVEMENTS WHEN EDITING A FIELD IN dBASE

When editing a dBASE file, use the following commands:

- **^HOME** takes you to the beginning of the first field in the allowable fields for editing.

- The **END** key takes you to the last character of the current field.

- **^END** takes you to the beginning of the last field.

- The **up-arrow** key takes you to the previous legal field, and won't complete the save when pressed at the first field.

- The **down-arrow** key takes you to the next legal field and won't complete a save when pressed at the last field.

- The **right-arrow** key takes you one character to the right, continues to the next field when pressed at end of a field entry, and won't complete a save when pressed at the last character of the last field.

- **^Y** deletes the rest of the current field.

- **^C** terminates the system without saving the current entry.

- **^W**, or **PgUp** or **PgDn** terminate the current field and save current values. This usually skips the cursor to the **<W>**rite to file command.

- **Esc** terminates an entry without saving the current field.

- **^U** (the **UNDO** key) returns a field to its original contents before your current edit. It doesn't restore the contents once the field has been **<W>**ritten to file.

ADDING NEW DATA TO YOUR dBASE FILE

You may want to add data to the existing file. This is done by using the **APPEND** command, which opens the file and allows you to add one or more records to the end.
At the dBASE prompt:

Type: USE ITEMDB<RETURN>

Type: APPEND<RETURN>

Response: (dBASE opens the file)

Enter three new items into the database. For example, a **Chair with Arms**, a **Leather Chair** and a **Side Chair**.

PRINTING REPORTS FROM dBASE

Data are only useful when put to work. Printing a report on the data is the most common need. You may print an entire data file by using the **LIST** command.

Type: USE ITEMDB<RETURN>

Type: LIST<RETURN>

That displays the entire file to the screen; or

Type: SET PRINT ON<RETURN>

Type: LIST<RETURN>

That prints everything, or you may set up a sort-by-parameter and print a selected report from the data. For example:

Type: `USE ITEMDB<RETURN>`

Type: `LIST ALL FOR QTY1<RETURN>`

Response: (dBASE lists items whose quantity field exceeds 1.)

A more sophisticated report can be used by invoking the **REPORT** command. It works as follows.

Type: `REPORT FORM BOM<RETURN>`

Response: `ENTER OPTIONS, M=LEFT MARGIN, L=LINES/PAGE, W=PAGE WIDTH`

Type: `M=0,W=70<RETURN>`

Response: `PAGE HEADING? (Y/N)`

Type: `Y<RETURN>`

Response: `ENTER PAGE HEADING:`

Type: `BILL-OF-MATERIALS REPORT<RETURN>`

Response: `: DOUBLE SPACE REPORT? (Y/N)`

Type: `N<RETURN>`

Response: `ARE TOTALS REQUIRED? (Y/N)`

Type: `N <RETURN>`

Response: `COL WIDTH, CONTENTS`
`        001`

Type: 10,ITEMNO<RETURN>

Response: ENTER HEADING

Type: TAG CODE<RETURN>

Response: 002

Type: 30,MISC1<RETURN>

Response: ENTER HEADING

Type: DESCRIPTION<RETURN>

Response: 003

Type: 10,CTGRYNO<RETURN>

Response: ENTER HEADING

Type: CATEGORY<RETURN>

Response: 004

Type: <RETURN>

Response: (dBASE sends the report to the screen.)

You've created your report form; now you may send the output to a printer using the **REPORT** command.

Type: SET PRINT ON<RETURN>

Type: USE ITEMDB<RETURN>

Type: REPORT FORM BOM<RETURN>

Response: (dBASE prints your report.)

If you want to sort by a parameter, use the **REPORT** command as follows:

Type: USE ITEMDB<RETURN>

Type: REPORT FORM BOM ALL FOR QTY1 TO PRINT<RETURN>

Response: (dBASE prints only items with quantities greater than 1.)

USING THE dBASE PROGRAMMING LANGUAGE

Using the dBASE commands at the dot prompt limits you to one command at a time. Many things aren't possible to do, for example heavily formatted reports. That makes the dBASE programming language important, particularly because it allows the creation of an input screen, won't intimidate the novice user, and will create fancy formatted reports.

In the final version of the bill of materials, you'll concentrate on creating a program that runs under dBASE, but doesn't depend on the user to type in commands. You'll see menus and input lines much like any other application program. To demonstrate this powerful capability, let's illustrate the principle of a **Command** File or dBASE Program.

At the dBASE dot prompt:

Type: MODIFY COMMAND TEST<RETURN>

Response: (dBASE displays briefly **NEW FILE**, then gives you a blank screen on which to type.)

Type: ERASE<RETURN>

Response: ?

Type: `"I am a test program"<RETURN>`

Response: `???`

Type: `CTRL-W (Hold down the control key and type W.)`

You've now created your first dBASE program! Now

Type: `Do Test<RETURN>`

Response: `I am a test program`

Your programs are easily written or keyed in from the listings included in this book using a text editor. While dBASE includes a built-in editor, Wordstar or the CAD-Edit programs included on *The AutoCAD Database Diskette* will be much easier to use and are less limited.

BILL OF MATERIALS PROGRAM STRUCTURE

The bill of materials program you'll work with is based on the files used by the ei:MicroSpec and Turbo Designer systems, developed by the authors to provide a sophisticated CAD database management system linked to AutoCAD. The program structure is valid for many general purpose applications and, of course, can be modified easily or used as a model for a program of your own design.

The data structure is a single dBASE II file linked to a universal AutoCAD attribute structure. The attribute structure contains codes that uniquely identify each typical item in the drawing, and which link to a larger, more fully defined data form in your dBASE II program.

The two-tiered data allow as much information as you want to be linked to the block, but with a minimum amount in the drawing itself to prevent slow **REGENERATION** times and inflated file sizes.

The dBASE II file structure is defined below. Let's look at a flow chart of the program.

FLOW CHART

AUTOCAD: *create attribute with fixed structure link to an extract file with .txt template file created using the* **ATTEXT** *command.*

SDF file: *created from* **ATTEXT**

---

dBASE II: create programs with menus and procedures designed to make linking, editing and reporting easy or the user. Append the **SDF** *file to the* **DBF** *file.*

DBF file: *(itemdb.dbf) with expanded information structure. Append the* **SDF** *file to the* **DBF** *file.*

BOM.PRG: *the main menu program which controls the link to AutoCAD and allows the selection of sub-program for adding data, editing and reporting.*

BOMADD.PRG: *the sub-program for adding new data to the dBASE data file.*

BOMED.PRG: *the sub-program for editing data in the dBASE data file.*

BOMRPT.PRG: *the sub-program for creating and printing reports.*

dBASE FILE STRUCTURE

The dBASE file, structured as below with the definition of the fields, has the same structure as the one you created in the tutorial section above. Now, you're already starting to write your bill of materials program!

DATABASESTRUCTURE:ITEMDB.DBF

FLD	NAME	TYPE	WIDTH	DEC
001	STATUS	C	001	
002	ITEMNO	C	010	
003	QTY	N	009	002
004	CTGRYNO	C	010	
005	DESC	C	030	
006	IORA	C	001	
007	CLASS	C	002	
008	MISC1	C	040	
009	MISC2	C	040	
010	MISC3	C	040	
011	MISC4	C	040	
012	MISC5	C	040	
013	COST	N	009	002

ITEM FIELD DESCRIPTIONS

STATUS: Is this item New or Existing or used in Phase 1 or 2 of the project?

ITEMNO: The ID tag of the block or item.

QTY: How many does each instance of the block represent?

CTGRYNO: In what category does the item belong? It might be a room number or any other grouping.

DESCRIPTION: Describe the item. This is the same information contained in the **Catalog** description field and in the **Assembly** and **Category** item description fields. It's automatically retained from the catalog file if the catalog is used. It may be user-modified.

IORA: Identifies the block as an item or an assembly of parts.

CLASS: A grouping of items. The class code, defined in the class maintenance routine selected from the main menu, switches the **MISC** item field prompts to conform to the class of item being described.

MISC1: A user definable field.

MISC2: A user definable field.

MISC3: A user definable field.

MISC4: A user definable field.

MISC5: A user definable field.

COST: The cost or value of the item.

The next step is to write your own program or key in the programs included in this chapter.

HOW TO KEY LISTING

When you key in the program listings included here, use EDLIN, Wordstar in non-document mode, the dBASE screen editor or any text editor in non-document mode. The indentation doesn't have to be exactly as the listing shows but it's important that everything shown on a line remain on the same line. dBASE reads the code one line at a time and requires that a semi-colon end any line wrapped to another line. The lines that begin with asterisks indicate notes. dBASE ignores these. So it's O.K. for you to add your own notes. Just remember to begin the line with one or more asterisks.

HOW TO DEBUG YOUR LISTING

The most critical aspect of writing any computer program is the debugging process. In the case of keyed-in code from a book, debugging is usually the result of typing errors. Be careful to type the code exactly as it appears in the listing (with the aforementioned exception of the indenting).

If the program doesn't run, it most likely is affected by a typing error. Check everything with your text editor and try again. If you need extra help, a number of debugging techniques can be used.

If something's wrong, dBASE generally repeats the command line containing the error and lets you change it and continue. You must make a note of the error and go into the code and correct it.

If the error is more serious, you can interrupt the program by pressing **<ESCAPE>**, or **CONTROL-C**. In the worst case, start over. Nothing bad will happen—reboot the computer and start again.

Several dBASE commands will help you find a bug. **TALK, STEP** and **ECHO**—those commands can be added to the first line or two of your programs and dBASE will help debug itself. When you've found the problem, delete those commands and your program returns to normal.

TALK automatically displays the result of every dBASE operation on the screen. The programs in this book all SET TALK OFF. Just SET TALK ON, and do your debugging. Then SET TALK OFF before saving your program for later use.

ECHO is similar to **TALK**. It prints every command line on the screen as it happens. The result is gibberish on your data screen. This command is a powerful way to see what's going right as well as what's going wrong. Add the line SET ECHO ON to the first of your programs and run them.

STEP is the most powerful tool. When you SET TALK ON and ECHO ON, as well as SET STEP ON, the computer will execute one line at a time, and stop and wait for you to press **<RETURN>**.

Now, reverse all the added debugging commands and you're in business. Let's begin.

PROGRAM LISTINGS

The first module in the set of programs which make up the bill of materials program is the main menu program which calls all the other options. When a subprogram has finished running, control of the program is returned to the master BOM.PRG for further instructions. The code listings below contain detailed comments the first time a procedure is used. This should enable you to learn what the program is doing and can help you to translate the program design into other database languages.

MAIN MENU

BOM.PRG — This is the main menu program for your bill of materials system. It presents the basic options, calls other programs, contains a routine to import data from an AutoCAD file and also performs other housekeeping functions. This is the database structure for the ITEMDB.DBF file which contains the bill of materials information:

```
***    DATABASE STRUCTURE: ITEMDB.DBF
*** FLD     NAME          TYPE WIDTH DEC
*** 001     STATUS        C    001
*** 002     ITEMNO        C    010
*** 003     QTY           N    009   002
*** 004     CTGRYNO       C    010
*** 005     DESC          C    030
*** 006     IORA          C    001
*** 007     CLASS         C    002
*** 008     MISC1         C    040
*** 009     MISC2         C    040
*** 010     MISC3         C    040
*** 011     MISC4         C    040
*** 012     MISC5         C    040
*** 013     COST          N    009   002
SET TALK OFF
ERASE
CLEAR
```

*** The following commands set the dBASE environment.
```
STORE 'Y' TO run
@ 5,17 SAY 'TURBO DESIGNER BILL OF MATERIALS PROGRAM'
@ 24,22 SAY 'DO YOU WISH TO CONTINUE ?';
GET run PICTURE '!'
READ
```

*** This writes a message to the screen and waits for a
*** response from the keyboard. The "@5,17" means
*** at line 5 and column 17 display the message "Turbo
*** Designer Bill of Materials program." The quote marks
*** tell dBASE it is a line of text, not commands.

```
    IF run = 'Y'
```
*** An IF sequence must end with a related ENDIF
```
        ERASE
        ELSE
        ERASE
        QUIT
    ENDIF
```
*** The next function writes the main menu to the screen
*** and waits for a response. Depending on the response,
*** the program runs the appropriate subprogram or
*** function.
```
DO WHILE t
```
*** A DO WHILE sequence must end with an ENDDO.
```
    ERASE
    @ 3,34 SAY "MAIN MENU"
    @ 5,24 SAY "(0) Exit to operating system"
    @ 7,24 SAY '(1) Add new items to Item List'
    @ 9,24 SAY '(2) Edit records in Item List'
    @ 11,24 SAY '(3) Print a Report'
    @ 13,24 SAY '(4) Append from AutoCAD SDF file'
    @ 15,24 SAY '(5) Return to Dot Prompt'
    @ 17,24 SAY 'Enter Desired Action'
    WAIT TO choice
        DO CASE
```
***A DO CASE must end with an ENDCASE.
```
            CASE choice = '0'
                ERASE
                QUIT
            CASE choice = '1'
                DO BOMADD
            CASE choice = '2'
                DO BOMED
            CASE choice = '3'
                DO BOMRPT
            CASE choice = '4'
    ERASE
        STORE t TO a
    DO WHILE a
    STORE '                    ' TO cdfile
```
*** The next sequence prompts the user to specify the
*** name of the file to read into the dBASE program from AutoCAD.

```
        @5,15 SAY 'What SDF file do you wish to append?';
      GET cdfile PICTURE  '!!!!!!!!!!!!!'
          READ
IF cdfile = '              '
      STORE f TO a
        ELSE
```
*** The next sequence trims the blanks from the file and
*** stores it in a temporary file.
```
          STORE TRIM(cdfile) TO tcdfile
          USE itemdb
```
*** The USE command activated the item database file
*** The APPEND command adds the AutoCAD information to
*** a temporary file, then to the main item database file.
```
          APPEND FROM &tcdfile SDF
```
*** The next sequence creates a new index file for dBASE.
*** The index helps dBASE more quickly find a data record
*** without searching through unorganized data.
```
          INDEX ON   itemno TO Nitem
          RELEASE cdfile
          RELEASE tcdfile
          ERASE
        ENDIF
    ENDDO
      CASE choice = '5'
        CANCEL
    ENDCASE
ENDDO t
```

SPECIFYING AND EDITING RECORDS

BOMED.PRG — This next module allows you to easily
specify and edit the bill of materials files one record at a time.
It allows the user to access the files by their item code rather
than just by the record number, as would be readily available using the dBASE dot prompt.

```
ERASE
USE ITEMDB INDEX NITEM
STORE t TO more
DO WHILE more
  STORE t TO right
```

```
DO WHILE right
  STORE 'Y' TO ya,mor
  STORE '            ' TO mitemno
  @ 2,0 SAY 'Which Item Code do you;
    wish to edit?  '
  GET mitemno
  READ
  STORE mitemno TO token
  SET EXACT ON
  FIND &token
  IF # = 0
    @ 24,0
    @ 24,0 SAY 'That Item Code does not;
      exist--try again?';
    GET ya PICTURE '!'
    READ
      If ya = 'Y'
        LOOP
      ELSE
        STORE 'N' TO mor
        STORE f TO more
      ENDIF ya = 'Y'
  ENDIF # = 0
  CLEAR GETS
  SET EXACT OFF
  IF ya = 'Y'
```

*** The following series of "@ says" writes labels
*** to the screen to identify the fields presented
*** for editing.

```
    @ 4,0 SAY 'Item Code'
    @ 4,25 SAY Itemno
    @ 5,0 SAY 'Status'
    @ 5,25 SAY Status
    @ 6,0 SAY 'Quantity'
    @ 6,25 SAY Qty
    @ 7,0 SAY 'Category'
    @ 7,25 SAY Ctgryno
    @ 8,0 SAY 'I or A'
    @ 8,25 SAY Iora
```

```
@ 9,0 SAY 'Class'
@ 9,25 SAY Class
@ 10,0 SAY 'Description'
@ 10,25 SAY Desc
@ 11,0 SAY 'Misc1'
@ 11,25 SAY Misc1
@ 12,0 SAY 'Misc2'
@ 12,25 SAY Misc2
@ 13,0 SAY 'Misc3'
@ 13,25 SAY Misc3
@ 14,0 SAY 'Misc4'
@ 14,25 SAY Misc4
@ 15,0 SAY 'Misc5'
@ 15,25 SAY Misc5
@ 16,0 SAY 'Cost'
@ 16,25 SAY Cost
STORE 'Y' TO yes
@ 24,0
@ 24,0 SAY 'Is this the record you are;
  looking for? ';
GET yes PICTURE  '!'
READ
  IF yes = 'Y'
    STORE f TO right
  ENDIF yes = 'Y'
  ELSE
    STORE f TO right
  ENDIF ya = 'Y'
ENDDO right
 If ya = 'Y'
   STORE t TO allok
 DO WHILE allok
   STORE Itemno TO mitemno
   STORE Status TO mstatus
   STORE QTY TO mqty
```

```
STORE Ctgryno TO mctgryno
STORE Iora TO miora
STORE Class TO mclass
STORE Desc to mdesc
STORE Misc1 TO mmisc1
STORE Misc2 TO mmisc2
STORE Misc3 TO mmisc3
STORE Misc4 TO mmisc4
STORE Misc5 TO mmisc5
STORE Cost TO mcost
@ 4,25 GET mitemno
@ 5,25 GET mstatus
@ 6,25 GET mqty
@ 7,25 GET mctgryno
@ 8,25 GET miora
@ 9,25 GET mclass
@ 10,25 GET mdesc
@ 11,25 GET mmisc1
@ 12,25 GET mmisc2
@ 13,25 GET mmisc3
@ 14,25 GET mmisc4
@ 15,25 GET mmisc5
@ 16,25 GET mcost
READ
STORE 'N' TO ya
@ 24,0
@ 24,0 Say 'Any more changes ?  'GET;
  ya PICTURE '!'
READ
CLEAR GETS
STORE ya <> 'N' TO allok
ENDDO allok
```
***This puts screen entries into files.
```
REPLACE Itemno WITH mitemno, Desc WITH mdesc
REPLACE Status WITH mstatus, Qty WITH mqty
REPLACE Ctgryno WITH mctgryno, Iora WITH miora
REPLACE Class WITH mclass, Misc1 WITH mmisc1
REPLACE Misc2 WITH mmisc2, Misc3 WITH mmisc3
```

```
      REPLACE Misc4 WITH mmisc4, Misc5 WITH mmisc5
      REPLACE Cost WITH mcost
    ENDIF ya = 'Y'
    @ 23,0
    IF mor = 'Y'
      @ 23,0 'Are there more to edit (Y/N)?    ;
      GET mor PICTURE  '!'
      READ
      STORE  (mor = 'Y') TO more
    ENDIF more <> 'Y'
    INDEX ON itemno TO nitem
    CLEAR GETS
    ERASE
ENDDO more
RELEASE more, right, token, mor, ya, yes
RELEASE msitemno, mstatus, mqty, mctgryno
RELEASE mclass, mdesc, mmisc1, mmisc2
RELEASE allok, miora, mcost, mmisc5
RELEASE mmisc3, mmisc4
RETURN
```

ADDING NEW RECORDS

BOMADD.PRG — The **BOMADD.PRG** allows the user to add new records to the database file from the keyboard rather than from an AutoCAD file. This permits you to create and extend a specification rather than just depend on the drawing database to access your project data.

```
Use itemdb
INDEX on itemno to NITEM
Use itemdb index nitem
STORE t TO more
DO WHILE more
  STORE '               ' TO mitemno
  STORE ' ' TO miora
  STORE '  ' TO mclass
  STORE ' ' TO mstatus
  STORE 0.00 TO mqty
  STORE '           ' TO mctgryno
  STORE '                              ' TO mdesc
  STORE '                              ' TO mmisc1
  STORE '                              ' TO mmisc2
  STORE '                              ' TO mmisc3
  STORE '                              ' TO mmisc4
  STORE '                              ' TO mmisc5
  STORE 0.00 TO mcost
  ERASE
  @ 24,0
  @ 24,0 SAY 'Enter blanks for Item Code when;
    you want to quit.'
*** This gets data to be added to database, first checking
*** Item Code to see if it's a duplicate.
  @ 2,25 SAY '< < < MASTER ITEM FILE > > >'
  @ 4,0 SAY 'Item Code                    ' GET;
    mitemno
  @ 5,0 SAY 'Status'
  @ 6,0 SAY 'Quantity'
  @ 7,0 SAY 'Category'
  @ 8,0 SAY 'I or A'
```

```
@ 9,0 SAY 'Class'
@ 10,0 SAY 'Description'
@ 11,0 SAY 'Misc11'
@ 12,0 SAY 'Misc12'
@ 13,0 SAY 'Misc13'
@ 14,0 SAY 'Misc14'
@ 15,0 SAY 'Misc15'
@ 16,0 SAY 'Selling Price'
READ
STORE mitemno <> ' ' TO more
if mitemno <>  '            '
  store t to more
else
  store f to more
  ERASE
endif
STORE f TO found
IF more
    STORE TRIM(mitemno) TO token
  SET EXACT ON
  FIND &token
IF #  <> 0
  @ 5,25 SAY Status
  @ 6,25 SAY Qty
  @ 7,25 SAY Ctgryno
  @ 8,25 SAY Iora
  @ 9,25 SAY Class
  @ 10,25 SAY Desc
  @ 11,25, SAY Misc1
  @ 12,25 SAY Misc2
  @ 13,25 SAY Misc3
  @ 14,25 SAY Misc4
  @ 15,25 SAY Misc5
  @ 16,25 SAY Cost
STORE 'Y' TO same
  @ 23,0
  @ 23,0 SAY 'The above Item Code already exists.;
      Is it a duplicate?';
```

```
     GET same PICTURE '!'
       READ
       IF same = 'Y'
         STORE t TO found
       ENDIF same
     ENDIF # = 0
ENDIF more
  SET EXACT OFF
IF more .AND. .NOT. found
  STORE T to again
  DO WHILE again
    @ 5,25 GET mstatus
    @ 6,25 GET mqty
    @ 7,25 GET mctgryrno
    @ 8,25 GET miora
    @ 9,25 GET mclass
    @ 10,25 GET mdesc
    @ 11,25 GET mmisc1
    @ 12,25 GET mmisc2
    @ 13,25 GET mmisc3
    @ 14,25 GET mmisc4
    @ 15,25 GET mmisc5
    @ 16,25 GET mcost picture;
        '99999999999.99'
    READ
    STORE 'N' TO OK
    @ 23,0
    @ 23,0 SAY 'Do you want to change;
        anything? '
    GET OK PICTURE '!'
    READ
    IF OK = 'N'
      STORE f TO again
    ENDIF OK
      CLEAR GETS
    ENDDO again
    IF mitemno <>   '          '
      APPEND BLANK
```

```
      REPLACE Itemno WITH mitemno, Desc WITH mdesc
      REPLACE Misc1 WITH mmisc1, Misc2 WITH mmisc2
      REPLACE Misc3 WITH mmisc3, Misc4 WITH mmisc4
      REPLACE Cost WITH mcost
      REPLACE Misc5, WITH mmisc5, cost WITH mcost
      REPLACE Class WITH mclass
      REPLACE qty WITH mqty, Ctgryno WITH  mctgryno
      REPLACE Iora WITH miora
        ELSE
          STORE f TO more
     ENDIF mitemno <>  '            '
   ENDIF .NOT.   found
 ENDDO more
RELEASE more, mitemno, mdesc, mclass
RELEASE mctgryno, mqty, RELEASE mstatus
RELEASE mmisc1, mmisc2, mmisc3, mmisc4, mmisc5
RELEASE mcost, miora, token, found, again, ok
CLEAR GETS
RETURN
```

CREATING REPORTS

BOMRPT.PRG—Predesigned reports are important for the casual dBASE user not familiar with the dot prompt and are essential for a complex formatted report. This module is the most likely candidate for customization and expansion. You should be able to pick up the basic principles from this module for extension.

```
STORE '                               ' TO header
@ 5,10 SAY 'ENTER HEADER TO BE PRINTED';
   GET header PICTURE;
      '!!!!!!!!!!!!!!!!!!!!!!!!!!!!!!!!!'
   READ
   STORE TRIM(header) TO theader
@10,10 SAY 'TURN ON PRINTER AND LINE UP PAPER'
@12,10 SAY 'PRESS ANY KEY TO CONTINUE........'
WAIT
ERASE
SET FORMAT TO PRINT
SET PRINT ON
SET SCREEN OFF
SET TALK OFF
*** The next line sets up a loop which adds a number
*** to the variable and checks the count after
*** every line is printed.  When the line count
*** reaches 48 lines, it sends a page feed and
*** starts a new page.
STORE 99 TO LINECNT
STORE 1 TO PAGENO
USE ITEMDB INDEX NITEM
DO WHILE .NOT. EOF
   IF LINECNT > 48
      ERASE
      @ 1,20 SAY 'YOUR COMPANY NAME'
      @ 3,25 SAY 'MASTER ITEM LIST'
      @ 3,65 SAY 'DATE ' + DATE ()
      @ 4,20 SAY theader
      @ 4,65 SAY 'PAGE ' + STR(PAGENO,3)
      STORE 6 TO LINECNT
      STORE PAGENO+1 TO PAGENO
```

```
      ENDIF
      @ LINECNT,1 SAY ' '
      @ LINECNT+1,1 SAY 'ITEM NO:        ' + ITEMNO
      @ LINECNT+2,1 SAY 'STATUS:         ' + STATUS
      @ LINECNT+3,1 SAY 'QTY USED:       ' + STR(QTY,7)
      @ LINECNT+4,1 SAY 'CATEGORY:       ' + CTGRYNO
      @ LINECNT+5,1 SAY 'I OR A:         ' + IORA
      @ LINECNT+6,1 SAY 'CLASS:          ' + CLASS
      @ LINECNT+7,1 SAY 'DESCRIPTION:    ' + DESC
      @ LINECNT+8,1 SAY 'MISC1:          ' + MISC1
      @ LINECNT+9,1 SAY 'MISC2:          ' + MISC2
      @ LINECNT+10,1 SAY 'MISC3:         ' + MISC3
      @ LINECNT+11,1 SAY 'MISC4:         ' + MISC4
      @ LINECNT+12,1 SAY 'MISC5:         ' + MISC5
      @ LINECNT+13,1 SAY 'COST:          ' + STR(COST,9,2)
      STORE LINECNT + 14 TO LINECNT
      SKIP
   ENDDO EOF
   EJECT
   SET FORMAT TO SCREEN
   SET SCREEN ON
   SET PRINT OFF
   RELEASE header, theader, linecnt, pageno
   RETURN
```

HOW TO RUN BOM.PRG

Type: dBASE bom<RETURN>

Response: ..screen shot of main menu (see Figure 1).

```
MAIN MENU
(0) Exit to operating system
(1) Add new items to Item List
(2) Edit records in Item List
(3) Print a Report
(4) Append from AutoCAD SDF file
(5) Return to Dot Prompt
Enter Desired Action
```

Figure 1: Main menu for the Bill of Materials program.

SUMMARY

This concludes the lesson in using dBASE to edit and print a bill of materials and to create a program to maintain a bill of materials database. Of course, you can create far more complex programs. A number of third-party CAD bills of materials programs also have been developed to work with AutoCAD and other CAD systems. Such programs can result in productivity gains limited only by your imagination.

chapter 5 AUTOLISP PROGRAMMING

IN THIS CHAPTER

In Chapters 3 and 4, you learned the basics of attributes and how to create a simple bill of materials program. In this chapter, you'll learn some of the basic concepts of LISP and how to write programs in AutoLISP so that you can extract and use data from AutoCAD drawings. These data include the blocks and attributes you've learned how to create in the previous chapter. When finished, you'll have learned just how simple LISP really is and how easy it is to understand and write AutoLISP programs.

AUTOLISP OVERVIEW

LISP stands for **LIS**t Processing, a simple, yet deceptively powerful language for handling symbolic data (words as opposed to numbers).

Because it's such a versatile and powerful language, LISP is the language of choice among Artificial Intelligence researchers.

If computer programming were like sculpture, then LISP would be like a sculptor's clay to most other computer language's stone. With LISP you can add a little piece here and a little dab there until you get a result that works. If you don't like the result, you can remove pieces and squeeze other parts around until the work pleases you—this is a modeling concept. Many programming languages use the building block concept where you must add building blocks and chisel away at them. If the result doesn't work, then too bad. You have to throw away a lot of what you did and start over—just as if you were carving in stone.

AutoLISP is a subset of Common LISP with many additional built-in graphics handling functions. AutoLISP was designed by Autodesk to extend AutoCAD's power by allowing you great latitude in creating an even more powerful drafting package for specific applications.

Because AutoCAD was designed to be a powerful general purpose drafting system, it wasn't possible, or practical, to include every type of useful feature for each drafting discipline. AutoLISP was created to fill that gap. For example, AutoCAD has no command for drawing parallel lines simultaneously—a useful feature for drawing walls on building plans. However, several AutoLISP programs make drawing double wall lines as easy as drawing ordinary lines[*].

But what will AutoLISP do for you? Why should you spend a lot of time learning an obscure specialized computer language? The answer is in two words—power and money.

First, the power. Even very simple AutoLISP functions add more power to AutoCAD. Imagine if everything that you put into your drawing was tracked automatically? Later in this chapter, you'll learn how to keep track of any item that you specify in a drawing with only ten simple lines of AutoLISP code.

And, of course, there's money. You can save by doing your drafting faster with the aid of AutoLISP routines and you can *earn* by being more productive. The next four chapters will show you how AutoLISP can save hours every week by eliminating repetitive, error-prone tasks.

---

[*]   For example, the wall drawing routines in TURBO DESIGNER™ and AutoCAD AEC®.

Of course, you can skip the explanation of how AutoLISP works, and just use the examples, which were designed to allow you to modify and build on them to suit your own purposes. However, that would be impossible to do without some basic understanding of AutoLISP. So, we encourage you to plow ahead and gain some facility for using AutoLISP—you will find it well worth the effort.

This chapter presents the basics of AutoLISP in a practical, hands-on fashion with many useful programming examples that will help you to understand and use AutoLISP effectively in your own work.

LEARNING ABOUT AUTOLISP

LISP is probably one of the simplest, yet most powerful programming languages around. However, the general consensus is that LISP is very difficult to learn, when quite the opposite is often true.* LISP is simple because it's a language that consists of only three elements: the *atom*, the *list* and the *function*.

The best way to start learning AutoLISP is to sit down and start playing with it on your computer as you follow along with the examples in this chapter. The first few one-line examples can be typed directly on AutoCAD's **Command** line and the result will be displayed as soon as you press **<RETURN>**.

The longer examples can be typed into any text editor or word processor, saved under any filename (with an **.LSP** extension) and loaded into AutoCAD and executed.

To simplify matters even further, see Appendix D, which will teach you to set up a text editor to use while you're running AutoCAD to simplify program writing and debugging.

---

* LOGO, the computer language developed to teach young children programming, is a subset of LISP.

You also can use SideKick™ or one of the other memory resident text editors for writing your AutoLISP code, but remember to always use the **F1** key to flip your screen out of the graphics mode before you call any of those programs. Otherwise, you may lock up your computer.

BASIC CONCEPTS

ATOMS: The basic unit of any LISP program is called the **ATOM**. Just as atoms were once thought to be the smallest possible units of matter, a LISP atom is simply the smallest possible unit in a LISP program. An atom can be a word, a symbol* or a number. It can have a meaning assigned to it (in which case the atom can also be called a variable or a function name) or it can simply stand for itself (with no other meaning assigned it). For example, consider the following lists:

```
'(furniture chairs tables desks lamps beds)


'(chairs side-chairs easy-chairs
     typing-chairs)


'(77 83 5.25678 44 33 1)
```

All the words or numbers (such as chairs, easy-chairs or 44) in the above lists are atoms, and because each of those lists begins with a quote (the list is called a "quoted list"), the atoms are called literals (i.e., they hold no additional value other than that of the word itself).

Think of an atom as being the same thing as a variable name in another computer language, such as BASIC. An atom usually acts the same way as a variable does.

---

*   An atom is often referred to as a SYMBOL.

For many purposes, you can use an atom like you would use a variable name in another language. But an atom can be much more than a variable name, because, while you can only assign a *value* to a variable name, you can *bind* almost anything to an atom. Not only can you assign a simple value to an atom, such as **(setq a 6)**, you can bind lists to atoms like this:

Type: `(setq b '(furniture chairs tables desks))`

Response: `(furniture chairs tables desks)`

In addition, when you assign a value to an atom, you can assign a different value to that atom within a function, and when that function is finished, the atom is rebound to the value it was set to before that function was run.

LISTS: A **LIST** is simply a group of atoms (or even a single atom) that is contained within a pair of parentheses. Lists must be constructed in a particular way to make sense to the LISP Interpreter. A list can be made up of other lists or combinations of lists and atoms as in the examples below:

`()`

This list is called an empty list or a **nil** list. Even though the list has nothing in it (which is why it's called a **nil** list), it's still a list because it's set off by a pair of parentheses.

`'(table)`

This list consists of a single atom surrounded by parentheses.

`'(desks files)`

This list contains two atoms.

`'((desks files) (chairs stools))`

This list contains two **SUBLISTS** each of which contain two atoms. A sublist is simply a list contained or nested inside another list. Lists can be nested inside other lists to almost any depth.

```
'(furniture (chairs stools side-chairs))
```

This list contains an atom and a sublist that consists of three atoms.

```
'((beds (single-bed murphy-bed)) (lamps) 97)
```

This list contains two sublists and an atom. The first sublist contains an atom and another sublist inside it that contains two atoms.

As you can see from the examples above, lists can be nested to great depths, and be quite complex—that may be why a lot of people think LISP is a difficult language.

AutoLISP programs will run much faster if complex, nested lists are used. However, for the purposes of illustration, you'll only be working with simple lists in these examples.

FUNCTIONS: A **FUNCTION** is defined as a LISP program.* A function may be called by another LISP program and executed, or it can be executed directly from the **Command** line in AutoCAD.

Functions are similar to programs, functions, procedures or subroutines in other computer languages.

---

*   In various books about LISP, there's some disagreement about the definition of a function. Some books call functions *procedures*. Other books call a function a type of *procedure* that does not have a side effect. Because the *AutoLISP Programmer's Reference* **only** talks about functions, we'll refer to everything as a function regardless of side effects. We'll discuss side effects a little later in this chapter.

A function always returns a *result*. Think of a function as a black box, with a hole in either end, that performs a process. You stick the raw materials in one end of the black box, and the finished product comes out the other end. If you want to add the numbers **2** and **4**, you stick those numbers (called arguments) in the black box called **+** (**PLUS**) and the result, **6**, comes out the other end.

Many functions are already built into AutoLISP, such as the common math functions **+ - * /** and the logical operators **<, >, =, /=.** * LISP's real power, however, is its ability to let you define your own functions to suit a specific application. Below is an example of a simple AutoLISP function that takes any number given to it and multiplies it by **10**.

Let's try it—hit the **F1** key, get into AutoCAD's text mode and:

Type: (defun tentimes (number) (* number 10))

Response: ((NUMBER) (* NUMBER 10))

This function can be called from another function with the following function call (which is simply another list that contains the name of the function and the value from which the function will derive an answer):

Type: (tentimes 2) <RETURN>

Response: 20

AutoCAD should print **20** on the next line. If not, retype the function.

If you got **20**, then congratulations. You've just successfully written your first AutoLISP program! Now, let's call the new function using other numbers as arguments:

Type: (tentimes 20) <RETURN>

---

*   Those built-in functions are called LISP *primitives.*

Response: 200

Type: (tentimes 3.7) <RETURN>

Response: 37

Let's look at that function in detail to see how it works. Here's the same function formatted to conform to accepted LISP programming practices:*

```
(defun tentimes (number)
  (* number 10)
)
```

The function is just a list that contains two atoms, **defun** and **tentimes**; a sublist that contains the atom **number** and another sublist that contains the three atoms *, **number** and **10**.

What does all this mean? The first atom, **defun**, is a built-in LISP function that indicates this list will be a definition of a function. The next atom, **tentimes**, is simply the name you've chosen to call the function that you're defining.

The first sublist that contains the single atom **number** is called the *argument list*. In this case, our function will take only one argument. An *argument* is an independent variable that takes the value given it when the function is called, and uses that value within the function.

The argument can be named anything. You could call it **Ralph**, but the word **number** was used as a reminder of the type of variable that would be used in that function.

---

* You don't have to follow the indenting conventions you find in this function or any other function in this book. The only spacing that's absolutely necessary in LISP code is *one space* to separate each atom in a list. We do, however, think that following standard conventions of indention helps enormously in making the code more readable, clarifying the intent of the programmer and making the code easier to debug.

The next line in that function contains the actual formula for multiplying a given number by 10. That formula could be expressed in algebra as:

```
answer=number * 10
```

But in LISP it's expressed as:

```
(* number 10)
```

That is, multiply the variable called **number** by **10**.

Isn't it easy? And that's all there is to LISP. You now know almost everything there is to know about the structure and syntax of LISP.

Now that we've gotten our feet wet with a simple LISP function, let's take a little closer look at the mechanics of the LISP Interpreter. Other computer languages have many different grammatical forms, called syntax, that vary with the type of operation you want to perform. LISP, on the other hand, has only one syntactical form—the function call. For example, if you want to say **x=2+4** in LISP, you would:

Type: `(setq x (+ 2 4))`

Response: 6

Let's examine the above list or expression more closely. If you understand how it works, you'll have a better grasp of how LISP actually works.

First, look at the list **(+ 2 4)**. This is called a sublist. Inside the LISP Interpreter is a section called the List Evaluater.* Whenever the List Evaluater sees a list that doesn't have a single quote in front of the list, it tries to evaluate that list. The List Evaluater takes the atom of the deepest sublist (in this case the symbol **+**) and checks to see if there is a function available called **+**. If it finds a func-

---

* An EVALUATER is a machine that evaluates; an
   EVALUATOR is a person who evaluates.

tion called **+**, it then will pass the numbers **2** and **4** (called *arguments*) to that function and the function called **+** will be evaluated. The function called **+** will probably say:

```
TAKE THE VALUE OF THE FIRST ARGUMENT AND
      PLACE IT IN
   A LOCATION IN MEMORY CALLED "a"
      WHILE THERE ARE MORE ARGUMENTS
         INCREMENT THE VALUE OF LOCATION "a"
            BY THE VALUE OF THE NEXT ARGUMENT
RETURN THE VALUE OF LOCATION "a" TO THE
      EVALUATER
```

In this case, the value returned from evaluating the function called **+** is **6**. When the first sublist has been evaluated, the sample expression now looks like this to the List Evaluater:

```
(setq x 6)
```

The List Evaluater now looks for a function called **setq**. The function **setq** says:

```
SET THE VALUE OF THE ATOM NAMED IN THE FIRST
   ARGUMENT TO THE VALUE OF THE SECOND ARGUMENT.
```

AutoLISP will always return the value of the last evaluated function to the **Command** line. In order to check the value of **x**, you can type this on the **Command** line:

Type: !x <RETURN>

Response: 6

AutoLISP will print **6** on the next line. Typing **!** (an exclamation point) followed by the name of any atom on the **Command** line will display the value that has been bound to that atom by a function. Try typing **!y**. AutoLISP should display **nil**, which means that there is no value bound to the atom called **y**.

Let's see what happens when you quote a list. Type the same list into the **Command** line, but put a quote in front of the sublist like this:

Type: (setq x ' (+ 2 4)) <RETURN>

Response: (+ 2 4)

If you type **!x**, **(+ 2 4)** will be displayed. That means that because the list **(+ 2 4)** was quoted, it wasn't evaluated by the List Evaluater and it simply set the value of **x** to the list.** To see what a really long list looks like, press **F1** to flip the screen to text mode and:

Type: !ATOMLIST

That **ATOMLIST** is the list of all the atoms that have some value attached to them. Most of those atoms are names of the built-in AutoLISP functions.

---

* Actually there's no atom called **y** because **y** was never defined as an atom. If at one time you had assigned a value to **y** using the **setq** function and then later set the value of **y** to **nil** then the atom called **y** would still exist in the computer's memory.

** If, at a later time, you wanted the value of 2 + 4, you could say (EVAL X) and then the List Evaluater would evaluate the list that is bound to the atom **x**.

SOME RULES ABOUT CONSTRUCTING LISTS

In LISP, a list can either be part of the program or data to be operated on by the program. The same list can even be data and part of the program simultaneously. Certain rules, however, must be observed to properly operate lists when you construct them for a LISP program.

Atoms within lists and lists should always be separated by one or more spaces.

The first atom of any list that may be evaluated must be the name of a valid function.* The list

```
(1 2 3 4 5)
```

will not evaluate unless there is a function called **1**. On the other hand, the list:

```
(+ 1 2 3 4 5)
```

will evaluate to **15**, but it's still a useless list, because the result of this evaluation hasn't been passed to either an atom or another list for further evaluation, as it has in the following two examples:

```
(setq answer (+ 1 2 3 4 5))
```


```
(setq answer (* 10 (+ 1 2 3 4 5)))
```

which brings us to the next rule.

You must always pass the result of a function evaluation to be the argument of another function or to an atom, unless the purpose of the evaluated function is its side effect.

---

* Either the name of a built-in function or a function that has been previously defined by **defun**.

What is a side effect? Common LISP doesn't have side effects. You normally pass arguments to a function such as **(setq c (+ a b))** and the result of evaluating that function is returned.

AutoLISP has many functions that are evaluated solely for their side effects and the result of the evaluation is often ignored. For example, when the function

```
(command "line" pt1 pt2 "")
```

is evaluated, the purpose is to invoke the AutoCAD command processor to draw a line between **pt1** and **pt2**—that's the side effect of the function called **command**. However, the result returned by this function (**nil**) is always ignored.[*]

If you don't want a list to be evaluated, quote the whole list and then **setq** that quoted list to an atom such as:

```
(setq ylist '(89 121))
```

so that when you want to look at that list, it has been defined as **ylist**.

That's really all you need to know about the structure and syntax of LISP and AutoLISP. The only other important thing to know about AutoLISP is how the various built-in functions work and how to write your own functions to solve your particular application problems.

---

[*] To better illustrate a side effect, think of your digestive system as a LISP function. The raw material your digestive system operates on is food (the arguments passed to the function). The direct result produced by the function of your system digesting this food and converting it into energy is waste (the value of which is **nil**). The side effect of this function, however, is to produce the energy to operate your body.

PRACTICAL TIPS ON USING AUTOLISP'S BUILT-IN FUNCTIONS

This section features practical exercises on using some of the more common AutoLISP functions. You should follow along by typing in these examples on AutoCAD's **Command** line so you can see the actual results. You're encouraged to experiment with the structure and variables to see what other kinds of results are possible with some of these functions.

The first thing to do is to **setq** the values to a few atoms so that we can use the values bound to those atoms instead of having to retype them each time. These atoms will be reused for the rest of the examples in this section. Type the following line at the **Command** line:

Type: `(setq a 1.0 b 2.0 c 3.0 d 4.0 e 5.0) <RETURN>`

Response: `(1.0 2.0 3.0 4.0 5.0)`

You'll notice that here we've set the value of several atoms with one **setq** function. Many of the built-in AutoLISP functions, such as **setq** and most of the arithmetic functions, allow the use of multiple arguments.

The advantage of **setq**ing several atoms with one function call is that it's much faster for the List Evaluater to evaluate five pairs of arguments in one function call than to evaluate five separate function calls.

Now let's explore how some of those functions function!

ARITHMETIC FUNCTIONS

AutoLISP has many built-in math functions, and in this section you'll play with some of the basic arithmetic functions, such as add, subtract, multiply and divide.

In math, there are basically three kinds of mathematical notation:

1. Algebraic or infix notation, the one we learned in high school algebra, in which the operator symbol is in the middle of the expression (i.e., 2+2).

2. Postfix notation, in which operator symbol appears at the end of the expression (i.e., 2 2 +), as used in Hewlett-Packard calculators and Forth.

3. Prefix notation, in which the operator appears at the beginning of the expression: (+ 2 2). LISP appears to use prefix notation in its math operations, but the math symbol is merely the name of the function called when that particular list is evaluated, as it is the first element in the list. Keeping this fact in mind, you'll see how easy it is to set up complex math formulas in LISP. Take this simple list to evaluate:

Type: (+ 2 4) <RETURN>

Response: 6

If you think like the List Evaluater, you'll say "ADD to 2 the value of 4," or if you use the atoms that you've previously **setq**ed, the list will read:

Type: (+ b d)

Response: 6

or "ADD to the value of **b** (**2**) the value of **d** (**4**)." With all the arithmetic functions, we can pass an almost unlimited number of arguments and the List Evaluater will evaluate all the atoms down to a single result. For instance, the following list:

Type: (+ a b c d e)

Response: 15

will be evaluated as "ADD to the value of **a** the value of **b** and to that result ADD the value of **c** and keep repeating that until there are no more arguments in the list."
    The SUBTRACT function operates the same way:

Type: (− e a)

Response: 4

The List Evaluater says "SUBTRACT from the value of **e** (5) the value of **a** (1)" and returns the result of 4. More complex subtraction is evaluated the same way:

Type: (- e a b a)

Response: 1

The List Evaluater says "SUBTRACT from the value of **e** (5) the value of **a** (1) and then from that result SUBTRACT the value of **b** (2) and keep repeating that until there are no more arguments."

If only one argument is given to the SUBTRACT function, it will subtract the value of that argument from **0**:

Type: (- e)

Response: -5

"SUBTRACT the value of **e** from **0**" will return a **-5**.

MULTIPLICATION and DIVISION functions are evaluated in exactly the same way:

Type: (* e c)

Response: 15

"MULTIPLY the value of **e** (5) by the value of **c** (3)."

Type: (* e c d b)

Response: 120

"MULTIPLY the value of **e** (5) by the value of **c** (3) and MULTIPLY that result by the value of **d** (4) and keep repeating that until there are no more arguments in the list."

Type: (/ e b)

Response: 2.5

"DIVIDE the value of **e** (5) by the value of **b** (2)"

Can you evaluate the following list by yourself?

Practice: (/ e b d c)

Hint: the answer is 0.20833.

Now, let's try playing List Evaluater and evaluate more complex lists. Remember, you always evaluate the most deeply nested list first (See if you can figure out this one before you type it in):

```
(setq answer (- (* (/ e b c) (* c a e) b)
  c (+ e d c b a)))
```

Evaluate the deepest level of sublists and you get this:

```
(setq answer (- (* 0.833333 15 2) 3 15))
```

Evaluate the next level of lists for this:

```
(setq answer (- 25 3 15))
```

LIST MANIPULATING FUNCTIONS

This section briefly explains how several important list manipulation functions work, and then shows how those functions can be used to build and access a database made up of lists.

As mentioned earlier, a list can either represent a program or data. Because this book is about linking AutoCAD with databases, we'll be concerned mostly with lists as data or databases in this section.

TAKING THINGS APART WITH CAR AND CDR

Car and **cdr** are LISP functions that take apart a list. **car** will return the first element of any list to which it's applied:

Type: (car '(furniture (chairs tables)))

Response: `furniture`

   Type: `(car '((chairs tables) furniture))`

Response: `(chairs tables)`

   cdr will return *all but* the first element of a list:

   Type: `(cdr '(furniture (chairs tables)))`

Response: `((chairs tables))`

   Type: `(cdr '((chairs tables) furniture))`

Response: `(furniture)`

   You can also combine **car** and **cdr** to extract other elements of a list:

   Type: `(car (cdr '(furniture (chairs tables))))`

Response: `chairs`

   Many other functions related to **car** and **cdr** will extract other elements of a list.
   For example, the function **cadr** will extract the second element of a list:

   Type: `(cadr '(furniture tables chairs))`

Response: `tables`

   There are actually a ridiculous number of functions, such as **caadr, caaadr, caaaadr, caddr, cadddr, caddddr,** for extracting various elements of a list. Those can be dangerous functions to use, because many times in LISP you may not know the exact order of the elements of a complex list and you can end up extracting the wrong element. It's been found that by only using the functions **car, cdr** and sometimes **cadr,** you can do an adequate job of taking a list apart.

LAST

Last is a handy function, because it will return the last element in a list, as in:

Type: `(last '(furniture tables chairs))`

Response: `chairs.`

Last is not used for disassembling a list because there isn't a corresponding function that will return *all but the last* element of a list.

REVERSE

Reverse will return the list in reverse order:

Type: `(reverse '(furniture tables chairs))`

Response: `(chairs tables furniture).`

PUTTING THINGS TOGETHER WITH LIST, APPEND AND CONS

Now that you know how to take lists apart with **car** and **cadr**, let's learn how you can make lists with **list**, **append** and **cons**. Each of those functions will return a different type of list, so it's important to know the difference in how each of them operates. Many hours have been wasted trying to track down a problem in a LISP function, only to find that the wrong function had been used to build a list.

These explanations and words of caution should save you at least a few sleepless nights. Try typing these examples, along with your own variations, into AutoCAD's **Command** line so you can see the results yourself.

The first thing you'll do is **setq** some variables to use in the following examples:

Type: `(setq fruit '(apples oranges))`

Response: `(apples oranges)`

Type: `(setq vegetables '(carrots peas))`

Response: `(carrots peas)`

Type: `(setq nuts '(walnuts almonds))`

Response: `(walnuts almonds)`

LIST

The **list** function will take any number of elements (either atoms and/or lists) and string them together into one list. For example:

Type: `(list fruit nuts)`

Response: `((apples oranges) (walnuts almonds))`

Type: `(list 'fruit 'nuts)`

Response: `(fruit nuts)`

Type: `(list fruit 'fruit)`

Response: `((apples oranges) fruit)`

If you want to get fancy and create a list that contains apples and peas, all you have to do is:

Type: `(list (car fruit) (cadr vegetables))`

Response: `(apples peas)`

This list contains the first element (**car**) of the list bound to the atom fruit and the second element (**cadr**) of the list bound to the atom vegetables.

What do the following lists return?

`(list 'fruit (car fruit) (cadr fruit))`

```
(list (car vegetables) (cdr nuts))

(list (cadr fruit) '(car nuts))

(list (list 'fruit (car fruit) (cadr fruit))

(list 'vegetables (car vegetables) (cdr
   vegetables)) (list 'nuts (car nuts)
   (cadr nuts))
```

APPEND

The **append** function takes only lists as arguments and strings the elements of those lists together as in the following examples:

Type: `(append fruit nuts)`

Response: `(apples oranges walnuts almonds)`

Here, you make a list using **list**:

Type: `(setq newlist (list fruit nuts))`

Response: `(fruits nuts)`

Then use **append** to append **newlist** to **vegetables**:

Type: `(append newlist vegetables)`

Response: `((apples oranges) (walnuts almonds) carrots peas)`

As you can see from the above example, **append** will only go one level deep into a list. That is, it will only strip off the top level of parentheses of each list before appending the lists together into a new list.

If you want a simple list that just contains the six atoms, do this:

Type: (append fruit nuts vegetables)

Response: (apples oranges walnuts almonds carrots peas).

CONS

The function **cons** is short for **cons**truct. **Cons** will add a new element (atom or list) to the front of a list—one element at a time. For example:

Type: (cons fruit nuts)

Response: ((apples oranges) walnuts almonds)

or

Type: (cons 'vegetables vegetables)

Response: (vegetables carrots peas)

Cons will only accept two arguments—the new first element and the list to which it will be added. Notice that unlike **list** and **append**, **cons** doesn't create a new list. That's very important when you want to create a list while in a loop, as shown in the following example (see also the complete example on page 98).

Say you want to create a loop that will execute ten times, and each time the loop executes you want to add a number to a list called **numberlist**. Starting with the number **1**, each number in the list will be twice as big as the previous number. The result of this function will be a list that looks like this:

(512 256 128 64 32 16 8 4 2 1)

Start out by defining **numberlist** as an empty or **nil** list:

(setq numberlist ())

Now set a counter variable to **1** for the first pass in the loop:

(setq count 1)

Then set up the loop to **repeat** ten times:

```
(repeat 10
```

The first thing to do in the loop is to **cons** the value of the atom **count** to the list **numberlist**:

```
(setq numberlist (cons count numberlist))
```

Now double the value of the atom **count**:

```
(setq count (* count 2))
```

Finally, close the loop with a closing parenthesis to balance the open one in front of the function **repeat**:

```
)
```

The **numberlist** will look like this the first four times the loop repeats:

```
1.   (1)
2.   (2 1)
3.   (4 2 1)
4.   (8 4 2 1)
```

And so on...

THE DIFFERENCES BETWEEN LIST, APPEND AND CONS

List, **append**, and **cons** build lists in different ways, and unless you clearly understand the differences between those functions, you'll have difficulty in writing code that will build and manipulate lists in a predictable way.

The next example illustrates a function that's too long to type on the AutoCAD **Command** line; now is a good time to learn how to save, load and call LISP functions.

Type the following function in a text editor in a non-document mode:

```
(defun makelist ()
  (setq numberlist ())
  (setq count 1)
  (repeat 10
    (setq numberlist (cons count numberlist))
    (setq count (* count 2))
    (print numberlist)
  )
)
```

Next, save this file in your AutoCAD subdirectory under the filename **MAKELIST.LSP**.

Enter the AutoCAD drawing editor, and at the **Command** line:

Type: `(load "makelist")` <RETURN>

Response: `MAKELIST`

If you've correctly typed in this function, AutoCAD will print **MAKELIST** on the next line, which means your function has properly loaded. To call and execute this function:

Type: `(makelist)` <RETURN>

Response: **Numberlist** should print ten times rapidly on the screen, growing longer each time. That means the loop is executing properly. When **numberlist** stops flashing it should read:

`(512 256 128 64 32 16 8 4 2 1)`

This is a simple list of ten atoms.

If you substituted the line:

`(setq numberlist (list count numberlist))`

for:

`(setq numberlist (cons count numberlist))`

in our **makelist** function, **numberlist** would look like this:

```
(512 (256 (128 (64 (32 (16 (8 (4 (2 (1
   ())))))))))
```

That would be a difficult list to manipulate.

If you substituted the line:

```
(setq numberlist (append count numberlist))
```

you would get an error message because **append** can only append a list to another list, and you've tried to append an atom called count to the list.

If, however, you add a line before the **append** function to change the atom count to a list, then the function will work:

```
(setq countlist (list count))
(setq numberlist (append countlist
   numberlist))
```

Now **numberlist** will look like this:

```
(512 256 128 64 32 16 8 4 2 1)
```

Exactly the same form of list you used with **cons** in the first example.

And finally, if you **cons countlist** to **numberlist** in the example, **numberlist** will look like this:

```
((512) (256) (128) (64) (32) (16) (8) (4) (2)
   (1))
```

Now you know how to take apart and build lists. What's the point of all of this? Because all the data you'll be gathering, manipulating and changing will be contained in lists of various types, you must have a good grasp of how those lists are constructed. Then you'll be able to write AutoLISP code that can access and manipulate the information.

ASSOCIATION LISTS AND ASSOC

An association list is a list structured so that it can be accessed by the **assoc** function. Let's play with the association list:

Type: `(setq food '((fruit apples oranges)`
`     (vegetables carrots peas) (nuts walnuts`
`     almonds)))`

Response: `((fruit apples oranges) (vegetables carrots`
`     peas) (nuts walnuts almonds))`

Let's examine the structure of the list. The whole association list is **setq**ed to the atom called **food**, consisting of three sublists, each containing three atoms. The first atom in each sublist is called the *key* or *index*, and in this particular association list, the second and third atoms in each sublist relate to the first atom. Apples and oranges are fruits; carrots and peas are vegetables; and walnuts and almonds are nuts.

Type: `(assoc 'fruit food)`

Response: `(fruit apples oranges)`

If you want to just retrieve the data in the association list:

Type: `(cdr (assoc 'fruit food))`

Response: `(apples oranges)`

Think of the association list as a database and each of the sublists as individual records in that database. The first atom in the sublist would be that record's index and any other atoms that follow the index atom in that sublist would be individual data fields.

That's exactly how AutoCAD's drawing database is structured. Each drawing entity, whether it be a **LINE**, **ARC**, **CIRCLE**, **TEXT** or **BLOCK**, is structured as an association list that, in turn, is indexed by an entity name.

SUMMARY

This chapter covered a lot of new territory. You've discovered the power of using AutoLISP for customizing AutoCAD applications, You learned the basic underlying principles of LISP and AutoLISP, and how LISP functions work. You actually used some of the built-in AutoLISP functions, and put lists together and took them apart. You added and extracted data from a list, and began to write and execute AutoLISP programs.

In the next chapter, you'll look at the structure of AutoCAD's database and how it relates to AutoLISP. You'll also learn how to write some simple practical programs that allow you to extract and organize meaningful information about your drawings.

chapter 6 THE DRAWING DATABASE AND AUTOLISP

IN THIS CHAPTER

In Chapter 5, you learned the basic concepts of AutoLISP and gained some hands-on experience in how it actually works. This chapter will give you an overview of how the AutoCAD drawing database is constructed and how to write simple AutoLISP routines to extract usable information from that data. You'll also expand your knowledge on how some of the more advanced AutoLISP functions work, and how you can take a simple AutoLISP function and expand it into a very useful application. So let's get started.

ANOTHER LOOK AT AUTOCAD'S DATABASE STRUCTURE

To see what an association list for an AutoCAD drawing entity looks like, you'll do the same exercise used in Chapter 2, but this time in a new context. Enter the AutoCAD drawing editor and draw one line from **1,4** to **6,6**. Press the **F1** key to put the screen into the text mode. Then, at the **Command** prompt:

Type: `(setq a (entget (entlast)))`.

AutoCAD should return with a list that looks like this:

Response: `((-1 . <Entity name : 60000014>) (0 . "LINE")`
`(8 . "0") (10 1.000000 4.000000) (11 6.000000`
`6.000000))`

This is an association list that contains five sublists and each sublist contains three atoms. The first atom in each sublist is called a *Group Code*. Each item of information about a drawing entity has its own unique Group Code. For example, the Group Code for entity type is **0** and the code for layer name is **8**.

You may notice in some of the sublists that the second atom is only a dot ".". The second and third atoms in those lists are known as dotted pairs. All you need to know about a dotted pair is that the dot only acts as a place holder, and when you access a sublist with a dotted pair like this:

Type: `(cdr (assoc '0 (entget e)))`

Response: `"LINE"`

only the atom **line** is returned.

What it all means:

(-1 . <Entity name: 60000014>)

This is the ENTITY NAME. It has a Group Code of **-1** and it's the unique index number for this drawing entity. The functions **entnext** and **entlast** will retrieve this number from the drawing database.

(0 . "LINE")

This is the ENTITY TYPE, in this case a line. Entity type has a Group Code of **0**.

(8 . "0")

This is the name of the **layer** on which the entity was drawn, in this case Layer **0**. Layer name has a Group Code of **8**.

(10 1.000000 4.000000)

This is the absolute **X Y** coordinate of the starting point of the line and has a Group Code of **10**.

(11 6.000000 6.000000)

This is the absolute **X Y** coordinate of the ending point of the line and has a Group Code of **11**.

The size of the entity association list will vary depending on the type of entity it describes.

Appendix C in the *AutoCAD Reference Manual* describes all the Group Codes assigned to different entity types. Those are the same numbers used as keys in the entity association list. Appendices A and B in this book offer complete, fully commented drawing databases with all the Group Codes, showing where they go and what they mean.

Here's a simple AutoLISP function that will list all the entity association lists in a drawing:

```
(defun c:entlst ()
  (setq e (entnext))    ;sets e to the first entity name
  (while e               ;loop as long as there are entities
    (print (entget e))    ;print the entity list
    (terpri)              ;new line
  (setq e (entnext e))    ;set e to next entity
  )
)
```

If you like, you can press **Control Q** to turn on the printer echo so you can print the drawing database to study its structure.

The AutoLISP program, **c:entlst**, is a basic loop structure that will look at every item in the drawing database. By inserting certain control statements in the middle of this loop structure, you can cause the program to look only for drawing entities that meet certain criteria.

For example, the following function called **blkcnt** will count the total number of blocks that have been inserted into a drawing.

Type the following function into your favorite text editor (ignoring any line that starts with a semicolon) and save it with the filename **BLKCNT.LSP**.

```
(defun blkcnt ()
;Resets the counter variable to 0.
   (setq cnt 0)
;Set E to the first entity in the drawing database
   (setq e (entnext))
;Begin the loop that looks at every drawing Entity
   (while e
;Set ENTTYP to the entity type of the current entity.
      (setq enttyp (cdr (assoc 0 (entget e))))
;If the current entity is a block INSERT then
      (if (equal enttyp "INSERT")
;Add one to the counter variable.
         (setq cnt (1+ cnt))
      )
;Set E to the value of the next entity in the database.
      (setq e (entnext e))
;Continue with the loop until there are no more entities.
   )
;After all of the entities have been looked at, print the
;total number of block insertions found in the drawing
   (princ "\nThere are ") (princ cnt)
   (princ " blocks in this drawing")
)
```

The function **blkcnt** has the same loop structure as the function **c:entlst**. However, their primary difference can be found in the conditional structure inside the loop, which states that if the entity type (Group Code 0) is named "INSERT," to count that entity as an inserted block and to add one to the counter variable. A simple routine at the end of the function prints out the total of **cnt** after that function has gone through the whole drawing database.

Now try running **blkcnt** on any drawing file containing blocks that you have by loading your desired drawing file and:

Type: (load "blkcnt") <RETURN>

Response: BLKCNT

Type: (blkcnt) <RETURN>

The function **blkcnt** can be further refined to only count blocks with a certain name. **blkcnt1** will only count blocks named **desk**. To use this example, you must have some blocks named **desk** in your drawing file. You could change the word **desk** in this function to the name of another block.

```
(defun blkcnt1 ()
   (setq cnt 0)
   (setq e (entnext))
   (while e
;Set blknm to the value of Group Code 2 for the current entity.
      (setq blknm (cdr (assoc 2 (entget e))))
      (setq enttyp (cdr (assoc 0 (entget e))))
;If entity type is INSERT and if the block name is desk
;for the current entity then
      (if (and (equal enttyp "INSERT")
            (equal blknm "DESK"))
;Add 1 to the counter variable.
         (setq cnt (1+ cnt))
      )
      (setq e (entnext e))
   )
   (princ "\nThere are ") (princ cnt)
   (princ " desks in this drawing")
)
```

The only change in this function is that now the entity type has to equal **insert** and the block name has to equal **desk** before the counter is incremented.

You could refine this function even more, and have it prompt you for the name of the block to count:

```
(defun blkcnt1a ()
  (setq cnt 0)
;String input with prompt for the name of the block.
  (setq blk (getstring "\nName of the block to
count: "))
;The function strcase turns a string into all upper case
;letters.  That ensures that you'll be matching an upper case
;word to an upper case block name in the database
  (setq blk2 (strcase blk))
  (setq e (entnext))
  (while e
    (setq blknm (cdr (assoc 2 (entget e))))
    (setq enttyp (cdr (assoc 0 (entget e))))
    (if (and (equal enttyp "INSERT")
         (equal blknm blk2))
      (setq cnt (1+ cnt))
    )
    (setq e (entnext e))
  )
  (princ "\nThere are ") (princ cnt)
  (princ " ") (princ blk)
  (princ "s in this drawing")
)
```

When you run that version of **blkcnt1**, you'll first be asked for the name of the block you wish to count in the drawing.

Suppose you want to count both desks and chairs in a drawing. All you need are a separate counter for desks, a separate counter for chairs, and another **IF** statement to look for chairs, as in the function **blkcnt2**:

```
(defun blkcnt2 ()
;Set counter for desk to 0
  (setq deskcnt 0)
;Set counter for chair to 0
  (setq chrcnt 0)
  (setq e (entnext))
  (while e
    (setq blknm (cdr (assoc 2 (entget e))))
    (setq enttyp (cdr (assoc 0 (entget e))))
;If the current entity is a block insertion, and it's a desk then
    (if (and (equal enttyp "INSERT")
         (equal blknm "DESK"))
;Add one to the desk counter.
      (setq deskcnt (1+ deskcnt))
    )
;If the current entity is a block insertion, and it's a chair then
    (if (and (equal enttyp "INSERT")
         (equal blknm "CHAIR"))
;Add one to the chair counter.
      (setq chrcnt (1+ chrcnt))
    )
    (setq e (entnext e))
  )
;Print the total number of desks and chairs to the screen
  (princ "\nThere are ") (princ deskcnt)
  (princ " desks and ") (princ chrcnt)
  (princ " chairs in this drawing")
)
```

You can set up any type of conditional statement to look for almost any type of entity in a drawing file. Using the structure presented here, you could even write a function that would delete all lines on Layer 53 that are less than 2" long.

The last example is a program that automatically writes out all the inserted blocks to the hard disk as drawing files, first checking to make sure the file isn't already there. That program performs many error trapping functions and even writes files to disk that list which drawing files were copied and which blocks were duplicates of drawings already on the hard disk.*

Blkwrite is significant because it demonstrates a fairly large, complex and complete AutoLISP program with several interesting programming techniques. The first technique checks your disk to see if a particular file exists:

```
(if (equal (setq l (open (strcat
      blkname ".dwg") "r")) nil)
   (<WRITES THE BLOCK>)
   (<DISPLAY MESSAGE THAT FILE EXISTS>)
)
```

The second routine will only accept certain characters from the keyboard for user input:

```
(setq a nil)
;creates lists of acceptable character codes
;these can be any ASCII codes that you desire.
;This list is for codes for RETURN button on
;cursor, RETURN on keyboard, space, N, Y,
;n and y.  One of these keys must be
;pressed to end the loop.
(setq ynlst '(0 13 32 78 89 110 121))
;If a key in this list is pressed, then
;the user has indicated a desire to continue
;with the routine.
(setq ylst '(0 13 32 89 121))
(terpri)
(prompt"\nDo you wish to write the block
      list out to a file?<Y>: ")
```

---

*   With the release of AutoCAD Version 2.6, which allows you to directly search the BLOCKS section of the drawing database, we've developed a simpler and faster version of **blkwrite** you'll find in the optional AutoCAD Database Diskette. The version of **blkwrite** presented here is still useful because it illustrates many important techniques for searching through the drawing database.

```
;this loop will continue until an acceptable key,
;listed in ynlst, is pressed
  (while (equal (member a ynlst) nil)
    (setq a (last (grread)))
  )
;If any key in ynlst is pressed, then the loop will end.
  (if (member a ylst)
;if Y or space or <RETURN> is pressed, then the
;next function will be called
    (<CALL NEXT FUNCTION>)
  )
```

You should find this last routine particularly valuable. This is a technique for displaying a default value with the user prompt. AutoCAD will accept that displayed default value if you press **<RETURN>** without entering anything. That default routine looks like this:

```
(setq fname (getvar "dwgname"))
(princ "\nEnter file name <")
(princ fname) (setq fname (getstring ">: "))
(cond ((equal fname "") (setq fname
    (getvar "dwgname"))))
```

INTRODUCTION TO BLKWRITE

This routine searches a drawing file for all **INSERTED** blocks and writes them out to a disk file if a drawing file of the same name doesn't already exist. A list of all the blocks written to disk will be generated and written to a disk file— with the same filename as the drawing file with the extension **.BLK**. If any duplicate filenames appear, another file will be written that lists all blocks in the drawing file that were *not* written to disk due to name duplication. That file will have the extension **.BEX**.

```
(defun C:blkwrite ( / e blocklist blkcnt a
       ynlst ylst l excptlist)
;finds the first entity in the database
   (setq e (entnext))
   (setq blocklist () excptlist () blkcnt 0)
;begins the search loop through the database
   (while e
;finds the name of the current entity
      (setq blkname (cdr (assoc 2 (entget e))))
```
;The body of this program is inside this conditional
;statement.   It will only execute if all of the following
;conditions are true for the current entity: 1. It is a block
;insertion.   2. The block hasn't been saved before.   3.
;The block isn't an "anonymous" block such as a hatch
;pattern.   4. A drawing doesn't exist on the hard disk
;with the same name as the block.

```
      (cond
        (
         (and
;Is current entity a block insertion?
          (equal (cdr (assoc 0 (entget e)))
             "INSERT")
;has current entity been saved before?
          (equal (member blkname blocklist) nil)
          (equal (member blkname excptlist) nil)
;is current entity an "anonymous" block?
          (not (equal (substr blkname 1 1) "*")))
;does a drawing file exist with the same name as the
;current entity?
          (if (equal (setq l (open (strcat
             blkname ".dwg") "r")) nil)
            (progn
;if all conditions are met, write the block to the hard disk
             (command "wblock" blkname blkname)
;add the block name to the blocklist
             (setq blocklist (cons blkname
                 blocklist))
             (terpri)
;increment the number of blocks saved and
             (setq blkcnt (1+ blkcnt))
```

```
;Display message to screen
                (princ "Block ") (princ blkname)
                (princ " written to disk")
            )
            (progn
;if drawing file already exists on disk, display message and
                (princ "\nDrawing file ")
                (princ blkname)
                (princ " already exists...")
                (close 1)
;add the name of the block to the exception list
                (setq excptlist (cons blkname
                    excptlist))
            )
          )
        )
      )
;go to next entity
      (setq e (entnext e))
    )
```

;The code in this section will only accept **Y**, **N**, space
;or **<RETURN>** from the keyboard. If **Y** or space or
;**<RETURN>** is pressed, the program continues. If **N** is
;pressed, then the program ends. This illustrates a
;good technique for error trapping data entry.

```
    (setq a nil)
```

;creates lists of acceptable character codes

```
    (setq ynlst '(0 13 32 78 89 110 121))
    (setq ylst '(0 13 32 89 121))
    (terpri)
```

;Displays the total number of blocks written to the disk

```
    (princ "A total of " ) (princ blkcnt)
    (princ " blocks were written to disk from
   this drawing file.")
    (prompt"\nDo you wish to write the block
        list out to a file?<Y>: ")
```

;this loop will continue until an acceptable key is pressed

```
    (while (equal (member a ynlst) nil)
      (setq a (last (grread)))
    )
    (if (member a ylst)
```

;if **Y** or space or **<RETURN>** is pressed, then the function

```
;named wrtlist is called
     (wrtlist blocklist excptlist)
  )
  (terpri)
  (gc)
)
;End of main function

;Start of function that will write the block lists
(defun wrtlist (blocklist excptlist /
        blkfilename f g h excptfilename)
;reverses the lists so they'll be in the order the
;blocks were written
  (setq blocklist (reverse blocklist))
  (setq excptlist (reverse excptlist))
;this routine allows you to enter any filename for the block
;list file, with the default name the same as the current
;drawing name.  This is a good example of how to set
;default values and have them appear on the prompt line.
  (setq fname (getvar "dwgname"))
  (princ "\nEnter file name <")
  (princ fname) (setq fname (getstring ">: "))
  (cond ((equal fname "") (setq fname
      (getvar "dwgname")))))
  (setq blkfilename (strcat fname ".blk"))
;if the block filename doesn't already exist, then
  (if (equal (setq g (open blkfilename "r"))
       nil)
;this section writes the .BLK file.  This is how to write a
;text file with AutoLISP.
    (progn
      (setq f (open blkfilename "w"))
      (print "Blocks written to disk from
          drawing file " f)
      (princ (getvar "dwgname") f)
      (while blocklist
        (print (car blocklist) f)
        (setq blocklist (cdr blocklist))
      )
      (close f)
;this section writes the .BEX exception file
        (cond ((not (equal excptlist nil))
```

```
            (setq excptfilename (strcat
                fname ".bex"))
            (setq h (open excptfilename "w"))
            (print"Duplicate file name on disk for
                these blocks from " h)
            (princ (getvar "dwgname") h)
            (while excptlist
              (print (car excptlist) h)
              (setq excptlist (cdr excptlist))
            )
            (close h))
        )
    )
```
;if a **.BLK** file exists with the chosen filename, then a
;message is displayed and this **function** will then call itself
;to give the user a chance to enter a new filename.
;This is called recursion.
```
    (progn
        (close g)
        (princ "\nThis filename already exists,
            please redo")
        (terpri)
        (wrtlist blocklist excptlist)
    )
    )
)
```
;end of the block file list writing function

SUMMARY

In this chapter, you learned how AutoCAD's drawing database is structured and how to write programs in AutoLISP that can extract meaningful data from the drawing database. You've also modified and expanded a simple AutoLISP function to extract different types of information from the drawing database. You've learned what a more complex AutoLISP program looks like and how to add error trapping and user interface routines to your AutoLISP applications.

In Chapter 7, you'll examine the drawing database in even more detail, and learn exactly how attributes are linked to blocks in the drawing. You'll learn how to extract attribute information from your drawings with AutoLISP. Finally, you'll see some practical examples of how AutoLISP drawing database programs are used in the real world.

chapter 7 UNDERSTANDING THE DRAWING DATABASE

IN THIS CHAPTER

In the last two chapters, you explored some of the basic principles of AutoLISP and learned how to access the drawing database. In this chapter, you'll examine AutoCAD's database structure in more detail and see just how powerful AutoLISP can be when it comes to extracting all types of information from an AutoCAD drawing database.

You'll learn more about how some of the advanced AutoLISP functions work, and you'll use those functions in writing your own database extraction routines. In addition, you'll see how AutoLISP can be used in many different day-to-day applications.

Finally, you'll begin to write some advanced AutoLISP code to utilize some of those concepts in real world applications.

THE DRAWING DATABASE CONCEPT

In Chapter 6, you took a look at AutoCAD's drawing database when you ran the function **entlst**. What you saw was a database description of a drawing formatted as a LISP association list. What does that mean? To answer that, let's define some terms.

As explained in Chapter 2, a database is simply a collection of information about a related subject organized in a way that's accessible to the user. Let's look again at the conceptual drawing database in more detail.

A drawing database is structured exactly the same way as any other database. Its purpose is to describe a drawing in a non-graphic way. A drawing database file is made up of records of alphanumeric descriptions called *drawing primitives* (AutoCAD calls these *drawing entities*).

A drawing primitive is a basic shape or form used in a drawing. **LINE**, **ARC**, **CIRCLE**, **POINT** and **TEXT** are all examples of drawing primitives.

When you draw a line in AutoCAD, you're actually calling up a primitive called **LINE** and then defining the starting and ending points of that primitive. AutoCAD then places a description of that primitive in its database, and a graphic representation of that database record is displayed on the screen.

Let's look again at the example of our simplified *hypothetical* drawing database:

```
# <NAME    ><START><END  ><LAYER >
1 LINE        0,0      0,2       0
2 LINE        0,2      2,2       0
3 LINE        2,2      0,2       0
4 LINE        0,2      0,0       0
5 CIRCLE      1,1      1         6
```

That database describes a square 2" on a side with a circle of 1" radius inscribed in the square. Notice how similar the database looks to the mailing list example we showed you in Chapter 2. The only difference between this sample drawing database and AutoCAD's drawing database is that the latter contains more fields.

Now is a good time to look at the AutoCAD drawing database. To do that, get into AutoCAD's drawing editor and:

Draw a square, using the **LINE** command from **0,0** to **0,2** to **2,2** to **0,2**. Finally, type **C <RETURN>** to close the square.

Draw a 1" radius circle with the center of the circle at **1,1**. Well, it looks like the **CHAIR** from Chapter 2.

Now let's load and run our old friend **entlst** from Chapter 6. Press **F1** to flip your screen into the text mode, and:

Type: (load "entlst")

Response: ENTLST

Type: entlst

But, now, when you run **entlst** to look at your drawing database, it doesn't look like our hypothetical example. That's because AutoLISP takes each database record and formats that record into an association list so the record can be used by AutoLISP. If you reorganize the *hypothetical* drawing database records into association lists, they'll look like this:

```
((# . 1) (NAME . "LINE") (START 0 0) (END 0
2) (LAYER . "0"))
((# . 2) (NAME . "LINE") (START 0 2) (END 2
2) (LAYER . "0"))
((# . 3) (NAME . "LINE") (START 2 2) (END 2
0) (LAYER . "0"))
((# . 4) (NAME . "LINE") (START 2 0) (END 0
0) (LAYER . "0"))
((# . 5) (NAME . "CIRCLE") (START 1 1) (RAD .
1) (LAYER . "6"))
```

The actual AutoCAD association list for the first record would be:

```
((-1 . <Entity name: 60000014>) (0 . "LINE")
  (8 . "0")(10 0.000000 0.000000)
  (11 0.000000 2.000000))
```

Now you can begin to see the similarity. At this point, the only difference between our sample and AutoCAD's record for our **CHAIR** drawing is the names for the fields. **#** is **-1**, **NAME** is **0**, **START** is **10**, **END** is **11** and **LAYER** is **8**.

Those numbers are called *Group Codes*. The AutoCAD field names are numbers because they're faster and more efficient to access than names.

By using the **assoc** function (covered in Chapter 5), you can access any field (in this case sublist) in this record. If you wanted to find out what layer this line was on, you would use the Group Code for "layer name" (which is 8) as the association key to extract the layer name from the first record of the drawing database. This is how you would do it:

First, find the name of the first record in the database:

Type: `(setq e (entnext))`

Response: `<Entity name 600000014>`

The AutoLISP function **entnext**, if used without an argument, will retrieve the first record in the database.

Type: `(setq layer (cdr (assoc 8 (entget e))))`

Response: `"0"`

AutoCAD's record database structure is much longer than indicated here because many entity types require more information to describe them than a line does. A complete list and description of all the drawing database's field names or Group Codes can be found in Appendix A.

DXF FILES AND ASSOCIATION LISTS

The structure and manipulation of **DXF** files will be covered in detail in Chapter 9. However, it's important here to point out the similarity between the drawing database association list and the **DXF** file format.

Neither the drawing database association list nor the **DXF** file is the actual AutoCAD drawing database—they're merely specially formatted versions of that database. The actual drawing database is encoded in binary format and is proprietary. You can, however, infer that the actual drawing database is structured quite closely to those file formats.

The **DXF** file format looks quite different than the association list format, but as you can see, they are almost functionally identical. The entities section of a **DXF** file looks like this for the single line example you've been using:[*]

```
ENTITIES      ;Start of entities section
   0          ;Start of entity (entity name follows)
LINE          ;Name of entity
   8          ;Group code for layer (layer name follows)
0             ;Name of layer
  10          ;Start X coordinate follows (Group Code)
0.0           ;Start X coordinate
  20          ;Start Y coordinate follows (Group Code)
0.0           ;Start Y coordinate
  11          ;End X coordinate follows (Group Code)
0.0           ;End X coordinate
  21          ;End Y coordinate follows (Group Code)
2.0           ;End Y coordinate
   0          ;Start of file separator
ENDSEC        ;End of (entities) section
   0          ;Start of file separator
EOF           ;End of file
```

This format is used because the **DXF** file format is primarily designed to be read by another program, and the one line/one field format is the easiest to read from a disk file.

Notice that the entity type and layer field names are the same as in the association list format. Only the **START Y** and **END Y** coordinate fields are new here. Because the association list format can hold the **X Y** coordinates as pairs and **X** and **Y** can be individually addressed by using **car** and **cadr**, there's no need for separate **Y** fields in that format. The **DXF** format is designed to be read by such sequential

---

[*] You can create this **DXF** file yourself by loading your previous drawing example into the AutoCAD drawing editor and typing DXFOUT **RETURN RETURN RETURN**. Now exit the drawing editor and load the **DXF** file into your text editor (the **DXF** file will have the same name as your drawing file with a **.DXF** extension).

file reading statements as **LINE INPUT** in BASIC and **READLN** in Pascal. In addition, an entity name is not generated in the **DXF** file format, because it wasn't expected that a file search would be done on such files.

Now that you have a fundamental grasp of how AutoCAD's drawing database is structured, you'll be shown how to access and modify the drawing database with the help of AutoLISP.

THE PROGRAMMING ENVIRONMENT

If you haven't already done so, read the section in Appendix D about the ACAD.PGP files. It describes how to set up a small text editor so you can write, test, run and edit your AutoLISP programs without ever having to leave the AutoCAD drawing editor. By spending ten minutes or so to set up this facility, you won't have to wait while you load and end AutoCAD just to re-edit your program.

GATHERING INFORMATION

First, take a look at the information you'll be modifying in the AutoCAD database.

Let's make a simple drawing block with attributes. Start a new AutoCAD drawing and make a block that consists of two attributes by following the directions in Chapter 3, pages 22-29. Set the text to be 9" high and centered. The first attribute tag will be **ROOMNO** and should be visible with no default value. The second attribute tag should be **EMPNAME** and also should be visible, but with a default value of **VACANT**. Draw a box around the **ROOMNO** tag and save the block under the name **ROOMTAG**.

INSERT that block into the drawing three times using different room numbers and names. Don't forget to save the sample drawing—you'll use it again in the next chapter.

Turn the printer on, press **Control Q** to turn the printer echo **ON** and load and run the **entlst** AutoLISP function from the last chapter, page 105. Your output should look like this (the following is prettyprinted for legibility):

```
(
(-1 . <Entity name: 600000A0>)  ;Unique ID number
0 . "INSERT")                    ;Entity type (Insert block)
(8 . "0")                        ;Layer Name
(66 . 1)                         ;Attributes follow flag
(2 . "ROOMTAG")                  ;name of this Block
(10 58.000000 129.000000)        ;insertion point for Block
(41 . 1.000000)                  ;X scale factor
(42 . 1.000000)                  ;Y scale factor
(50 . 0.000000)                  ;rotation angle
(43 . 1.000000)                  ;Z scale factor
(70 . 0)                         ;column count for MINSERT
(71 . 0)                         ;row count for MINSERT
(44 . 0.000000)                  ;clmn spacing for MINSERT
(45 . 0.000000)                  ;row spacing for MINSERT
)
```

Attribute records always immediately follow the **INSERT** or block record they're attached to if field **66** (attributes follow flag) has a value of **1**.

```
(
(-1 . <Entity name: 600000B4>)  ;Unique ID number
(0 . "ATTRIB")                   ;Entity type
(8 . "0")                        ;Layer name
(10 20.000000 115.571400)        ;insertion point for text(left)
(40 . 9.000000)                  ;Height for attribute text
(1 . "John Jones")               ;Attribute value
(2 . "EMPNAME")                  ;Attribute tag
(70 . 0)                         ;column count for MINSERT
(73 . 0)                         ;row count for MINSERT
(50 . 0.000000)                  ;Attribute text rotation angle
(41 . 1.000000)                  ;X scale factor for attrib text
(51 . 0.000000)                  ;Obliquing angle for attrib text
(7 . "SIMPLEX")                  ;Text STYLE of attribute[*]
(71 . 0)                         ;Text generation flag (normal)
(72 . 1)                         ;Text Justification type (centered)
```

---

* Not the name of the font file.

```
(11 57.500000 115.571400)  ;alignment point for text
                                          (centered)
)
```

The following list is the second attribute record attached to the block. Because that record is almost identical to the last record, you won't need the comments.

```
(
(-1 . <Entity name: 600000C84>)
(0 . "ATTRIB")
(8 . "0")
(10 46.785710 131.000000)
(40 . 9.000000)
(1 . "100")
(2 . "ROOMNO")
(70 . 0)
(73 . 0)
50 . 0.000000)
(41 . 1.000000)
(51 . 0.000000)
(7 . "SIMPLEX")
(71 . 0)
(72 . 1)
(11 57.500000 131.000000)
)
```

The record **seqend** (or **SEQ**uence **END**) always appears at the end of a linked series of records. The purpose of this record is to signal that the end of a multiple record entity has been reached and also to contain the entity name for the first entity in that series. Currently, only two types of entities consist of more than one record: **BLOCK** or **INSERT** with attached attributes; and **POLYLINES**.

```
(
(-1 . <Entity name: 600000DC>)
(0 . "SEQEND")          ;entity type (SEQuence END)
(8 . "0")               ;layer name
(-2 . <Entity name: 600000A0>);name of first entity
                                      in this series
)
```

ACCESSING THE DRAWING DATABASE WITH AUTOLISP

In Chapter 6, the first AutoLISP program example was a small function called **entlst**. **entlst** demonstrates the basic method that you'll be using to access and list the drawing database with AutoLISP. Let's examine **entlst** in greater detail so we can see what each line does:

```
(defun c:entlst ()
```

Defun is the function **def**ining **func**tion. When the List Evaluater sees **defun** at the beginning of the list, it doesn't evaluate that list. The **defun** list is placed in memory and it's only evaluated when the name of the defined function is called by another function.

c:entlst is the name of this particular function. The **C:** before the function name means this function can be called from the AutoCAD **Command** line as if it were a regular AutoCAD command.* If this function were just called **entlst**, it could only be called from within a list, surrounded by parentheses, like this: **(entlst)**.

```
(setq e (entnext))
```

entnext is an AutoLISP function that will return the name of a drawing entity in the AutoCAD drawing database. **entnext** called without an argument, as in this case, will return the name of the first entity in the database. In this line, the atom **e** is set to the value of the first entity name in the drawing database. If an argument is supplied with **entnext** (the argument must be a valid entity name), **entnext** will return the next entity name in the database after the argument name supplied.

If the end of the database is reached and there are no more entities, **entnext** will return **nil** (or no value).

---

*   Contrary to popular myth, neither the **C:** nor the function
      name has to be typed in upper case letters.

```
(while e
```

while defines a basic while loop. While the atom **e** contains a value, the list that starts with the function **while** will continue to be evaluated. Because **while** will only operate as long as **e** has a value, when the end of the database is reached, the atom **e** will have no value (**nil**) and the **while** loop will no longer be evaluated.

```
(print (entget e))
```

entget retrieves the association list that contains all the information about the entity name represented by the atom **e**. The argument for that function must be the name of a valid entity retrieved by **entnext**.

print simply prints the list **entget e** to the screen.

```
(terpri)
```

terpri stands for **ter**minal **pri**nt, which prints a blank line on the screen. That function is used to increase the readability of the list.

```
(setq e (entnext e))
```

This line sets the value of **e** to the next entity name in the database so you can look at that entity when the **while** loop repeats. As mentioned earlier, the function **entnext**, when called with the name of a drawing entity as an argument, will return the name of the next entity in the database. If there are no more entities in the database, the atom **e** will have no value (or **nil**) and the loop won't continue.

```
    )
  )
```

Those two closing parentheses close the **while** loop and the function definition respectively.

FINDING BLOCKS WITH ATTRIBUTES

You've looked at the data structure of a block with linked attributes, and you've also examined in greater detail how the function **entlst** works. Now you'll modify and expand **entlst** to find only the blocks in the drawing database that have attributes. Remember: if Group Code **66** is set to **1** in an entity record of an INSERT entity type, that means the block has attributes attached.

Here's the new function:

```
(defun findatt ()
;Sets e to the first record in the database
   (setq e (entnext))
;Starts the loop to look at every entity in the database
   (while e
;Sets enttyp to Group 0 (Entity type) and blknm to the
;Block name for current entity
      (setq enttyp (cdr (assoc 0 (entget e))))
      (setq blknm (cdr (assoc 2 (entget e))))
;If current entity is a Block Insertion and the attributes
;follow flag is set then
      (if
        (and
          (equal enttyp "INSERT")
          (equal (cdr (assoc 66 (entget e))) 1)
        )
;The function progn is used here because normally only
;the first "result is true" list is evaluated in the IF function.
;We want every list within the progn function evaluated if
;the result is true.
        (progn
;Print the block name
          (print blknm)
          (terpri)
        )
      )
;Do the loop again if there are more entities.
   (setq e (entnext e))
   )
)
```

If you load and call the function, **findatt**, from within the sample drawing you did earlier in this chapter, you'll see that the name of every block that contains attributes is printed on the screen. **findatt** first looks only for INSERT records that contain the Group Code of **66** set to **1** (the attributes follow flag) then prints the name of the block it finds in that record.

This is interesting, but not very useful. You really would like to see the attribute tags and attribute values for each block. So, how do you do that?

Here's the strategy. When you've found an INSERT record that contains a Group Code of **66** set to **1**, you then know that, at least, the next record contains an attribute linked to that block. In fact, every record between INSERT and **seqend** will be an attribute linked to that block. Now, all you have to do is write a function that steps through and reads every record between INSERT and **seqend**. Again, you can use the basic structure of **entlst** to write this function.

```
(defun attriblst (ent name)
  (while (not (equal name "SEQEND"))
    (if (equal name "ATTRIB")
      (progn
        (setq attag (cdr (assoc 2
            (entget ent))))
        (setq attval (cdr (assoc 1
            (entget ent))))
        (princ "\nThe Value of attribute ")
        (princ attag)
        (princ " is ")
        (princ attval)
        (terpri)
      )
    )
  (setq ent (entnext ent))
    (setq name (cdr (assoc 0 (entget ent))))
  )
  (setq ent ent)
)
```

Now, you must modify **findatt** so it will call **attriblst**. You do that by replacing the line:

```
(print blknm)
```

with:

```
(setq e (attriblst e blknm))
```

and deleting:

```
(terpri)
```

Type both of these functions together in a text editor in a non-document mode and save the file under the name **FIND-ATT.LSP**. To run this function:

Type: (load "findatt") <RETURN>

Response: ATTRIBLST[*]

Type: (findatt)

Response: The value of attribute ROOMNO is 100
The value of attribute EMPNAME is John Jones

and so on.

The function **attriblst** is a little different from the function **findatt**. You could have included the body of this function inside of the loop of **findatt** and achieved the same result, but this is an example of how to pass arguments back and forth between functions.

Following the function name **attriblst** is the sublist:

```
(ent name)
```

---

[*] The name of the last function in the file.

These are the arguments on which this function operates. When you call this function with:

```
(setq e (attriblst e blknm))
```

The atom **ent** takes on the value of the atom **e**, and the atom **name** takes on the value of the atom **blknm**. When the function is finished, it then returns the result of the last list in the function evaluated to the function that called it. In that function, the last list evaluated is:

```
(setq ent ent)
```

The result of that list is returned to **setq e** in the calling function.

PRACTICAL APPLICATIONS

Now you know how to look at any piece of information in an AutoCAD drawing database. What are the practical uses for this? Remember, you now can extract just about any type of information contained in the drawing database. Below are a few ideas of how you can use the programming techniques and tools you've learned.

WALL QUANTITY TAKEOFF

If you wanted to calculate the lineal feet of wall in a building floor plan, you would draw walls, and only walls, on a layer reserved for walls. Call that layer **WALL**. Now, all you have to do is write a function that looks through the drawing database for all **LINE** entities on layer **WALL**; total up their lengths and divide that total by two (because it takes two lines to draw one wall). You could even draw different types of walls on different layers and keep track of the quantity of each wall type by layer.

Here's a simple example of an AutoLISP function that will find the total length of all walls drawn on a layer named **WALL**. This function is based on **entlst**.

```
(defun wallcnt ()
  (setq wlencnt 0)
  (setq e (entnext))
  (while e
    (setq enttyp (cdr (assoc 0 (entget e))))
    (setq layname (cdr (assoc 8 (entget e))))
    (if
      (and
        (equal enttyp "LINE")
        (equal layname "WALL")
      )
      (progn
        (setq stpt (cdr (assoc 10 (entget e))))
        (setq enpt (cdr (assoc 11 (entget e))))
        (setq wlen (distance stpt enpt))
        (setq wlencnt (+ wlen wlencnt))
      )
    )
  (setq e (entnext e))
  )
  (setq wlencnt (/ wlencnt 2)
  (princ "\nThere are ")
  (princ wlencnt)
  (princ " Lineal feet of wall in this drawing")
)
```

A FASTER METHOD OF QUANTITY COUNT

In Chapter 3 you learned how to extract attributes by using the **attext** command, then reading the attribute file into a database program to produce reports. If all you want is a quick count of, say, chips in a particular integrated circuit board, it would be much faster to use the function **blkcnt2** in Chapter 5. The blocks you count by using that method don't even need attributes attached to them.

A QUICKER WAY OF PRODUCING REPORTS

If you were to slightly modify our last function, **findatt**, to write the information line to a disk file instead of to the screen, you would have a simple report of all the attribute tags and their associated values. You can, of course, format the output in different ways. You can write the results of **attriblst** to a disk file by making the functions **attriblst** and **findatt** look like this:

```
(defun findatt ()
;User prompt for filename
   (setq filenm (getstring
       "\nEnter filename for report: "))
;Set the value of F to the filename of the file to be
;written to.  "w" means to open the file in the write mode.
   (setq f (open filenm "w"))
   (setq e (entnext))
   (while e
      (setq enttyp (cdr (assoc 0 (entget e))))
      (setq blknm (cdr (assoc 2 (entget e))))
      (if
        (and
          (equal enttyp "INSERT")
          (equal (cdr (assoc 66 (entget e))) 1)
        )
        (setq e (attriblst e blknm))
      )
   (setq e (entnext e))
   )
;Close the file that you have previously opened.
   (close f)
)


(defun attriblst (ent name)
   (while (not (equal name "SEQEND"))
     (if (equal name "ATTRIB")
       (progn
          (setq attag (cdr (assoc 2
             (entget ent))))
          (setq attval (cdr (assoc 1
             (entget ent))))
;These princ functions have been changed so that they
;will print to file F specified in the file OPEN function
          (princ "\nThe Value of attribute " f)
          (princ attag f)
```

```
        (princ " is " f)
        (princ attval f)
    )
  )
(setq ent (entnext ent))
  (setq name (cdr (assoc 0 (entget ent))))
)
(setq ent ent)
)
```

NEW INFORMATION FROM THE DATABASE

The authors were asked by a geological engineering firm to develop a program that would list all the intersection points for an irregularly spaced grid. We did this by taking each gridline (a **LINE** entity on a layer named **GRID**) and comparing it with every other gridline for an intersection by using the AutoLISP function **inters**. We, then, put each coordinate into a list with **cons** and when the comparison was done, the list was sorted for order using the **min** function. Next, we saved the sorted list to a disk file so it could be processed by another program.

TRACK ENTITIES THAT ARE NOT BLOCKS

In another example, we were asked to develop a program that would check to see if all of the polylines in a drawing were closed properly; if they weren't properly closed, the program was to automatically close them. An example of the program can be found in the AutoCAD Database Diskette.

The applications are almost endless. Every bit of information contained in your drawing is now accessible and can be tracked. You're only limited by your imagination.

In the next chapter, you'll get to the good part—how to change the information in the database by using a powerful function called **subst**; and how to use that function in creating an AutoLISP program that will automatically update your drawings from an outside database.

SUMMARY

By now you should know what a database is, and the similarities and differences between a drawing database and other types of databases. You've examined AutoCAD's drawing database structure in great detail and you've learned how to extract any type of information from the drawing database. You've been exposed to some of the more powerful and advanced AutoLISP functions and to some potential applications for using AutoLISP for extracting data from the drawing database.

chapter 8 MODIFYING THE DRAWING DATABASE

It's one thing to be able to write a program that reads and makes reports based on AutoCAD's drawing information. But actually being able to change that drawing with a program that you wrote is something else again.

In this chapter, you'll learn how to write AutoLISP functions that will actually change the contents of a drawing, based on information that isn't contained in that drawing. With a very powerful AutoLISP function called **subst**, those changes will be made automatically.

You'll also explore the LISP concept of property lists and how they can be used to extend the usefulness and utility of AutoCAD in many different applications.

Finally, you'll be taken step-by-step through an actual AutoLISP programming project recently completed by the authors.

CHANGING THE DATABASE WITH ENTMOD AND SUBST

Subst will **subst**itute one expression (an atom or a list) for another expression in a list. The best way to explain how this function works is to try it:

Type: `(setq a '(fruit apples oranges)) <RETURN>`

Response: `(fruit apples oranges)`

Now:

Type: `(subst 'pears 'oranges a) <RETURN>`

Response: `(fruit apples pears)`

As you can see, **subst** substitutes pears for oranges in the list. If you

Type: `!a`

Response: `(fruit apples oranges)`

you get your original list back. In order to permanently change the list, set the value of the new list like this:

Type: `(setq a (subst 'pears 'oranges a))`

Response: `(fruit apples pears)`

Now

Type: `!a`

Response: `(fruit apples pears)`

You also can use multiple instances of **subst** to substitute expressions at almost any level of nesting in a list. However, it's a bit more complex. Let's try an example:

Type: (setq b '((fruit apples oranges)
           (nuts walnuts almonds)))*

Response: ((fruit apples oranges)
           (nuts walnuts almonds))

Now substitute pears for oranges:

Type: (setq c (subst (subst 'pears 'oranges
           (car b)) (car b) b))

Response: ((fruit apples pears) (nuts walnuts almonds))

This looks a lot more complex than it actually is. Let's examine the list inside out. The inner list:

Type: (subst 'pears 'oranges (car b))

Response: (fruit apples pears)

That's easy enough: you're substituting **pears** for **oranges** in the first sublist (**car**) of list **b**. Now, take the new sublist **(fruit apples pears)**, and substitute it for the old sublist in the main list. Below is the same way of stating this:

Type: (subst '(fruit apples pears) '(fruit apples
oranges) a)

Practice: Using the last example, substitute **cashews** for **almonds**.

Entmod is a special AutoLISP function that is called after an entity is changed with **subst**. **Entmod** simply tells AutoLISP that you've modified a particular entity. You'll see how this is used to modify the drawing database later.

---

* You should type all this on one line at the **Command** prompt. We have broken these lists into two lines because the pages of this book aren't wide enough.

Here's a quick example that will show you graphically how AutoLISP can modify the database. First, draw a line in AutoCAD from **0,0** to **0,40**:

Type: `LINE <RETURN> 0,0 <RETURN> 0,40`
`<RETURN><RETURN>`

Response: A vertical line is drawn.

Be sure you're **ZOOMED** out enough so you can see the whole line, and watch the line as you press **<RETURN>**:

Type: `(entmod (subst (subst 20 40 (assoc 11`
`(entget (entlast)))) (assoc 11`
`(entget (entlast))) (entget (entlast))))`

Response: `((-1 . <Entity name: 60000208>) (0 . "LINE")`
`(8 . 0)(10 0.000000 0.000000)`
`(11 0.000000 20))`[*]

Did you notice how the line was instantly halved in length? Now you have the power to do practically anything you want with your drawing database.

Because this is a book about linking AutoCAD drawing files to outside databases, all the examples concentrate on that result. But, as you've seen in the previous example, it's easy to manipulate the graphic elements, too.

GUIDELINES FOR MODIFYING DRAWING DATABASES

Before you get involved in modifying your drawings with AutoLISP, you should know about certain limitations:

---

[*]   The modified entity association list.

You *can't* add an entity record to the database except at the end of the list and then only by using the **command** function.

- You *can't* change an entity record's type (i.e., you can't change a **LINE** into a **POLYLINE**). You have to delete the desired entity record with **entdel** and then add a new entity to the drawing with the **command** function[*].

- You *can't* change an entity record's **TEXT STYLE**, **LINETYPE**, **SHAPE** or **BLOCK NAME**, unless the definitions you're changing them to exist in the tables section of your drawing. An exception to this rule is the **LAYER NAME**. A desired **LAYER NAME** *does not* have to exist in the table section to be used.

- **entdel** *will not* delete an ATTRIB subentity record linked to an INSERT record nor will it delete a VERTEX subentity record linked to a POLYLINE record. One technique for removing VERTEXes from a POLYLINE involves stepping through the desired POLYLINE record and adding the coordinates of all the vertices bound to a list using **cons**; deleting the undesired VERTEX coordinates from the coordinate list; deleting the old POLYLINE record with **entdel** and then creating a new POLYLINE with the desired vertices with the **command** function.

- You *can't* ADD an ATTRIB subentity record to an INSERT entity record nor can you ADD a new VERTEX to a POLYLINE entity record.

- You *can't* change the ATTRIBUTE TAG in an ATTRIB subentity record, since that tag is a reference to an ATTDEF entity in the blocks section of the drawing database.

---

[*]   This new entity then, of course, will be at the end of the drawing database.

- You *can't* add a field to an entity record if that field *does not* already exist. For example, if an entity did not have an ELEVATION assigned to it (Group Code 38) when it was created, then the Group Code won't even show up as a field in the database—thus you could not change it with subst. You could, however, add an ELEVATION by using the **CHANGE** command with the following form: (COMMAND "CHANGE" <entity name> "" "P" "E" <desired elevation goes here> ""). This is also true for **THICKNESS**, **LINETYPE**, **BYLAYER** and **COLOR BYLAYER**

MODIFYING YOUR DRAWING WITH AN OUTSIDE DATABASE

INTRODUCTION

Throughout the rest of this chapter, you'll go step by step through a programming project which illustrates some of the techniques for developing an AutoLISP program to find and modify specific drawing entities from the drawing database.

You're encouraged to carry out the examples on your own computer. Don't just believe that these functions work—try them out for yourself. You're also encouraged to experiment with the examples. Try different values. How does the illustrated function work on different list structures? Maybe you can rewrite the illustrations to suit your own purposes or to solve your own problems.

THE PROBLEM

A large, growing corporation has a huge office building. And since this is a growing corporation, they find they have to move their employees around within the building quite frequently. They don't do this because they need to keep the people in the personnel and the facility planning departments occupied, and give them a greater sense of importance than they deserve. No, this corporation moves their employees around because it's a company in flux. Change is the only constant. Whole new departments spring from the ground overnight and existing divisions are decimated wholesale to staff these new endeavors. New employees are drafted from the ranks of the competition by press gangs of executive headhunters with large bounties for every warm body procured. For this is a company driven by great hopes to accomplish even greater deeds. Within the walls of this seemingly ordinary corporate headquarters lies the legendary *Raiders of the Lost Market Share*.

The head of the Facilities Department of this large and still un-named corporation has a real problem on his hands. He has a difficult time keeping track of all of the people (not to mention the furniture) in this huge office building. All of the employee location information is kept and maintained in a regular alphanumeric database, but since the people in the Facilities Department are visually oriented, they need a visual way of keeping track of their people (and furniture).

So they decide that the solution to their dilemma is to create an AutoCAD drawing of the building floorplan and INSERT blocks containing the Employee Information Attributes into the floorplan drawing.

This works for awhile, but turns out to not to be the ideal solution. For you see, just as soon as the Facilities Department finishes a floorplan and inserts all of the employees names into the right workstations, the powers-that-be decide that a new department needs to be formed or an old division needs to have new life-blood injected into it.

It just doesn't seem fair. As soon as they have all the right names in the right places on the drawing, Corporate decides that all the people should be moved around to different locations, and the Facilities Department has to spend a lot of time updating their drawings.

The problem is this: when the floorplans were first done in AutoCAD, it was decided to label all of the private offices and open plan workstations with a unique location number and the name of the employee currently occupying that space. Here's how they did it.

First, they made up a block, similar to Figure 1, with two visible attributes. The block was called **ROOMTAG** and the attribute tags were called **ROOMNO** and **EMPNAME**. Next, they inserted the **ROOMTAG** block at every private office and work station, entering at the prompts, the Room (or workstation) Number and employees' name.

Sometimes the information was extracted from the drawing file using the ATTEXT (**att**ribute **ext**ract) command and that data was used in other databases.

It was very difficult to keep the employee location information up-to-date and accurate in the drawing database, and it was not easy to update the employee location information in the drawing.

When employee moves were decided upon, they were usually worked out in advance on a regular database program. Here was one place where all of the employee locations were accurately maintained.

The problem was, that although you could extract alphanumeric database information from an AutoCAD drawing file, there was no easy way to put that database information into an AutoCAD drawing.

THE PROBLEM SUMMARY

The question: Is it possible to take outside database information and use it to update an already existing drawing without having to manually enter every piece of data? The answer: Yes. Here's how it's done:

THE SOLUTION

First, you need a little preparation. Take the sample drawing file you made at the beginning of this chapter, and insert the **ROOMTAG** block five times using room numbers **100**, **110**, **120**, **130**, **140** and **150**. Save the drawing file.

Next, using a text editor in non-document mode, type the following lines exactly as shown (with two spaces between the number and the name):

```
100   JONES
110   SMITH
120   BROWN
130   GREEN
140   MUSTARD
150   SCARLETT
```

Finally, save this file under the filename **TEST.SDF**. That's the sample data file you'll be using to update the roomtags. The file is in a standard Space Delimited File format that can be output by most database and spreadsheet programs.

READING THE DATA FILE

First you need to write a function that will read this data file and format the **SDF** format into an association list. That function might look like this:

```
(defun extfile ()
;Creates an empty list called FILELIST.
   (setq filelist ())
;Opens the test file in the read mode.
   (setq file (open "TEST.SDF" "r"))
;Reads the first line in the file.
   (setq record (read-line file))
;Starts a loop that will continue until the whole file is read.
   (while record
;Sets the value of ROOMNO to the first 3 characters in the line.
      (setq roomno (substr record 1 3))
;Sets the value of EMPNAME to the rest of the line.
      (setq empname (substr record 6))
;Sets the value of RECLIST to a list of ROOMNO and EMPNAME.
      (setq reclist (list roomno empname))
;Adds the list RECLIST to the list FILELIST.
      (setq filelist (cons reclist filelist))
;Reads the next line of the file and
      (setq record (read-line file))
;begins again if there are more lines in the file
   )
;Closes the database file.
   (close file)
)
```

The result of running that function would be an association list that looks like this:

```
(("150" "SCARLETT") ("140" "MUSTARD")
   ("130" "GREEN") ("120" "BROWN")
   ("110" "SMITH") ("100" "JONES"))
```

Now, you'll modify the function **attriblst** so it will build an association list from the blocks and the linked attributes using the **ROOMNO** attribute tag as the key. This function will be called **bldprop** and will look like this:

```
(defun bldprop (e)
;Creates an empty list called dblist.
   (setq dblist ())
;Begin a search loop through all entities from INSERT to
;SEQEND*
   (while (not (equal (cdr (assoc 0
       (entget e))) "SEQEND"))
       (cond
;If attributes follow flag is set, then this entity is INSERT and
        ((cdr (assoc 66 (entget e)))
;reset dblist and recordlist
           (setq dblist ())
           (setq recordlist ())
;add the entity name for this INSERT to recordlist
           (setq recordlist (cons (cdr
               (assoc -1 (entget e))) recordlist))
;add the BLOCK name to the front of RECORDLIST**
           (setq recordlist (cons (cdr
               (assoc 2 (entget e))) recordlist))
;add recordlist to dblist***
           (setq dblist (cons recordlist dblist))
```

---

* These entities, by their location, will be ATTRIBs.

** **Recordlist** now looks like this: ("ROOMTAG" entity name: 600000014)

*** **Dblist** now looks like this: (("ROOMTAG" entity name: 600000014))

```
              )
;If the entity is an ATTRIB
          ((equal (cdr (assoc 0 (entget e)))
              "ATTRIB")
;reset recordlist
          (setq recordlist ())
;add this attribute value to recordlist
          (setq recordlist (cons (cdr (assoc 1
              entget e))) recordlist))
;add this attribute tag (EMPNAME) to the front of recordlist
          (setq recordlist (cons (cdr (assoc 2
              (entget e))) recordlist))
;add recordlist to the front of dblist *
          (setq dblist (cons recordlist dblist))
;If this attribute tag is ROOMNO
          (if (equal (cdr (assoc 2 (entget e)))
              "ROOMNO")
;then set the value of KEY to the attribute value of this
;entity.
              (setq key (cdr (assoc 1 (entget e)))))
          )
       )
     )
;Looks for the next entity in the database
     (setq e (entnext e))
;and if the next entity is not a SEQEND to go through this
;loop again.
    )
;After all the attributes for this block have been found:
;Reverse the order of dblist so that it will be in the
;order that we want it **
    (setq dblist (reverse dblist))
```

---

*   **Dblist** now looks like this: (("EMPNAME" "John Jones")
      ("ROOMTAG" Entity name: 600000014))

**   **Dblist** now looks like this:(("ROOMTAG" Entity name:
      600000014) ("EMPNAME" "John Jones") ("ROOMNO" "100"))

```
;Add the value of KEY to the front of dblist *
   (setq dblist (cons key dblist))
;Finally, add dblist to the front of proplist
   (setq proplist (cons dblist proplist))
)
```

All this function does is look through the drawing database for ATTRIBUTE records every time a block with attributes is found by the function **findatt**. It then creates a property list, which is essentially an association list of association lists. When this function is called from within your test drawing, the list it produces will look something like this:

```
(
("150"
("ROOMTAG" <Entity name: 600001B8>)
("EMPNAME" "vacant")
("ROOMNO" "150")
)
("140"
("ROOMTAG" <Entity name: 60000168>)
("EMPNAME" "vacant")
("ROOMNO" "150")
)
etcetera
)
```

This looks similar to the drawing database you examined in the last chapter. It's actually an abbreviated version of that list that contains only the essential information you need. The **proplist** becomes an index of every occurrence of a ROOMTAG block in the drawing database indexed by the ROOMNO. So, instead of searching through the entire database for a specific ROOMNO, you now can just look up the ROOMNO value in **proplist** and find the entity name of the block insertion that contains the searched for attribute value.

---

* **Dblist** now looks like this:("100" ("ROOMTAG" Entity name: 600000014) ("EMPNAME" "John Jones") ("ROOMNO" "100"))

Now you have two lists: the list of room numbers and names that we created from the database file, and the list of blocks and attributes from the drawing database. You still need a function that will look at a room number on the **filelist** and check **proplist** to see if there is a ROOMTAG with a room number that matches. If it does find a match, then it will use **subst** and **entmod** to change the value of the attribute EMPNAME to the new value found in **filelist**. Here's how that function should look:

```
(defun chgname ()
;Sets a working list inlist to be the value of FILELIST
   (setq inlist filelist)
;As long as there are items left in inlist, do this loop
   (while inlist
;Sets looklist to be the first sublist in INLIST
      (setq looklist (car inlist))
;Resets inlist to be inlist less the first sublist
      (setq inlist (cdr inlist))
;Sets ROOMNUM to be the first item in looklist and
;EMPNM to be the last item.
      (setq roomnum (car looklist))
      (setq empnm (last looklist))
      (cond
;If ROOMNUM from the outside data file is found in proplist
        ((assoc roomnum proplist)
;then set the value of chgattlist to the sublist in
;proplist that contains that key.
          (setq chgattlist (assoc roomnum
             proplist))
;Set CE to the value of the entity name of the INSERT
;entity from the chosen sublist.
          (setq ce (last (cadr chgattlist)))
;Start a loop that looks at entities in the drawing database
;beginning at the chosen INSERT entity and continuing until
;it reaches SEQEND.
          (while (not (equal (cdr (assoc 0
             (entget ce)))"SEQEND"))
;Sets ATTAG to whatever is found for Group Code 2 for
;this entity.
            (setq attag (cdr (assoc 2
               (entget ce))))
```

```
        (cond
;Checks to see if the attribute tag for this entity is
;EMPNAME.
              ((equal attag "EMPNAME")
;If it is, then it changes the attribute value of that attribute
;to the name from the outside database.
                 (entmod (subst (CONS '1 empnm)
                     (assoc 1) (entget ce))
                     (entget ce)))
;Updates the entity that has just been changed with subst.
                 (entupd ce)
              )
          )
          (setq ce (entnext ce))
      )
      )
    )
  )
)
```

Finally, you need to write a short function that will call all of these other functions. Let's put the whole thing together, and see how it works. The calling function is the main function that calls the other functions:

```
(defun c:update ()
  (extfile)
  (findatt)
  (chgname)
)
```

THE FINAL PROGRAM

Here's the whole program, again, without the comments. Presenting it like this should make it easier for you to see its overall structure.

Update starts the program running and calls the other functions:

```
(defun c:update ()
  (extfile)
  (findatt)
  (chgname)
)
```

Extfile reads the outside database:

```
(defun extfile ()
  (setq filelist ())
  (setq file (open "TEST.SDF" "r"))
  (setq record (read-line file))
  (while record
    (setq roomno (substr record 1 3))
    (setq empname (substr record 6))
    (setq reclist (list roomno empname))
    (setq filelist (cons reclist filelist))
    (setq record (read-line file))
  )
  (close file)
)
```

Findatt does the loop through the whole drawing database, and stops and calls **bldprop** when it finds a block with attributes:

```
(defun findatt ()
  (setq proplist ())
  (setq e (entnext))
  (while e
    (setq enttyp (cdr (assoc 0 (entget e))))
    (setq blknm (cdr (assoc 2 (entget e))))
    (if
      (and
        (equal enttyp "INSERT")
        (equal (cdr (assoc 66 (entget e))) 1)
      )
      (bldprop e)
    )
    (setq e (entnext e))
  )
)
```

Bldprop builds the property list from the drawing database:

```
(defun bldprop (e)
  (setq dblist ())
  (while (not (equal (cdr (assoc 0 (entget e)))
       "SEQEND"))
    (cond
      ((cdr (assoc 66 (entget e)))
        (setq dblist ())
        (setq recordlist ())
        (setq recordlist (cons (cdr
            (assoc -1 (entget e))) recordlist))
        (setq recordlist (cons (cdr (assoc 2
            (entget e))) recordlist))
        (setq dblist (cons recordlist dblist))
      )
      ((equal (cdr (assoc 0 (entget e)))
          "ATTRIB")
        (setq recordlist ())
        (setq recordlist (cons (cdr
            (assoc 1 (entget e))) recordlist))
        (setq recordlist (cons (cdr
            (assoc 2 (entget e))) recordlist))
        (setq dblist (cons recordlist dblist))
        (if (equal (cdr (assoc 2 (entget e)))
            "ROOMNO")
          (setq key (cdr (assoc 1 (entget e)))))
      )
    )
    (setq e (entnext e))
  )
  (setq dblist (reverse dblist))
  (setq dblist (cons key dblist))
  (setq proplist (cons dblist proplist))
)
```

Chgname is the function that actually updates the drawing database with new employee names for the roomtags.

```
(defun chgname ()
  (setq inlist filelist)
  (while inlist
    (setq looklist (car inlist))
    (setq inlist (cdr inlist))
    (setq roomnum (car looklist))
    (setq empnm (last looklist))
    (cond
      ((assoc roomnum proplist)
        (setq chgattlist (assoc roomnum
          proplist))
        (setq ce (last (cadr chgattlist)))
        (while (not (equal (cdr
            (assoc 0 (entget ce)))"SEQEND"))
          (setq attag (cdr (assoc 2
            (entget ce))))
          (cond
            ((equal attag "EMPNAME")
              (entmod (subst (CONS '1 empnm)
                (assoc 1 (entget ce))
                (entget ce)))
              (entupd ce)
            )
          )
          (setq ce (entnext ce))
        )
      )
    )
  )
)
```

Save this file under the name **UPDATE.LSP** and run it in your sample drawing:*

---

* If you find that this routine doesn't work the first time, exit AutoCAD, rename **ACAD.LSP** and try it again. That will make more memory available for this routine.

Type: (load "update") <RETURN>

Response: CHGNAME

Type: update <RETURN>

Response: Watch the names change on your drawing.[*]

We have attempted to keep these functions general in nature so you can use them with minor modifications in your own applications, similar to the way that we based some of the new functions on **entlst** . At this point, you've just barely scratched the surface of what you can do with AutoLISP in the linking of AutoCAD drawings and other types of databases. But now that you've learned how to establish a two-way link between AutoCAD and other types of databases, you can begin to get some idea of the power and possibilities of AutoLISP.

SUMMARY

This chapter has presented some state-of-the-art information and techniques about AutoLISP applications. In it you've learned to actually modify the data within the drawing database and to update the information in an AutoCAD drawing from an outside database.

In Chapter 9, you'll examine the drawing database from the entirely different perspective of the **DXF** file format. You'll also learn how to modify the AutoCAD **DXF** file with BASIC programs.

---

[*] On large drawings with several hundred block insertions to be linked into a property list, AutoLISP may run out of memory. If you run into that problem, the solution can be found in *The AutoCAD Database Diskette.*

chapter 9 UNDERSTANDING AND USING DXF FILES

In the last four chapters, you learned how to use AutoLISP to directly access and manipulate the AutoCAD drawing database. However, AutoLISP is only one of two important ways to read and change the drawing database. Another method is to read and write **DXF** (Drawing e**X**change Format) files. The **DXF** file of a drawing contains all the information in the drawing database for that drawing, formatted to be easily read by you or a computer.

In this chapter, you'll learn about **DXF** files, their many important uses, and how to read and understand them. Finally, you'll learn how to write useful programs in BASIC that will write, read and modify **DXF** files.

DXF OVERVIEW

DXF files were developed to allow users flexibility in managing data and translating AutoCAD drawings into file formats that could be read and used by other CAD systems. **DXF** has become the de facto standard of interchanging CAD drawing files for almost all microcomputer (and many larger) CAD systems. Almost every CAD system we're aware of has some sort of facility for reading and writing **DXF** files.

The **DXF** file standard has become ubiquitous—you can actually use the format without ever using AutoCAD! For example, we've translated many drawing files from CADvance directly to VersaCAD using **DXF** files without touching AutoCAD.

We've also used **DXF** files to import AutoCAD and VersaCAD drawings to be used as illustrations in Ventura Publisher documents. The layout and page formatting of this book was done with Ventura Publisher, and all the AutoCAD drawings were inserted into these pages by using **DXF** files.

WHAT YOU SEE IS NOT ALWAYS WHAT YOU GET WITH DXF

You should know that **DXF** file conversion from one CAD system to another is not 100 percent perfect. Other CAD systems don't always have the same entity types as AutoCAD, or the entity type is different enough that the translation doesn't always come across as you would expect.

For example, AutoCAD is the only CAD system that we know that allows you to *name* layers (in most other CAD systems, the layers are numbered). So when you export an AutoCAD drawing to another CAD system via a **DXF** file, the AutoCAD layer name gets translated into a seemingly arbitrary layer number in another system.

Even if you assign numbers to AutoCAD drawing layers before you translate the drawing, those layer numbers may not show up as the same layer numbers in the other CAD system. Conversely, when you import a **DXF** file from another CAD system into AutoCAD, the layer numbers in the AutoCAD drawing may not be the same numbers that were in the original AutoCAD drawing.

Another area of translation inaccuracy has to do with entity definitions. Most of the time, the drawing that was translated from another CAD system will *look* the same as the original when viewed on the display screen, but there will be many differences in the entity definitions that may make the resultant drawing file difficult or impossible to use. That's caused by different CAD systems having different drawing primitives and different ways of describing those graphic primitives in their drawing database.

For example, VersaCAD has a primitive called a **REC-TANGLE**; AutoCAD does not. When a VersaCAD drawing is translated to AutoCAD, any instances of **RECTANGLE** primitives appear in AutoCAD as a block called **UNITSQUARE** (a 1" x 1" square scaled to the size of the original **RECTANGLE** primitive). However, because a rectangle is an unequally scaled square, the block **UNITSQUARE** will always have different **X** and **Y** scales. Because the **X** and **Y** scales of the **UNITSQUARE** block are different, you won't be able to **EXPLODE** that rectangle for editing.

That could be a major problem if you were planning to edit the drawing. One solution to this particular problem would be to **EXPLODE** all the **RECTANGLE** primitives in VersaCAD before making the translation.

Blocks from AutoCAD will only translate to their individual component parts in VersaCAD. Symbols in VersaCAD will show up as individual entities in AutoCAD. Symbols from CADvance, however, will show up as blocks in AutoCAD and vice versa.

POLYLINES don't exist in VersaCAD, so they'll show up in VersaCAD as individual lines. **POLYLINE CURVES** and **ELLIPSES** from AutoCAD will show up as straight **LINE** segments in VersaCAD.

LINES in CADvance look like **POLYLINES** to AutoCAD, so all lines in a CADvance drawing show up in AutoCAD as **POLYLINES**. Unfortunately, the **POLYLINE** structures from CADvance won't be properly **CLOSED** (the starting vertex and ending vertex of a CADvance **POLYLINE** square, for example, will have the same coordinates).

POLYLINE ARCS and **CURVES** won't be translated properly into Ventura Publisher. A **POLYLINE ARC** will show up as a straight **LINE**, and a **CURVE** will show up as **LINE** segments.

Most CAD systems' **DXF** translators will make a stab at translating everything they find in a **DXF** file, but some don't even try. Unless you know that in advance, the results can be disastrous. For example, one translator (used for translating **DXF** files to a CALMA system) will only translate **POLYLINES** and ignore everything else. In that case, a preprocessor program must be written to convert every entity in an AutoCAD drawing into a **POLYLINE** before the file can be translated to the CALMA format.

Those are just a few examples of some problems you may encounter in making **DXF** file translations. But by the time you read this book, many of the problems might be fixed. Currently, several software houses are aware of the problems with their translators, and they are taking steps to fix them. Remember that microcomputer-based CAD is less than ten years old, and universal standards aren't created overnight. You can expect **DXF** to become a much more powerful and accurate tool in the future.

WHAT YOU *CAN* DO WITH A DXF FILE

You now know what **DXF** files were designed for, and how they can and can't be used. Now you'll learn how to write and modify **DXF** files.

Why, you may ask, would you want to know how to read and write a **DXF** file? A fair question. One of the examples in this chapter is a BASIC program that will create a **DXF** file from a text file. That file then can be loaded into the AutoCAD drawing editor to give you a drawing that consists of the text file converted to AutoCAD text. Now, you have a block of text in your drawing that was easier to put in than by typing directly into the drawing file.

Here are a few other ideas for programs to read and write **DXF** files:

Keep Track of Different Items in a Drawing—You could write a program that can read a **DXF** file and count instances of certain types of entities that you specify. As an example of this, you could keep track of the number of nuts and bolts in an assembly drawing.

Changing Entities in a Drawing—Since a **DXF** file is a complete file of the drawing, you could write a program to change any of the properties of such entities as **LAYER**, **LINETYPE** or **COLOR**.

Performing Calculations—A structural drawing of a building could be translated to a **DXF** file, and then read by a program that would perform stress calculations on the elements of that drawing. The results of the calculations could then be used to create a new **DXF** file to be read by AutoCAD for a visual evaluation of the results.

Generating Charts in AutoCAD—A program can be written to generate graphs of certain mathematical functions. The results of those functions could be used to produce a **DXF** file and to be loaded into AutoCAD to view or plot the results.

NC and Tool Path Generation—Computer controlled machine tools use a special computer language called **NC**, or numeric control—which instructs the machine tool to follow a particular path when cutting a part. The part is based on a geometric description of the drawing. For example, in **NC** code, a line from 0,0 to 2,5 is represented by the following code:

```
G00X2.0Y5.0
```

An AutoCAD drawing contains all the essential information for creating a tool path; the **DXF** file which contains this geometric information can be translated into **NC** code. Each entity in the **DXF** file is translated into the corresponding entity in **NC** code.

While this mammoth subject is outside the scope of this book, third-party **DXF** file translators and AutoLISP-based products are available which perform **NC** translation and tool path tasks.

Altering Drawings from the Database — Sophisticated programs like Synthesis can read a user-created
master drawing, then create a **DXF** file from that drawing.
Modifications are then made to drawing entities and dimensions according to your specifications. For example, if you
need 50 versions of a window, programs like Synthesis
allow you to manipulate entities to create those 50 windows
from one basic drawing. This kind of programming is quite
complex, and falls outside the range of *The AutoCAD
Database Book*. However, the material presented in this
and previous chapters should give you enough information
to determine whether your money would be well spent on
third-party parametric programming software.

WHY USE DXF?

Many of these applications can be accomplished using
AutoLISP. So why go to all the trouble of producing a **DXF**
file, operating on it with another program, then reading **DXF**
back into another drawing file? There are at least three
basic reasons for operating on a **DXF** file with an outside
program, instead of using AutoLISP:

Speed—If you're searching through a large drawing
database to count or modify entities, you'll find that
AutoLISP can be quite slow. Here's a BASIC version of
blkcnt[*] that, when compiled, will run at least five times
faster than the AutoLISP version.

```
10 CNT=0
20 INPUT "ENTER THE NAME OF THE DXF FILE TO
     READ";INFILE$
30 INFILE$=INFILE$+".DXF"
40 OPEN "I",1,INFILE$
50 WHILE IN$"EOF"
60     LINE INPUT #1,IN$  'read line from DXF
70 'If block INSERT then count it.
```

---

[*] The **blkcnt** routine appears in Chapter 6.

```
80     IF IN$="INSERT" THEN CNT=CNT+1
90     IF IN$="EOF" THEN CLOSE 'close file at end
100 WEND
110 PRINT "THERE ARE" CNT "BLOCKS IN THIS
    DRAWING"
120 END
```

Memory Size—With AutoLISP, you're limited (at least presently) to 45K of memory for both the AutoLISP program and any memory necessary to hold intermediate data and results. * This isn't a lot of memory, and if your data manipulations are at all complex, you'll find that you'll quickly run out of memory (*node space* in AutoLISP).

Complete Database Access—With AutoLISP, you are limited to access and modify only the data in the Entities Section of the drawing database. With AutoCAD Version 2.6, you now can look at other sections of the drawing database, such as **BLOCKS** and **TABLES**, but you won't be able to modify anything in those sections. With a **DXF** file, you have access to the entire drawing database and the freedom to make any changes necessary for your application.

One of the programming examples in this chapter is a BASIC program that adds a new entity to the beginning of the Entities Section of the **DXF** file. That would be impossible to do with AutoLISP, because you wouldn't be able to change the order of the entities in the database.

---

* Even though the function VMON (Virtual Memory ON) will page unused functions in and out of memory, you're still stuck with the memory limitation of 45K to do all of your list processing. The only way to get around that memory limitation is to use UNIX or wait for OS/2.

LOOKING AT A DXF FILE

So far, we've discussed what can be done with a **DXF** file. But what does it look like? Let's find out.

Because the complete **DXF** file for even the simplest drawing (one entity) is at least eight pages long (and would make this book look padded), we're not going to reproduce one here. Instead, you can make your own:

Start a new AutoCAD drawing and call it TEST. Draw a **LINE** from **0,0** to **9,9**. Then,

Type: DXFOUT<RETURN>

Response: File name:<TEST>

Type: <RETURN> (The file will be named TEST.DXF)

Response: Enter decimal places of accuracy (0 to 16) (or entities) <6>

Type: <RETURN>

When the **DXF** file has been completed, **END** the drawing and exit AutoCAD. At this point, you can either load TEST.DXF into a text editor to look at, or you can print it out for a reference copy. To print this file, be sure your printer is turned on (otherwise your program may crash)* and have at least eight pages of continuous paper in your printer. Now, at the DOS prompt:

Type: COPY TEST.DXF PRN <RETURN>

Pretty long isn't it—especially for just one line. Let's take a closer look.

---

*   And that would be bad.

The first six pages down to the first **ENDSEC** are called the Header Section, which describes the AutoCAD drawing environment that existed when the **DXF** file was created. Very little of this information is necessary for your immediate purposes, and you can find an adequate explanation of these variables in Appendix C of the *AutoCAD Reference Manual.*

The next section is called the Tables Section, which contains information about LINETYPEs (LTYPE), LAYERs, text STYLEs and VIEWs that you may have defined in your drawing. Because this is a simple drawing, only the defaults, CONTINUOUS linetype, LAYER 0 and STANDARD text have been defined in the table. If an entity were to have a HIDDEN LINETYPE and be drawn on a LAYER called FLOOR, then HIDDEN linetype and layer FLOOR would have to be defined in this section.

The third section is the Blocks Section, where the entity description for each block in the drawing resides. That section is discussed in greater detail later. Because there were no blocks in the TEST drawing, there's nothing in the Blocks Section.

The section of most concern at this point is the Entities Section. Your Entities Section should look like this (without the comments):

0	Indicates the start of a file separator
SECTION	Start of a file section
2	Indicates name will be on the next line
ENTITIES	Name of the section
0	Start of an entity—type follows
LINE	The type of entity
8	Indicates LAYER name follows
0	Name of layer that this entity resides
10	Next line will be starting X coord.
0.0	Starting X coord.
20	Next line will be starting Y coord
0.0	Starting Y coord.
11	Next line will be ending X coord.
9.0	Ending X coord.

21	Next line will be ending Y coord.
9.0	Ending Y coord.
0	Next line will be a file separator
ENDSEC	The end of the Entities Section
0	Next line will be a file separator
EOF	Indicates the end of the DXF file

If you changed the format of this entity record to a more conventional data format, it might look like this:

0	8	10	20	11	21
LINE	0	0.0	0.0	9.0	9.0

or:

TYPE	LAYER	START X	START Y	END X	END Y
LINE	0	0.0	0.0	9.0	9.0

Now the entity data start to look like a more conventional database format. If you had continued your lines to draw a diamond, the database would look like this:

TYPE	LAYER	START X	START Y	END X	END Y
LINE	0	0.0	0.0	9.0	9.0
LINE	0	9.0	9.0	18.0	0.0
LINE	0	18.0	0.0	9.0	-9.0
LINE	0	9.0	-9.0	0.0	0.0

You may have noticed that everything in the Entities Section appears in groups of two—a number, followed by a description. Those two items are, in fact, called *groups*. The first item is the Group Code, which indicates both the type of value the group contains and the general use of the group (a Group Code of **0** to **9** indicates that the value of that group will be a string; a Group Code of **10** to **59** indicates that the value will be a real number; and a Group Code of **60** to **79** indicates an integer value for the group).

Appendix C of the *AutoCAD Reference Manual* includes descriptions of all of the Group Codes. Appendix B of this book provides commented **DXF** listings for all AutoCAD drawing entities.

REVISING DXF FILES

Now that you've seen how readable a **DXF** file can be, let's modify the TEST.DXF file. Start by loading the **DXF** file into a text editor and add the following lines *just before* the **0** in front of ENDSEC (be sure to add the leading spaces where indicated):

```
0
LINE
  8
0
 10
9.0
 20
9.0
 11
18.0
 21
0.0
  0
LINE
  8
0
 10
18.0
 20
0.0
 11
9.0
 21
-9.0
  0
LINE
  8
0
 10
```

```
 9.0
 20
-9.0
 11
 0.0
 21
 0.0
```

Now, save your new **DXF** file, then enter AutoCAD and start a new drawing called TEST2:

Type: DXFIN <RETURN>

Response: File Name <TEST2>

Type: TEST <RETURN>

Your new **DXF** file will now be loaded. If all goes well and there are no typos in your file, AutoCAD will accept your **DXF** file and then you can see what you've done. If it's a diamond, congratulations! You've just written your first **DXF** file, and you've done an AutoCAD drawing without using AutoCAD. Think of all the money you can save by not having to spend $2850 on AutoCAD to make drawings!

Of course, it's very tedious to write a **DXF** file by hand. This exercise demonstrates how simple the **DXF** file structure really is. If you want more practical experience with **DXF** files, go to Appendix B, pick out a few entity types, add them to your **DXF** file and see what happens when you load that file into AutoCAD.

Let's try another experiment. There's nothing special about the current AutoCAD environment, so let's see if you can eliminate a good percentage of your **DXF** file. First, make a back-up copy of your TEST.DXF file, load your **DXF** file into your text editor again and do a **BLOCK DELETE** of the Header Section of your file—all the way down through ENDSEC. Save the **DXF** file, and now load it into a **NEW** AutoCAD drawing.

It still works, doesn't it? That's because the Header Section mostly determines how the drafting environment variables are set. Because all the variables in a drawing file have default values to begin with, the Header Section only changes those variables that are different from the default values in the **DXF** file. Since you didn't change any of the drafting variables in your TEST drawing, all header file variables were default variables anyway.

The only known Header Section that's valuable to keep track of in some cases is the variable called $INSBASE. That variable is the coordinate for the insertion point of a drawing that's used as a block inserted into other drawings. You'll use the $INSBASE variable in one of the examples.

Let's try something a little more radical. Take your back-up **DXF** file and delete every variable group in the Header Section *except* the $INSBASE part. Your Header Section should look like this:

```
0
SECTION
  2
HEADER
  9
$INSBASE
 10
0.0
 20
0.0
  0
ENDSEC
```

Now, go into your AutoCAD drawing editor and do a DXFIN for this file. It still works! That means the only information you really need in your Header Section is variables that aren't set to default values.

Let's do something even more radical. Take your **DXF** file, and delete everything *except* the Entities Section. Your **DXF** file should look something like this:

```
0
SECTION
  2
ENTITIES
. . . . .        (listing of line entities)
. . . . .
  0
ENDSEC
  0
EOF
```

Now load the **DXF** file into your AutoCAD editor and see what happens. Even that works. You've now reduced your **DXF** file size from 3441 bytes to 291 bytes. So what's the purpose of all the information we've just eliminated?

Header Section—The Header Section, mentioned earlier, contains all the drawing variables that were current when the **DXF** file was created. That can be useful when you're using the **DXF** file for file translations. However, when reading and creating **DXF** files with a program other than another CAD program, you don't really care what the current layer or snap resolution is.

Tables Section—Any **LINETYPE**, **LAYER** or **TEXT** Style referenced in either the Entities Section or the Blocks Section must first be defined here. If AutoCAD finds a reference to a **LAYER** name, **LINETYPE** or **TEXT** style in either the Entities Section or the Blocks Section that hasn't been defined in the Tables Section, it will reject the whole **DXF** file. The format for the Tables Section is explained in Appendix B.

Blocks Section—The Blocks Section contains all the Block Definitions used in the drawing. It's similar in structure to the Entities Section. Each Block Definition starts with the name **BLOCK** followed by a list of all entities that make up that block (including **INSERT** references to other blocks that may be nested within that block) and ending with the name **ENDBLK**.

Programs that write **DXF** files usually won't write Block Definitions because they would tend to add unnecessary complexity to the program. On the other hand, programs designed to read **DXF** files must be capable of properly interpreting the Block Section. The Block Section Format, including the Attribute Definition Structure, is addressed in Appendix B.

With this chapter and Appendix B as a guide, you should be well on your way to mastering the structure of **DXF** files. Now, let's concentrate on how to write programs in BASIC to read and write **DXF** files.

A FEW WORDS ABOUT USING BASIC

After much discussion, we decided to use BASIC to present the concepts and programs in this chapter. Obviously, BASIC wasn't our first choice, but because everyone reading this book probably has at least a nodding acquaintance with BASIC, and because everyone has BASIC (it usually comes with your computer), it's the most accessible computer language to use.

HOW TO USE THE PROGRAM EXAMPLES IN THIS CHAPTER

The programs in this section have been debugged and tested, and are simple versions meant to be illustrative, as well as useful. They were designed so that you could try them out and modify them for your own purposes when you understand how they operate. Each was written to solve a real problem for a client. The actual program listings were merged into this chapter from the program files to minimize the possibility of typographical errors.

This isn't a tutorial on how to use BASIC—we assume that you either have some familiarity with it, or can read one of the 10,000 books about BASIC already available.

TYPING IN THE PROGRAMS

If you've never had the opportunity or inclination to try BASIC, here's a quickie tutorial to get you started. If you don't already know how to load the BASIC editor that came with your computer, the following instructions will guide you through that procedure.

If you have an IBM PC:

Type: BASICA <RETURN>

Response: Ok

If you have an IBM PC compatible or a "Clone":

Type: GWBASIC <RETURN>

Response: Ok

Now you're in the BASIC Program Editor.

Type: AUTO 10 <RETURN>

Response: 10

Now you've started the Automatic Line numbering feature, and you can type in each line of the BASIC program (minus the line number).

After you've typed in the whole program:

Type: SAVE "[the program name]" <RETURN>

Response: Ok

Type: RUN

And, if you haven't made any typographical errors, your program will run.

MODIFYING A DXF FILE WITH BASIC

Below is a simple program that illustrates methods of reading, modifying and writing a **DXF** file with a BASIC program. The program also demonstrates something you can't do with AutoLISP—namely add to or change the order of the drawing entities in the drawing database.

THE PROBLEM

We were involved in a project where we had to translate many drawing symbols from AutoCAD to VersaCAD via **DXF**. With AutoCAD, you can put the Insertion Base Point of a block anywhere you want, and that coordinate will show up in a Header Record called $INSBASE. VersaCAD, on the other hand, wants to use the first point in its drawing database as the **Handle (Insertion Base) Point**. Of course, none of the Insertion Bases on the AutoCAD drawings was the first drawing entities.

THE SOLUTION

We wrote a simple program (shown below) that would take a **DXF** file from AutoCAD, find the coordinates of the Insertion Base Point ($INSBASE), then add a Point Entity with the same coordinates as the Insertion Base Point to the beginning of the Entities Section of the **DXF** file.

That program (called DXFFIX) reads a **DXF** file, line by line, then writes each line out to a temporary file.

When it reaches the variable $INSBASE (Line 210), it goes to a subroutine that stores the coordinates of that record to variables.

When it reaches the beginning of the Entities Section (Line 240), it goes to another subroutine that writes a Point Entity at the beginning of the Entities Section with coordinates that match those of $INSBASE. DXFFIX then reads the rest of the **DXF** file and writes it to the temporary file. After the complete file is read, the program erases the old **DXF** file and renames the temporary file to the name of the old **DXF** file.

```
10 '
20 'This section reads the DXF file that the
30 'user names and then opens that file to read.
40 'It then opens a temporary output file called
50 'TEMP.TMP hold the new DXF file as it is written.
60 INPUT "FILE TO READ";INFILE$
70 INFILE$=INFILE$+".DXF"
80 OUTFILE$="TEMP.TMP"
90 OPEN "I",1,INFILE$
100 OPEN "O",2,OUTFILE$
110 '
120 'This section is a While Loop that reads
130 'each line of the DXF file and then writes
140 'that line out to the temporary file.
150 'If the line is of interest, it is sent
160 'to a subroutine.
170 WHILE IN$<>"EOF"
180    LINE INPUT #1,IN$ 'read line from DXF
190 'If Start of $INSBASE section is found
200 'go to subroutine that gets coordinates
210    IF IN$="$INSBASE" THEN GOSUB 390
220 'If Entities Section is reached, go to
230 'subroutine that inserts the point in the list
240    IF IN$="ENTITIES" THEN GOSUB 560
250    PRINT#2,IN$ 'Write line to temp file
260    PRINT IN$ 'Write line to screen
270    IF IN$="EOF" THEN CLOSE 'close file at end
280 WEND
290 'Kill old DXF file and rename temp file to
300 'name of old DXF file.
310 KILL INFILE$
320 NAME OUTFILE$ AS INFILE$
330 END
340 '
350 'This subroutine reads the Insertion Base
360 'coordinates and puts them into variables
370 'BASE3$ and BASE5$.   Notice that the DXF
380 'values are strings and not numbers.
390 BASE1$=IN$
400 LINE INPUT #1,BASE2$
410 LINE INPUT #1,BASE3$      'X Coordinate
420 LINE INPUT #1,BASE4$
```

```
430 LINE INPUT #1,BASE5$    'Y Coordinate
440 LINE INPUT #1,BASE6$
450 PRINT#2,BASE1$
460 PRINT#2,BASE2$
470 PRINT#2,BASE3$
480 PRINT#2,BASE4$
490 PRINT#2,BASE5$
500 IN$=BASE6$
510 RETURN
520 '
530 'When the Entities Section is reached,
540 'this subroutine will add a POINT Entity
550 'to the beginning of the Entities Section.
560 PRINT#2,IN$
570 PRINT#2,0
580 PRINT#2,"POINT"
590 PRINT#2,8
600 PRINT#2,"0"
610 PRINT#2,10
620 PRINT#2,BASE3$   '$INSBASE X Coordinate
630 PRINT#2,20
640 PRINT#2,BASE5$   '$INSBASE Y Coordinate
650 LINE INPUT #1,IN$
660 RETURN
```

This program illustrates the basic methods of **DXF** file reading and writing. To utilize this program, you can substitute other types of entities to add to the new **DXF** file.

CREATING A DXF FILE FROM OTHER SOURCES

This program takes a text file produced on a text editor and formats the text into a **DXF** file. You have absolute control over the size of the text and the width of the columns with this program. You can specify the height of the text in either inches or points. You can even specify that the text be formatted into multiple columns.

HOW THE PROGRAM WORKS

When you format text with a word processor, all the characters are the same width. So, when you request right justification on a document, the word processor simply adds extra spaces to a line until that line flushes out to the right margin.

With proportional type and AutoCAD text fonts, that process is a little more involved. Each character in a type font takes up as much space as is necessary for that character—an **M** or a **W** takes up more space on a line than an **I** or a **P**. If you were to take a formatted word processor file and insert it into a drawing file with a proportional type font, it's likely you would end up with lines too short or too long for the column width you thought you had specified. For example, a line with 40 upper case letters would be more than twice as long as a line with 40 lower case characters.

This program reads a text file one character at a time. It then takes that character and gets the width of that letter from a shape width file .SWD (a shape width file for Simplex appears in Appendix C). It then places that character in a line of text in a **DXF** file and adds the width of that letter to a variable. It continues adding characters from the text file to that line until the line is almost full. At that point, when the program reaches a space (indicating the end of a word), it starts a new line of text in the **DXF** file.

---

*   Each letter in an AutoCAD font file is created on a grid.
Each individual unit of measurement in this grid is called a
vector. Vectors have no inherent length, except in relation-
ship to a scale applied to the font. The letter **M**, for example,
may be 25 vectors high by 25 vectors wide or the letter **I** may
be 25 vectors high by 6 vectors wide. An SWD file is merely
a file that contains the ASCII code and the vector width for
each character for a particular font. Because the character
width varies from font to font, each font needs its own SWD
file.

This program is a little more sophisticated than most AutoCAD text formatting programs because it takes into account the fact that each letter is a different width. The program gives you control of the line width independent of the line width in the text file. Here's the listing for this program with comments:

```
10 ON ERROR GOTO 3120
20 CCOUNT=0:ROT$="0":W$="":Y$="":L$=""
30 VCOUNT=0:WVCOUNT=0:XLOC=0:YLOC=0:LS$=""
40CDEPTH=0:COLDIST=0:CWP=0:CWI=0:PSIZE=0:HGT=0
50 SCREC$="Y"
60 CLS:KEY OFF
70 DIM CWARRAY(256)
80 DIM INARRAY$(82)
90 DIM OUTARRAY$(200)
100 GOSUB 1640
110 IF CDEPTH>0 AND COLDIST=0 THEN GOTO 3200
120 IF SCREC$="Y" OR SCREC$="y" THEN CLS
130 '
140 'LOAD CHARACTER WIDTH ARRAY
150 'This routine loads an array with all of the
160 'character width information from the .SWD file
170 'Each cell number is the ASCII code of a character,
180 'and the contents are the width of that character in
190 'vectors
200 OPEN "I",1,FILE1$
210 WHILE EOF(1) <> -1
220     INPUT#1,P,CW
230     CWARRAY(P)=CW
240 WEND
250 CLOSE
260 GOSUB 360 'to calculate vector length
270 OPEN "I",2,FILE2$ 'open text file
280 OPEN "O",3,FILE3$ 'open DXF file
290 GOSUB 2060 'to write Table Section of DXF
300 GOSUB 550 'to main subroutine
310 PRINT "TEXT FILE TRANSLATION
    COMPLETE...Press any key to continue"
320 A$=INKEY$: IF A$="" GOTO 320
30 CLS
340 END
```

```
350 '
360 'CALCULATE VECTOR LENGTH
370 'This routine calculates the actual vector
380 'length based on the text height and information
390 'in the SWD file (CWARRAY).
400 IF PSIZE >0 THEN HT=PSIZE*.0138
    *(CWARRAY(0)/CWARRAY(10))
410 VLEN=HGT/CWARRAY(0)
420 'Calculates column width in inches if column width
430 'was expressed as picas.
440 IF CWP>0 THEN CWI=CWP*.1656
450 'Calculates the number of vectors in a line
460 IF CWI>0 THEN TVEC=INT(CWI/VLEN)
470 'Calculates the height of the letters if
480 'the height was expressed in points.
490 HGT=INT(HGT*1000):HGT=HGT/1000
500 HGT$=STR$(HGT):HGT$=MID$(HGT$,2,5)
510 'Calculates the distance between each line of text
520 LFLEN=VLEN*CWARRAY(10)
530 RETURN
540 '
550 'INPUT CHARACTERS
560 'This subroutine reads the data file
570 'one character at a time and then sends
580 'them to a subroutine that checks its
590 'length and adds it to a string
600 WHILE EOF(2) <> -1
610     AR$=INPUT$(1,#2)
620     GOSUB 670 'to character sort routine
630 WEND
640 GOSUB 1510 'to print the last line routine
650 RETURN
660 '
```

This section takes each character and decides what to do with it.

```
670 'CHARACTER SORT ROUTINE
680 'This routine looks at each character and figures
690 'out what to do with it.
700 '
710 'If letter is a vertical bar, then do the end
```

```
720 ' of paragraph routine.   Get next letter.
730 IF AR$=CHR$(124) THEN GOSUB 1150:GOTO 1020
740 ' If letter is a space and it's the beginning of
750 ' a line, then ignore it and get the next letter.
760 IF AR$=CHR$(32) AND VCOUNT=0 THEN GOTO
    1020
770 ' If letter is a period and it's the beginning of
780 ' a line, then next letter will be a control character.
790 ' Set the FLAG and get the next letter.
800 IF AR$=CHR$(46) AND VCOUNT=0 THEN
    FLAG=1:GOTO 1020
810 ' If letter is UC M then put an "EM QUAD" space in
820 ' the line of text. Reset flag.   Get the next letter.
830 IF AR$=CHR$(77) AND FLAG=1 THEN
    L$=CHR$(228):GOSUB 1040:FLAG=0:GOTO 1020
840 ' If letter is not a space and not a line feed and
850 ' not a vertical bar and not a carriage return and not
860 ' a tab, then add the letter to the word being formed.
870 ' Get the next letter.
880 IF AR$<>CHR$(32) AND AR$<>CHR$(10) AND
    AR$<>CHR$(124) AND AR$<>CHR$(13) AND
    AR$<>CHR$(9) THEN L$=AR$:GOSUB 1040:GOTO
    1020
890 ' If letter is a space and it is not at the beginning
900 ' of a line, then add it to the end of the word being
910 ' formed, add that word to the line of text, start a
920 ' new word and get the next letter.
930 IF AR$=CHR$(32) AND VCOUNT>0 THEN
    L$=AR$:GOSUB 1040:GOSUB 1260:GOTO 1020
940 ' If letter is a carriage return and it is not at the
950 ' beginning of a line, then add a space to the end of
960 ' the word being formed, add the word to the line of
970 ' text, start a new word and get the next letter.
980 '
990 IF AR$=CHR$(13) AND WVCOUNT>0 THEN
    L$=CHR$(32):GOSUB 1040:GOSUB
    1260:GOTO 1020
1000 IF AR$=CHR$(13) THEN GOTO 1020
1010 IF AR$=CHR$(10) THEN GOTO 1020
1020 RETURN
1030 '
```

The following routines format each character into a word, and then each word into a line until the line has been filled; it then starts a new line.

```
1040 'LETTERS INTO WORDS
1050 'This subroutine sets each valid letter into a
1060 'word and keeps track of the vector length of
1070 'that word.
1080 W$=W$+L$
1090 VCOUNT=VCOUNT+CWARRAY(ASC(L$))
1100 WVCOUNT=WVCOUNT+CWARRAY(ASC(L$))
1110 L2$=L$
1120 L$=""
1130 RETURN
1140 '
1150 'SHORT LINE PROCESS
1160 'If the end of a paragraph is reached before the
1170 'line is filled, then this routine is invoked
1180 IF WVCOUNT+TVCOUNT=>TVEC THEN GOSUB 1350
1190 TVCOUNT=TVCOUNT+WVCOUNT
1200 Y$=Y$+W$
1210 WVCOUNT=0
1220 IF TVCOUNT<TVEC THEN GOSUB 1350
1230 W$=""
1240 RETURN
1250 '
1260 'WORDS INTO LINES
1270 'Adds a completed word to the line of text
1280 IF WVCOUNT+TVCOUNT=>TVEC THEN GOSUB1350
1290 TVCOUNT=TVCOUNT+WVCOUNT 'adds word vector to
       line vector
1300 Y$=Y$+W$ 'adds word to line
1310 W$="" 'resets word variable
1320 WVCOUNT=0 'resets word vector count
1330 RETURN
1340 '
1350 'PRINT LINE
1360 'This subroutine prints the formatted line
1370 'to the DXF file
1380 '
1390 'Strips any spaces from beginning of line.
```

```
1400 IF LEFT$(Y$,1)=CHR$(32) THEN
       Y$=RIGHT$(Y$,(LEN(Y$)-1))
1410 IF LS$<>"" AND LEFT$(Y$,1)=LS$ THEN
       Y$=RIGHT$(Y$,(LEN(Y$)-1))
1420 GOSUB 2650 'write start of DXF text line
1430 PRINT #3,Y$ 'write the text line to the DXF file
1440 GOSUB 2950   'write the end of DXF text line
1450 IF SCREC$="y" OR SCREC$="Y" THEN PRINT Y$
1460 TVCOUNT=0 'reset line vector count
1470 Y$="" 'reset line variable
1480 VCOUNT=0 'reset vector count
1490 RETURN
1500 '
1510 'Print last line
1520 'This subroutine prints the last line in
1530 'the file.
1540 IF LEFT$(Y$,1)=CHR$(32) THEN
       Y$=RIGHT$(Y$,(LEN(Y$)-1))
1550 IF LS$<>"" AND LEFT$(Y$,1)=LS$ THEN
       Y$=RIGHT$(Y$,(LEN(Y$)-1))
1560 GOSUB 2650 'write start of DXF text line
1570 PRINT #3,Y$ 'write the text to DXF file
1580 GOSUB 2950 'write the end of the DXF text line
1590 GOSUB 3020   'write the end of the DXF file
1600 IF SCREC$="y" OR SCREC$="Y" THEN PRINT Y$
1610 CLOSE
1620 RETURN
```

The following section of the program produces data entry screens so that you can enter the information about text height, column width, column depth, etc.

```
1630 '
1640 'DATA ENTRY ROUTINE
1650 CLS
1660 TYP$="":CWI=0:HGT=0:MCOL$="":STL$="":
     FILE1$="":FILE2$=""
1670 FILE3$="":FILE4$="":CWP=0:PSIZE=0
1680 INPUT "Text Height to be specified in
     <I>nches or <P>icas: ";TYP$
1690 IF TYP$="I" OR TYP$="i" THEN GOSUB 1720
     ELSE GOSUB 1800
```

```
1700 RETURN
1710 '
1720 REM DATA ENTRY ROUTINE (for height in inches)
1730 CLS
1740 INPUT "Enter Column Width in inches:
                    ";CWI
1750 INPUT "Enter Text Height in decimal
     inches:        ";HGT
1760 INPUT "Do you wish multiple columns
     (Y or N):        ";MCOL$
1770 IF MCOL$="y" OR MCOL$="Y" THEN GOSUB
     1880 ELSE GOSUB 1940
1780 RETURN
1790 '
1800 REM DATA ENTRY ROUTINE for height in points
1810 CLS
1820 INPUT "Enter Column Width in Picas
     (1/6 inch):      ";CWP
1830 INPUT "Enter Type Size in Points
     (1/72 inch):         ";PSIZE
1840 INPUT "Do you wish multiple columns
     (Y or N):        ";MCOL$
1850 IF MCOL$="y" OR MCOL$="Y" THEN
     GOSUB 1880 ELSE GOSUB 1940
1860 RETURN
1870 '
1880 'MULTIPLE COLUMN INPUT
1890 INPUT "Enter Column depth in
     inches:              "; CDEPTH
1900 INPUT "Enter Gutter distance between
     Columns:       ";COLDIST
1910 GOSUB 1940
1920 RETURN
1930 '
1940 'REST OF INPUT ROUTINE
1950 INPUT "Enter the name of the text
     STYLE:            ";STL$
1960 INPUT "Enter the name of the FONT
     file:            ";FILE1$
1970 FILE4$=FILE1$
1980 FILE1$=FILE1$+".SWD"
1990 INPUT "Enter the name of the Text
```

```
        file to translate:";FILE2$
2000 INPUT "Enter the name for the .DXF
        file:          ";FILE3$
2010 FILE3$=FILE3$+".DXF"
2020 INPUT "IS THE ABOVE INFORMATION
        CORRECT? (Y or N)";CRCT$
2030 IF CRCT$="n" OR CRCT$="N" THEN GOTO 1640
2040 RETURN
```

This next section looks very long, but all it does is write the Tables Section of the **DXF** file to a disk file according to how the text is to be formatted.

```
2050 '
2060 'DXF TABLE SECTION WRITING ROUTINE
2070 'This routine writes the table section
2080 'of the DXF file.
2090 PRINT #3,0
2100 PRINT #3,"SECTION"
2110 PRINT #3,2
2120 PRINT #3,"TABLES"
2130 PRINT #3,0
2140 PRINT #3,"TABLE"
2150 PRINT #3,2
2160 PRINT #3,"LAYER"
2170 PRINT #3,70
2180 PRINT #3,2
2190 PRINT #3,0
2200 PRINT #3,"LAYER"
2210 PRINT #3,2
2220 PRINT #3,"TEXT"        'LAYER NAME
2230 PRINT #3,70
2240 PRINT #3,0
2250 PRINT #3,62
2260 PRINT #3,7
2270 PRINT #3,6
2280 PRINT #3,"CONTINUOUS"     'LINETYPE NAME
2290 PRINT #3,0
2300 PRINT #3,"ENDTAB"
2310 PRINT #3,0
2320 PRINT #3,"TABLE"
2330 PRINT #3,2
```

```
2340 PRINT #3,"STYLE"
2350 PRINT #3,70
2360 PRINT #3,2
2370 PRINT #3,0
2380 PRINT #3,"STYLE"
2390 PRINT #3,2
2400 PRINT #3,STL$ 'the name of the text style chosen
2410 PRINT #3,70
2420 PRINT #3,0
2430 PRINT #3,40
2440 PRINT #3,"0.0"
2450 PRINT #3,41
2460 PRINT #3,1
2470 PRINT #3,50
2480 PRINT #3,0
2490 PRINT #3,71
2500 PRINT #3,0
2510 PRINT #3,42
2520 PRINT #3,1
2530 PRINT #3,3
2540 PRINT #3,FILE4$   'name of SHX file for text
2550 PRINT #3,0
2560 PRINT #3,"ENDTAB"
2570 PRINT #3,0
2580 PRINT #3,"ENDSEC"
2590 PRINT #3,0
2600 PRINT #3,"SECTION"
2610 PRINT #3,2
2620 PRINT #3,"ENTITIES"
2630 RETURN
```

These subroutines will write the **DXF** entry for each line of text formatted to the disk file.

```
2640 '
2650 'DXF LINE START HEADER ROUTINE
2660 'This subroutine writes the lines
2670 'before the text string in the DXF file.
2680 '
2690 'If multicolumn option has been chosen,
2700 'the program goes to this subroutine and checks to see if
2710 'the column depth has been exceeded.
```

```
2720 IF CDEPTH >0 THEN GOSUB 2870
2730 PRINT #3,0
2740 PRINT #3,"TEXT"     'TEXT ENTITY
2750 PRINT #3,8
2760 PRINT #3,"TEXT"      'LAYER NAME
2770 PRINT #3,10
2780 PRINT #3,XLOC  'X Start of text
2790 PRINT #3,20
2800 PRINT #3,YLOC  'Y Start of text
2810 YLOC=YLOC-LFLEN 'move to next line
2820 PRINT #3,40
2830 PRINT #3,HGT$
2840 PRINT #3,1
2850 RETURN
2860 '
2870 'MULTICOLUMN SWITCH
2880 'If a column depth is specified, then
2890 'this subroutine will be called.
2900 NCDEPTH=0-CDEPTH
2910 IF YLOC<=NCDEPTH THEN
XLOC=XLOC+COLDIST+CWI
2920 IF YLOC<=NCDEPTH THEN YLOC=0
2930 RETURN
2940 '
2950 'DXF LINE END HEADER ROUTINE
2960 'This subroutine writes the 2 lines
2970 'after the text string in the DXF file.
2980 PRINT #3,7
2990 PRINT #3,STL$
3000 RETURN
3010 '
3020 'DXF FILE END ROUTINE
3030 'When the whole text file has been translated,
3040 'this routine writes the closing lines of the
3050 'DXF file.
3060 PRINT #3,0
3070 PRINT #3,"ENDSEC"
3080 PRINT #3,0
3090 PRINT #3,"EOF"
3100 RETURN
```

These are simply error trapping routines. They are included so that the program won't crash if you type in a wrong file name or input invalid data.

```
3110 '
3120 'FILE NOT FOUND ERROR TRAP
3130 CLS
3140 IF ERR=53 OR ERR=64 THEN PRINT "FILE
SPECIFIED NOT
     FOUND...PLEASE TRY AGAIN"
3150 PRINT
3160 PRINT
3170 PRINT "     Press any key to continue"
3180 A$=INKEY$: IF A$="" THEN 3180
3190 GOTO 100
3200 'DATA ENTRY ERROR TRAP
3210 CLS
3220 PRINT "INVALID DATA...PLEASE TRY AGAIN"
3230 PRINT
3240 PRINT
3250 PRINT "       Press any key to continue"
3260 A$=INKEY$: IF A$="" THEN 3260
3270 GOTO 100
```

HOW TO USE THIS PROGRAM

Because different text editors use different methods for ending a paragraph, you must add a *vertical bar* to the end of each paragraph and for each blank line in your text file (the vertical bar usually is found on the backslash key). That lets the program know the end of a paragraph is reached when it finds a vertical bar in the text file (see line 730).

You must have an **SWD** file available for the font you specify when you run this program. An **SWD** file for Simplex appears in Appendix C (with instructions on how to create it), and **SWD** files for Simplex, Complex and Italic are on the *AutoCAD Database Diskette*.

Now you can go into your BASIC Interpreter and run this program, answer the prompts and the program will produce a **DXF** file with the text formatted exactly to your specifications.   At this point, you can start a new drawing in AutoCAD and, after typing **DXFIN <RETURN>** you can load your **DXF** text file and view the results.

CREATING A DXF FILE FROM OTHER SOURCES

This program takes a text file produced on a text editor and formats the text into a DXF file. You have absolute control over the size of the text and the width of the columns with this program. You can specify the height of the text to be either in inches or points. You can even specify that the text be formatted into multiple columns.

HOW IT WORKS

When you format text with a word processor, all of the characters are the same width, so when you request right justification on a document, the word processor simply adds extra spaces to a line until that line flushes out to the right margin. With proportional type and AutoCAD text fonts this process is a little more involved. Each character in a type font takes up exactly as much space as

is necessary for that character—an M or a W takes up more space on a line than an I or a P. If you were to take a formatted word processor file and insert it into a drawing file with a proportional type font, it is very likely that you would end up with lines that are too short and lines that are too long for the column width that you thought that you had specified. For example, a line with 40 upper case letters would be more than twice as long as a line with 40 lower case characters.

This program reads a text file one character at a time. It then takes that character and gets the width of that letter from a shape width file .SWD (a shape width file for Simplex appears in the appendix). It then places that character in a line of text in a DXF file and adds the width of that letter to a variable. It continues adding characters from the text file to that line until the line is almost full. At that point, when the

Figure 1 Sample of formatted text output.

SUMMARY

In this chapter, you've discovered what a **DXF** file is and what it looks like. You've also learned some of the pitfalls of using the **DXF** file format to translate files from one CAD system to another. You've received some hands-on experience on how to modify and create **DXF** files.

Finally, you've explored some programming techniques in BASIC used in developing programs to modify and create **DXF** files. Appendix B provides detailed information on **DXF** file structure, which will aid you in creating and modifying your own files and programs.

APPENDICES

Appendix A: The AutoCAD Database Commented

Appendix B: DXF Database: Commented Listing

Appendix C: How To Create Your Own SWD Files

appendix A THE AUTOCAD DATABASE: REVEALED AND COMMENTED

To understand and manipulate the AutoCAD Drawing Database, you must have a complete knowledge of the database structure. The drawing database is complex, and available information on database structure is terse at best. Although we've spent almost two years writing programs to manipulate the AutoCAD Drawing Database, there are still times when we feel we haven't mastered all its fine points.

The next two Appendices contain a complete annotated listing of all AutoCAD drawing entities with variations that can be found in the AutoCAD Drawing Database. This Appendix contains the association list format of the database that's accessed and manipulated with AutoLISP. Appendix B contains the **DXF** file format of the same database. The drawing from which we generated these databases is shown in Figure 1.

We've found those listings to be extremely valuable for our own use. Now, instead of looking up the Group Codes in the *AutoCAD Reference Manual* and trying to figure out what they mean, you can look up the actual data structure for the entity type that interests you and immediately see what the exact structure looks like for that record type.

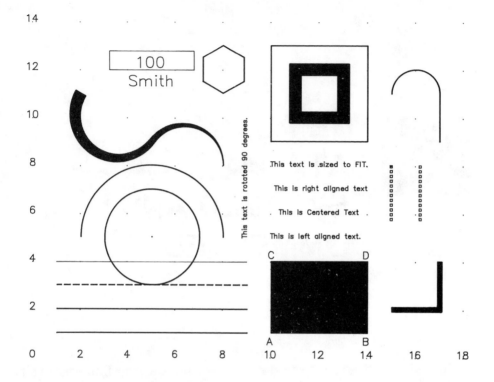

Figure 1: Plot of Sample Database

Since we began this project, AutoCAD Version 2.6 has been released, giving users the ability to access and read (only) the Tables Section of the Drawing Database in addition to providing several new entity types. We're including this new information on the 2.6 Version at the end of each Appendix so it won't be confused with the information about the earlier versions.

ASSOCIATION LIST FORMAT

This Appendix is the drawing database format you'll see when using AutoLISP. The association lists have been reformatted slightly so that the structure of each record becomes clear. The actual record appears in the left column and the appropriate comments for each field appear next to that field in the right column. Here's how the first LINE association list would actually look if you used AutoLISP code to retrieve the list:

```
((-1 . <Entity name: 60000014>) (0 . "LINE")
(8 . "0") (10 1.000000 1.000000) (11 9.000000
1.000000))
```

These records were actually generated from an AutoCAD drawing (Figure 1) by modifying our sample function **entlst** to write the association lists to a disk file. Then, we simply placed each field on a separate line and added our comments.

LINE

The first LINE listing is for a simple Line entity.

(	
(-1 . <Entity name: 60000014>)	Entity name (record index)
(0 . "LINE")	Entity type
(8 . "0")	Layer name for this entity.
(10 1.000000 1.000000)	Starting **X Y** coordinate pair.
(11 9.000000 1.000000)	Ending **X Y** coordinate pair.
)	

EXTRUDED LINE

This LINE listing is for a LINE that has a **Z** coordinate thickness and elevation. Notice that in this entity listing there are two new Groups—Group **38** and Group **39**. These Groups are valid Groups for all entity types, but will appear *only* in an entity that's been assigned an elevation and/or thickness that's non-zero. The example below illustrates how and where they'll show up in an entity association list. You can check any entity for a non-zero elevation value by this AutoLISP form:

```
(COND ((CDR (ASSOC 38 (ENTGET E))) (<do if
      condition is true>)))
```

AutoCAD Version 2.6 now has two new 3D entity types: 3DLINE and 3DFACE. We'll examine those entities at the end of this Appendix.

```
(
(-1 . <Entity name: 60000028>)      Entity name (record index)
(0 . "LINE")                        Entity type.
(8 . "0")                           Layer name for this entity.
(38 . 2.000000)                     If Group 38 exists in the
                                    entity list, then this entity
                                    has a Z elevation that is
                                    not zero and the second
                                    element of this list is the
                                    elevation.
(39 . 4.000000)                     If Group 39 appears in
                                    the list, then this entity
                                    has a Z thickness greater
                                    than zero. The second
                                    element in this list is the
                                    thickness.
(10 1.000000 2.000000)              Starting X Y coordinate
                                    pair.
(11 9.000000 2.000000)              Ending X Y coordinate
                                    pair.
)
```

LINE BY LINETYPE

This next LINE listing is for a line that has a linetype different than the one set for the layer on which this entity resides.

```
(
(-1 . <Entity name: 6000003C>)      Entity name (record index)
(0 . "LINE")                        Entity type.
(8 . "0")                           Layer name for this entity.
(6 . "HIDDEN")                      If Group Code 6 appears,
                                    the linetype for this entity
                                    isn't the same linetype
                                    set for the layer for this
                                    entity.
```

`(10 1.000000 3.000000)`	Starting **X Y** coordinate pair.
`(11 9.000000 3.000000)`	Ending **X Y** coordinate pair.
`)`	

LINE "BYCOLOR"

This last LINE listing has a different color than the one assigned to that entity's layer.

`(`	
`(-1 . <Entity name: 60000050>)`	Entity name (record index)
`(0 . "LINE")`	Entity type.
`(8 . "0")`	Layer name for this entity.
`(62 . 1)`	If Group Code **62** appears, then the color for this entity is different than the entity's layer color. Color number 1 is RED.
`(10 1.000000 4.000000)`	Starting **X Y** coordinate pair.
`(11 9.000000 4.000000)`	Ending **X Y** coordinate pair.
`)`	

POINT

The POINT is a very simple entity that has only one coordinate. The different available Point Modes are set with the variable $PMODE in the Header Section of the data file.*

`(`	
`(-1 . <Entity name: 60000064>)`	Entity name (record index)
`(0 . "POINT")`	Entity type.

---

* See 4.2 in the *AutoCAD Reference Manual* for more information about points.

`(8 . "0")`	Layer name for this entity.
`(10 5.000000 5.000000)`	X Y coordinate pair for this point.

`)`

CIRCLE

The CIRCLE has only two defining measurements, the **X Y** coordinates for the center and the **radius**.

`(`

`(-1 . <Entity name: 60000078>)`	Entity name (record index)
`(0 . "CIRCLE")`	Entity type.
`(8 . "0")`	Layer name for this entity.
`(10 5.000000 5.000000)`	Center X Y coordinate pair.
`(40 . 2.000000)`	Radius.

`)`

ARC

The ARC is described with a center, a radius, a starting angle and an ending angle. The arc is *always drawn **counter-clockwise*** from the starting angle to the ending angle. The actual coordinates for the starting or ending points of the arc can be found by using the **POLAR** function like this:

```
(setq start-point (polar center start-angle
    radius))
```

or:

```
(setq start-point (polar (cdr (assoc 10
    (entget e))) (cdr (assoc 50 (entget e)))
    (cdr (assoc 40 (entget e)))))
```

`(`

`(-1 . <Entity name: 6000008C>)`	Entity name (record index)
`(0 . "ARC")`	Entity type.

```
(8 . "0")                                 Layer name for this entity.

(10 5.000000 5.000000)                    Center point coordinates.

(40 . 3.000000)                           Arc radius.

(50 . 0.000000)                           Starting angle in radians.
```
Starting angle in radians. All angles in the AutoCAD drawing database are expressed in radians. There are 2 times PI radians (or 6.283185307 etc.) in a full 360 degree circle.

```
(51 . 3.141593)                           Ending angle in radians.

)
```

SOLID

A SOLID is a filled three- or four-sided figure, uniquely described by two opposing pairs of points rather than by four points around the perimeter (as a normal rectilinear shape would be described).

In Figure 1, the SOLID is properly defined by the first pair of points **A** and **B** (the base) and then by the second pair of points **C** and **D** (the top). If this were a square figure, rather than a SOLID, it would be correctly described by the following sequence of points: **A, C, D, B** and **A**. If the SOLID were to be triangular in form, it would be described with the first two points as the base (**10** and **11**), and the third point for the apex (**12**).

```
(

(-1 . <Entity name: 600000A0>)    Entity name (record index)

(0 . "SOLID")                     Entity type.

(8 . "0")                         Layer name for this entity.

(10 10.000000 1.000000)           First X Y coordinate point
                                  for base.

(11 14.000000 1.000000)           Second X Y coordinate
                                  point for base.
```

```
(12 10.000000 4.000000)
```
First **X Y** coordinate point for top.

```
(13 14.000000 4.000000)
```
Second **X Y** coordinate point for top.   If this SOLID were triangular in form, this group would not appear in the listing.

```
)
```

TEXT AND SHAPE

The next several listings will deal with various types of TEXT and SHAPE entities.

There's only one TEXT entity, but there are a number of variations of that entity based on how the text has been formatted in the drawing editor. These formatting variations of the TEXT entity can be very confusing, so we'll illustrate most of them explicitly by example listings.

In all the TEXT entity listings below, the text is the same height and style. Only format is different (i.e., CENTER, RIGHT, FIT etc.).

SHAPE entities look exactly like TEXT entities, except no text formatting information is contained in the record description. The .SHX format for text FONTS and SHAPES are identical. The only difference between the two files is that the FONT .SHX file contains letter forms, numbered to conform to the ASCII code for those letters, and a SHAPE .SHX file contains forms other than letters numbered arbitrarily. FONT files and SHAPE files can even be used interchangeably in a drawing for certain purposes (usually not a good practice).

It might be helpful at this point to explain just how TEXT and SHAPES are handled in AutoCAD's drawing database. The actual information on how each letter of text or each SHAPE is to be formed isn't in the drawing database, but is contained in a separate SHAPE file that has an extension .SHX. You can get an idea of how a SHAPE file looks and how it's constructed by looking in Appendix B of the *AutoCAD Reference Manual.*

The TEXT and SHAPE entities in the drawing database contain only information about sizing, scaling and formatting TEXT and SHAPES. When AutoCAD finds a TEXT or SHAPE entity in the drawing database, it looks for the .SHX file named in the entity record on your hard disk. It then extracts all appropriate data from that file and uses that information to actually construct the forms of the letters or SHAPES. Finally, that information is sent to your screen or plotter.

If the .SHX files referenced in your drawing aren't on your hard disk when you load your drawing into the drawing editor, and no alternate .SHX file is named, none of the text defined by that .SHX file will appear in your drawing.

The description of TEXT and SHAPE entities will become more apparent when you study the annotated listings below. The first TEXT listing will be addressed in greater detail than the subsequent records. For the remaining TEXT listings, we'll only comment at length on the variations.

LEFT TEXT

The first listing is for standard left justified text, the kind you get when you just pick a starting point in response to the TEXT command.

```
(
(-1 . <Entity name: 600000C8>)     Entity name (record index)

(0 . "TEXT")                       Entity type.

(8 . "0")                          Layer name for this entity.

(10 10.000000 5.000000)            Insertion point X Y coor-
                                   dinate for this line of text.
                                   This is the actual starting
                                   point of the line of text.
                                   This point is always at
                                   the beginning of the text
                                   string.

(40 . 0.200000)                    The body height of the
                                   upper case letters for this
                                   line of text.
```

```
(1 . "This is left
    aligned text.")
```

The actual text string for this entity. These characters will appear on your screen. This text string can have a maximum length of 255 characters.

```
(50 . 0.000000)
```

The rotation angle for this line of text in radians. The pivot point for this angle is always at the insertion point (Group **10**) which may be different from the starting point of the text (depending on the text formatting).

```
(41 . 1.000000)
```

Relative **X** scale, or width factor. Most of the time this will be **1.000000**. If, when you define your text style with the STYLE command,* you use a width factor other than 1, it will show up here.

```
(51 . 0.000000)
```

The obliquing angle of the text in radians. If you define this text style to have slanting letters, the angle of that slant would be in this group. If the characters aren't slanted, this number will be **0**.

```
(7 . "NORMAL")
```

The name assigned to the STYLE definition for this text style. In this example, the text style was named **NORMAL**. This is

---

*   See Section 4.10.1 of the *AutoCAD Reference Manual.*

NOT the name of the font file, which appears in the STYLE table in the Tables Section of the drawing database where the complete definition for the **NORMAL** text style is found (the name of the font file for **NORMAL** is SIMPLEX).

(71 . 0)

Text generation flag. This is a bit coded flag with the second (**2**) and third (**4**) bits capable of being set. If both bits are **0** then text will appear normal. If the second bit is set (**2**), then the text will appear mirrored in the **X** axis (left to right). If the third bit (**4**) is set, the text will appear upside down. Only one bit will be set at a time. See the beginning of Appendix B for more information about bit coded flags.

(72 . 0)

Text justification type flag. This is *not* a bit coded flag. The value of this number determines how the text is justified. In this example, **0** means the text will be left justified. We'll explain what other numbers mean in the other TEXT entity descriptions.

```
(11 0.000000 0.000000)
```

Alignment point. This is the **X Y** coordinate point where the text was inserted. Because this TEXT entity is left-justified, the point where the text was inserted and the insertion point are the same. This coordinate is **0,0**. See the other TEXT entity descriptions for more information.

```
)
```

CENTERED TEXT

The only difference between this TEXT entity listing and the preceding one is that this text is **centered** on an **alignment point** (Group **11**). Text always has a base point at the *beginning* of the TEXT entity (in this example, just before the **T** in "This"). If you specify **Center** alignment when inserting your line of text into the drawing, AutoCAD will calculate a point to the left of the center point half the length of your text string. This point is the actual insertion point for the TEXT entity.

```
(
(-1 . <Entity name: 600000DC>)
```

Entity name (record index)

```
(0 . "TEXT")
```

Entity type.

```
(8 . "0")
```

Layer name for this entity.

```
(10 10.357140 6.000000)
```

Insertion point **X Y** coordinate for this line of text. This is the actual starting point of the line of text.

```
(40 . 0.200000)
```

This is the body height of the upper case letters for this line of text.

```
(1 . "This is Centered Text")
```

The actual text string for this entity.

`(50 . 0.000000)`	The rotation angle for this line of text in radians.
`(41 . 1.000000)`	Relative **X** scale, or width factor.
`(51 . 0.000000)`	The obliquing angle of the text in radians.
`(7 . "NORMAL")`	Text STYLE for this entity.
`(71 . 0)`	Text generation flag.
`(72 . 1)`	Text justification type flag. The value of this number determines how the text is justified. In this example, **1** means that the text will be CENTERED.
`(11 12.000000 6.000000)`	The actual **centered** Insertion **X Y** coordinate of this text string. This is the point picked for inserting the text after the center option was picked in the TEXT command.
`)`	

RIGHT ALIGNED TEXT

If Right Aligned Text were specified, then the actual TEXT entity insertion point would be a point to the left of the alignment point *equal in distance to the total width* of the TEXT entity.

`(`	
`(-1 . <Entity name: 600000F0>)`	Entity name (record index)
`(0 . "TEXT")`	Entity type.
`(8 . "0")`	Layer name for this entity.
`(10 10.161900 7.000000)`	Insertion point **X Y** coordinate for this line of text. This is the actual starting point of the line of text.

`(40 . 0.200000)`	The body height of the upper case letters for this line of text.

`(1 . "This is right`
 	
`   aligned text")`
	The actual text string for this entity.

`(50 . 0.000000)`	The rotation angle for this line of text in radians.
`(41 . 1.000000)`	Relative **X** scale, or width factor.
`(51 . 0.000000)`	The obliquing angle of the text characters in radians.
`(7 . "NORMAL")`	Text STYLE for this entity.
`(71 . 0)`	Text generation flag.
`(72 . 2)`	Text justification type flag. The value of this number determines how the text is justified. In this example, **2** means the text will be RIGHT ALIGNED.
`(11 14.000000 7.000000)`	The actual *right* insertion **X Y** coordinate of this text string. This is the point picked for inserting the text after the right option was picked in the TEXT command.
`)`	

TEXT TO "FIT"

The difference between this TEXT entity listing and standard TEXT entity is that this text is fitted between a starting and ending point. After you pick a starting and an ending point, AutoCAD will adjust the **Relative X Scale Factor** (Group **41**) for this TEXT entity so that it will fit between the specified starting and ending points. An **alignment point**

(Group **11**), halfway between the starting and ending points, is also calculated. Again, text always has a base point at the *beginning* of the
TEXT entity (in this example, just before the **T** in "This"), or at the starting point for **Fitted Text**. This point is the actual insertion point for the
TEXT entity.

```
(
```

`(-1 . <Entity name: 60000104>)`	Entity name (record index)
`(0 . "TEXT")`	Entity type.
`(8 . "0")`	Layer name for this entity.
`(10 10.000000 8.000000)`	Insertion point **X** **Y** coordinate for this line of text. This is the actual starting point of the line of text.
`(40 . 0.200000)`	The body height of the upper case letters for this line of text. The height will remain the same no matter how much the text is "squeezed" to fit.
`(1 . "This text is` `   sized to FIT.")`	The actual text string for this entity.
`(50 . 0.000000)`	The rotation angle for this line of text in radians.
`(41 . 1.042184)`	Relative **X** scale, or width factor. This is the factor that changes when a TEXT entity is "stretched" or "squeezed" to fit between two points. In this example, the text had to be stretched slightly to fit, because the factor is slightly greater than 1.
`(51 . 0.000000)`	The obliquing angle of the text in radians.

```
(7  .  "NORMAL")
```
Text style for this entity.

```
(71  .  0)
```
Text generation flag.

```
(72  .  5)
```
Text justification type flag. The value of this number determines how the text is justified. In this example, **5** means that the text will be sized to FIT.

```
(11 14.000000 8.000000)
```
The actual **centered** insertion **X Y** coordinate of this text string. This is the point calculated by AutoCAD to be halfway between the starting and ending points picked for inserting the text after the **FIT** option was picked in the TEXT command.

```
)
```

ROTATED TEXT

This example is simply left-justified text rotated 90 degrees counterclockwise.

```
(
```

```
(-1  .  <Entity name: 60000118>)
```
Entity name (record index)

```
(0  .  "TEXT")
```
Entity type.

```
(8  .  "0")
```
Layer name for this entity.

```
(10 9.000000 5.000000)
```
Insertion point **X Y** coordinate for this line of text. This is the actual starting point of the line of text.

```
(40  .  0.200000)
```
The body height of the upper case letters for this line of text.

`(1 . "This text is rotated` `    90 degrees.")`	The actual text string for this entity.
`(50 . 1.570796)`	The rotation angle for this line of text in radians. In this case the text was rotated **90** degrees or **PI/2.**
`(41 . 1.000000)`	Relative **X** scale, or width factor.
`(51 . 0.000000)`	The obliquing angle of the text in radians.
`(7 . "NORMAL")`	Text STYLE for this entity.
`(71 . 0)`	Text generation flag.
`(72 . 0)`	Text justification type flag.
`(11 0.000000 0.000000)`	Alignment point. This is the **X Y** coordinate point where the text was inserted. Because this TEXT entity is left-justified, the point where the text was inserted and the insertion point are the same, and that coordinate is **0,0.**
`)`	

Two remaining text justification types that we haven't illustrated are **ALIGNED** and **MIDDLE**.

Aligned—is similar to FIT, except the text height (Group **40**) is adjusted to fit instead of the relative **X** scale factor (Group **41**). The text justification type (Group **72**) for ALIGNED is **3**.

Middle—is similar to CENTER except the text is centered with the alignment point (Group **11**) in both the **X** and the **Y** axis. The text justification type (Group **72**) for MIDDLE is **4**.

BLOCK INSERTION, ATTRIBUTE AND SEQEND

The following four entity association lists represent a Block insertion that contains two attributes. The only difference between this block insertion record and that of a block that doesn't contain attributes is that in the latter, Group **66** is set to **0**.

The actual list of entities that makes up any given block or attribute can be found in the Block Section of the Drawing Database. With Version 2.6, we now have access, via AutoLISP, to the information contained in the Block Section. Later in this appendix, we'll examine the Block Section of this drawing.

BLOCK INSERTION

```
(
(-1 . <Entity name: 6000017C>)    Entity name (record index)
(0 . "INSERT")                    Entity type.
(8 . "0")                         Layer name for this entity.
(66 . 1)
```

"Attributes Follow" flag. If this number is **1**, all the records that follow this record will be attributes attached to this block until a SEQEND entity type is reached. If this number is **0**, then no attributes are attached to this block.

```
(2 . "ROOMTAG")
```

The name of this block. If an INSERT record is found with a BLOCK name that starts with an asterisk (*), then that BLOCK is an "anonymous" block, created by an internal AutoCAD operation. Hatch patterns and arrowheads are examples of anonymous blocks.

`(10 5.000000 12.000000)`	The **X Y** coordinate of the insertion point for this instance of the BLOCK.
`(41 . 0.050000)`	The **X** scale for this insertion of this BLOCK.
`(42 . 0.050000)`	The **Y** scale for this insertion of this BLOCK.
`(50 . 0.000000)`	The rotation angle in radians for this BLOCK insertion.
`(43 . 0.050000)`	The **Z** scale for this insertion of this BLOCK.
`(70 . 0)`	Column count for MINSERT. If this or any of the next three Groups has a value other than **0**, then this INSERT was done with the MINSERT command, and this record represents multiple occurrences of the referenced BLOCK in the drawing file.*
`(71 . 0)`	Row count for MINSERT.
`(44 . 0.000000)`	Column spacing for MINSERT.
`(45 . 0.000000)`	Row spacing for MINSERT.
`)`	

---

* See Section 9.1.6 in the *Autocad Reference Manual* for more information about MINSERT

ATTRIBUTES

The next two listings are for the two attributes linked to the BLOCK insertion above. Notice the similarity to the TEXT entity listing. Because the attribute entity is primarily a carrier of textual data, it could be considered a specialized type of TEXT entity. All text formatting features available with the TEXT command are available with attributes. The actual attribute prompts that appear when this BLOCK is inserted are stored in the Block Section of the Drawing Database in an entity called ATTDEF.

```
(
(-1  .  <Entity name: 60000190>)
(0  .  "ATTRIB")
(8  .  "0")
(10  4.085714  11.328570)



(40  .  0.450000)
```

`(-1  .  <Entity name: 60000190>)`	Entity name (record index)
`(0  .  "ATTRIB")`	Entity type.
`(8  .  "0")`	Layer name for this entity.
`(10  4.085714  11.328570)`	Insertion point **X Y** coordinate for this attribute. This is the actual starting point of the text of this attribute.
`(40  .  0.450000)`	The body height of the upper case letters for this attribute. The original height of this text, when this attribute was defined, was 9". When we inserted the BLOCK attached to this attribute into the drawing, we scaled the block to .05X scale. AutoCAD automatically recalculated all the sizes of the attributes associated with that BLOCK to be the same relative size.[*]

---

[*] For a comparison, see this same block with attributes listed in Chapter 7.

(1 . "Smith")

The attribute value given this particular insertion of this attribute. This value is linked to the attribute tag "EMPNAME".

(2 . "EMPNAME")

The attribute tag, the key searched for when attributes are extracted using the ATTEXT command. The attribute tag remains the same for all instances of this attribute, while each instance can have different values linked to it. Think of the attribute tag as a FIELD NAME and the attribute value as the value contained in that field in a database record.

(70 . 0)

The attribute flag. It is a bit coded flag with the first (1), second (2) and third (4) bits capable of being set. If no bits are set in this Group (0), then the attribute will be visible. If the first (1) bit is set, it means that the attribute will be invisible. If the second (2) bit is set, then the attribute value will be a constant. If the third (4) bit is set, then verification will be required on input of any value for this attribute. Only one bit will be set at a time in this field. See the beginning of this Appendix for more information about bit coded flags.

(73 . 0)

The field length. We know of no way this group can be used at present.

(50 . 0.000000)

The rotation angle for this attribute text in radians.

(41 . 1.000000)

Relative **X** scale, or width factor.

(51 . 0.000000)

The obliquing angle of the attribute text in radians.

(7 . "STAND")

Text STYLE for this attribute entity.

(71 . 0)

Text generation flag. This group works the same way as Group **71** in the TEXT entity record.

(72 . 1)

Text justification type flag. The attribute text in this example is centered. This group has the same values as the TEXT entity Group **72**.

(11 4.975000 11.328570)

The actual **centered** insertion **X Y** coordinate of this attribute text string. This point picked for inserting the attribute text after the CENTER option was picked in the ATTDEF command when this attribute was defined.

)

The following ATTRIB listing is almost identical to the one above. We wanted to show you an example of how two (or more) attributes could be linked with the same Block INSERT record. We'll only comment on those fields that are different from the preceding ATTRIB record.

```
(
(-1 . <Entity name: 600001A4>)
(0 . "ATTRIB")
(8 . "0")
(10 4.439286 12.100000)
(40 . 0.450000)
(1 . "100")
```

The attribute value for the attribute tag ROOMNO. Notice that all numbers are carried as strings.

```
(2 . "ROOMNO")
```

The attribute tag to which the value "100" is linked.

```
(70 . 0)
(73 . 0)
(50 . 0.000000)
(41 . 1.000000)
(51 . 0.000000)
(7 . "STAND")
(71 . 0)
(72 . 1)
(11 4.975000 12.100000)
)
```

The next entity, SEQEND, only appears at the end of a series of attribute records (or, as we'll see later, at the end of a series of POLYLINE vertexes). SEQEND serves two purposes: 1) marks the end of a series of attributes linked to a Block insertion, and 2) contains the entity name (or record number) of the Block insertion to which it's linked.

There are two strategies for using SEQEND in searching for occurrences of Block insertions with attributes.

Strategy one: Knowing that every record between INSERT and SEQEND will be an ATTRIB record linked to the INSERT record, we can step through the database until we find an INSERT record and check that record to see if Group **66** is set to 1 (Attributes Follow Flag). Now we can examine every record after this INSERT record for specific attribute values until we reach the SEQEND record.

Strategy two: This involves looking for pairs of INSERT SEQEND records. When a pair of this type has been found, you can look at the Group **2** of SEQEND for the entity name of the INSERT record and use that entity name to go back to the beginning of the attribute list.

```
(
(-1  .  <Entity name: 600001B8>)
(0  .  "SEQEND")
(8  .  "0")
(-2  .  <Entity name: 6000017C>)


)
```

`(-1  .  <Entity name: 600001B8>)`	Entity name (record index)
`(0  .  "SEQEND")`	Entity type.
`(8  .  "0")`	Layer name for this entity.
`(-2  .  <Entity name: 6000017C>)`	Entity name (record index) of the INSERT entity to which this SEQEND is linked.

POLYLINES

A **POLYLINE** looks like a series of line and arc segments connected to form one continuous entity. Polylines have many properties not available for other entities:

- They can have a specified width, which can be varied from one end of a segment to the other to form a taper.

- Polyarcs or polyline arcs are polyline segments with "*Bulge Factor*" information added.*

- Vertexes can be moved, added to or subtracted from polylines.

- Curve fitting information can be added to any polyline.

- Ellipses and polygons are actually polyline structures.**

POLYLINES may look like a series of connected lines and arcs on the screen, but their database description is completely different from that of lines and arcs. A polyline actually consists of a series of points, and each point is called a *vertex*. AutoCAD takes the coordinate information for each vertex and draws lines between each vertex point (these aren't LINE entities).

Try to visualize the polyline data structure as a "connect-the-dot" picture with AutoCAD drawing in the lines between the dots when it displays a polyline on the screen. If you were to draw a square using lines, that square would consist of four LINE entities describing eight coordinate points (the starting point of each line would be identical to the ending point of the preceding line). If you draw the same square using polylines, you would have one polyline entity that consisted of four vertex subentities with each vertex describing one corner of that square.

The polyline data format consists of three parts. The first part is the Header Record entity, called polyline. The POLYLINE record signals the start of the polyline data structure and contains some general information about the polyline. The structure of this record is quite similar to the INSERT record followed by ATTRIB. The second part of the

---

*   See the section on tapered polyarcs for information on how the bulge factor
    is calculated.

** See the *AutoCAD Reference Manual* for more information about
    POLYLINES.

polyline data structure is a series of entity records called vertex. The vertex record contains the coordinates and other information about each vertex or point in the polyline. Finally the SEQEND entity appears as the last record in the polyline data structure to signal the end of that structure.

POLYLINE HEADER

(

(-1 . <Entity name: 600001CC>)	Entity name (record index)
(0 . "POLYLINE")	Entity type.
(8 . "0")	Layer name for this entity.
(66 . 1)	Vertex follows flag. Since the polyline header record cannot exist unless at least two vertex entities follow it, this flag would seem redundant. It does, however, follow a consistent data structure.
(70 . 1)	Polyline flag. This is a bit coded flag. Currently only the first bit (1) is capable of being set. If the bit is not set (0) then it means that this is an open polyline, and if the bit is set (1) (as in this example), this means that it's a closed polyline. When a polyline is defined as **Closed**, it will appear on the screen with a line connecting the last vertex in the polyline with the first vertex. A polyline is closed by using the C option in the PLINE command. If this

	flag were set to **0**, then this polyline would be U-shaped instead of a square.
(40 . 0.000000)	Default starting width. The only time that Group **40** is not **0** is either in the polyline record or at the specific vertex record, where the starting width is changed. The starting polyline width is assumed to be always the same until it is changed.
(41 . 0.000000)	Default ending width. The only time that Group **41** is not **0** is either in the polyline record or at the specific vertex record where the ending width is changed. The ending polyline width is assumed to be always the same until it's changed. The ending width of the current vertex becomes the starting width of the next vertex.
)	

VERTEXES

The following four vertex records describe a polyline square with the polylines having zero width:

(	
(-1 . name: 600001E0)	Entity name (record index)
(0 . "VERTEX")	Entity type.

(8 . "0")	Layer name for this entity. Theoretically, you could place each vertex of a polyline on a separate layer, but this doesn't seem to have any practical consequence.
(10 10.000000 13.000000)	**X Y** coordinate pair for this vertex.
(40 . 0.000000)	Starting polyline width. This is always **0**, unless the starting width is changed at this vertex.
(41 . 0.000000)	Ending polyline width. This is always **0**, unless the ending width is changed at this vertex.
(42 . 0.000000)	Polyline bulge factor. This Group is always **0**, unless it is describing a **POLYARC**.
(70 . 0)	Vertex flag. This is a bit coded flag where only the first (**1**) and second (**2**) bit is set. If the first bit (**1**) is set then it means that the next vertex record was added by AutoCAD as an extra vertex to create a smoother curve. If the second bit (**2**) is set, it means that a curve fit tangent has been defined, and that tangent information will appear in Group Code **50** below. Possible bit combinations for this flag are **1, 2** or **3**.

(50 . 0.000000)	Curve fit tangent direction in radians. This is always **0**, unless "Fit Curve" has been used on this polyline and the second bit (**2**) flag in Group Code **70** above has been set.*
)	

We'll only comment briefly on the following vertex records unless they're different from the preceding vertex record. These records are included to show how a complete polyline data structure would look.

(	
(-1 . <Entity name: 600001F4>)	Entity name (record index)
(	
(0 . VERTEX)	Entity type.
(8 . "0")	Layer name for this entity.
(10 14.000000 13.000000)	**X Y** coordinate pair for this vertex.
(40 . 0.000000)	Starting polyline width.
(41 . 0.000000)	Ending polyline width.
(42 . 0.000000)	Polyline bulge factor.
(70 . 0)	Vertex flag.
(50 . 0.000000)	Curve fit tangent direction in radians.
)	
(	
(-1 . <Entity name: 60000208>)	Entity name (record index)
(0 . "VERTEX")	Entity type.
(8 . "0")	Layer name for this entity.

---

*   See Section 5.4.1.1 in the *AutoCAD Reference Manual* for more information about curve fitting.

`(10 14.000000 9.000000)`	**X Y** coordinate pair for this vertex.
`(40 . 0.000000)`	Starting polyline width.
`(41 . 0.000000)`	Ending polyline width.
`(42 . 0.000000)`	Polyline bulge factor.
`(70 . 0)`	Vertex flag.
`(50 . 0.000000)`	Curve fit tangent direction in radians.

`)`

`(`

`(-1 . <Entity name: 6000021C>)`	Entity name (record index)
`(0 . "VERTEX")`	Entity type.
`(8 . "0")`	Layer name for this entity.
`(10 10.000000 9.000000)`	**X Y** coordinate pair for this vertex.
`(40 . 0.000000)`	Starting polyline width.
`(41 . 0.000000)`	Ending polyline width.
`(42 . 0.000000)`	Polyline bulge factor.
`(70 . 0)`	Vertex flag.
`(50 . 0.000000)`	Curve fit tangent direction in radians.

`)`

POLYLINE SEQEND

This SEQEND record is exactly the same record found at the end of a list of ATTRIB records. It marks the end of the list of vertex records that define a polyline.

`(`

`(-1 . <Entity name: 60000230>)`	Entity name (record index)
`(0 . "SEQEND")`	Entity type.

```
(8 . "0")
```

```
(-2 . <Entity name: 600001CC>)
```
Entity name (record index) of the polyline entity to which this SEQEND is linked.

```
)
```

WIDE POLYLINE

This next polyline record describes a closed polyline box in which the polyline has a width of .5". Note the starting and ending widths of .5" (Groups **40** and **41**) only appear in the polyline record and not in any subsequent vertex records. The only time these fields would *not* be **0** in a polyline or a vertex record is when the starting or ending widths are changed *in that record*. Those values are kept until changed in another record. Therefore, if you wish to change the width of a polyline with an AutoLISP routine using **subst**, you would have to change Group **40** and **41** records *only* at the vertex in which you want to change the width.

```
(
```

```
(-1 . <Entity name: 60000244>)
```
Entity name (record index)

```
(0 . "POLYLINE")
```
Entity type.

```
(8 . "0")
```
Layer name for this entity.

```
(66 . 1)
```
Vertex follows flag.

```
(70 . 1)
```
Polyline flag.

```
(40 . 0.500000)
```
Default starting polyline width. This is where the polyline starting width is defined.

```
(41 . 0.500000)
```
Default ending polyline width. This is where the polyline ending width is defined.

```
)
```

```
(
(-1 . <Entity name: 60000258>)      Entity name (record index)
(0 . "VERTEX")                       Entity type.
(8 . "0")                            Layer name for this entity.
(10 11.000000 10.000000)             X Y coordinate pair for
                                     this vertex.
(40 . 0.000000)                      Starting  polyline   width.
                                     This  field  returns  to  0,
                                     even though the starting
                                     width remains at .5.
(41 . 0.000000)                      Ending   polyline   width.
                                     This  field  returns  to  0,
                                     even  though  the  ending
                                     width remains at .5.
(42 . 0.000000)                      Polyline bulge factor.
(70 . 0)                             Vertex flag.
(50 . 0.000000)                      Curve fit tangent direction
                                     in radians.
)
(
(-1 . <Entity name: 6000026C>)      Entity name (record index)
(0 . "VERTEX")                       Entity type.
(8 . "0")                            Layer name for this entity.
(10 11.000000 12.000000)             X Y coordinate pair for
                                     this vertex.
(40 . 0.000000)                      Starting polyline width.
(41 . 0.000000)                      Ending polyline width.
(42 . 0.000000)                      Polyline bulge factor.
(70 . 0)                             Vertex flag.
(50 . 0.000000)                      Curve fit tangent direction
                                     in radians.
```

```
)
(
(-1 . <Entity name: 60000280>)    Entity name (record index)
(0 . "VERTEX")                    Entity type.
(8 . "0")                         Layer name for this entity.
(10 13.000000 12.000000)          X Y coordinate pair for
                                  this vertex.
(40 . 0.000000)                   Starting polyline width.
(41 . 0.000000)                   Ending polyline width.
(42 . 0.000000)                   Polyline bulge factor.
(70 . 0)                          Vertex flag.
(50 . 0.000000)                   Curve fit tangent direction
                                  in radians.
)
(
(-1 . <Entity name: 60000294>)    Entity name (record index)
(0 . "VERTEX")                    Entity type.
(8 . "0")                         Layer name for this entity.
(10 13.000000 10.000000)          X Y coordinate pair for
                                  this vertex.
(40 . 0.000000)                   Starting polyline width.
(41 . 0.000000)                   Ending polyline width.
(42 . 0.000000)                   Polyline bulge factor.
(70 . 0)                          Vertex flag.
(50 . 0.000000)                   Curve fit tangent direction
                                  in radians.
)
(
(-1 . <Entity name: 600002A8>)    Entity name (record index)
```

```
(0 . "SEQEND")                          Entity type.

(8 . "0")                               Layer name for this entity.

(-2 . <Entity name: 60000244>)          Entity    name    (record
                                        index) of the polyline en-
                                        tity to which SEQEND is
                                        linked.


)
```

SIMPLE POLYLINE WITH A POLYARC

This polyline structure is one straight line followed by a semi-circle
(180 degree half circle, the largest arc that can be created with a
single polyarc). The only difference between the first vertex record and
the second (other then the coordinates) is that the second vertex contains a **polyline bulge factor of 1.** The bulge factor is *1/4 of the tangent of the included angle of the arc.* If the bulge factor is **0**, then the
polyline segment that extends from that vertex will be straight. If the
bulge factor is **1**, as in this case, then the polyline segment will appear
as a semicircle. Later on, in the Tapered Polyarc Section, we will explain how to derive the arc information from the bulge factor.


```
(

(-1 . <Entity name: 600007A8>)          Entity name (record index)

(0 . "POLYLINE")                        Entity type.

(8 . "0")

(66 . 1)                                Vertex follows flag.

(70 . 0)                                Polyline flag.

(40 . 0.000000)                         Default   starting   polyline
                                        width.

(41 . 0.000000)                         Default   ending   polyline
                                        width.

)

(

(-1 . <Entity name: 600007BC>)          Entity name (record index)
```

`(0 . "VERTEX")`	Entity type.
`(8 . "0")`	Layer name for this entity.
`(10 17.000000 9.000000)`	**X Y** coordinate pair for this vertex.
`(40 . 0.000000)`	Starting polyline width.
`(41 . 0.000000)`	Ending polyline width.
`(42 . 0.000000)`	Polyline bulge factor.
`(70 . 0)`	Vertex flag.
`(50 . 0.000000)`	Curve fit tangent direction in radians.
`)`	
`(`	
`(-1 . <Entity name: 600007D0>)`	
`(0 . "VERTEX")`	Entity type.
`(8 . "0")`	Layer name for this entity.
`(10 17.000000 11.000000)`	**X Y** coordinate pair for this vertex.
`(40 . 0.000000)`	Starting polyline width.
`(41 . 0.000000)`	Ending polyline width.
`(42 . 1.000000)`	Polyline bulge factor. A bulge factor of **1** means that this polyline segment will be a semi-circle.
`(70 . 0)`	Vertex flag.
`(50 . 0.000000)`	Curve fit tangent direction in radians.
`)`	
`(`	
`(-1 . <Entity name: 600007E4>)`	Entity name (record index)
`(0 . "VERTEX")`	Entity type.

`(8 . "0")`	Layer name for this entity.
`(10 15.000000 11.000000)`	**X Y** coordinate pair for this vertex.
`(40 . 0.000000)`	Starting polyline width.
`(41 . 0.000000)`	Ending polyline width.
`(42 . 1.000000)`	Polyline bulge factor. The bulge factor if the preceding polyarc were continued back to the starting point of the polyarc (a full circle).
`(70 . 0)`	Vertex flag.
`(50 . 0.000000)`	Curve fit tangent direction in radians.

`)`

`(`

`(-1 . <Entity name: 600007F8>)`	Entity name (record index)
`(0 . "SEQEND")`	Entity type.
`(8 . "0")`	Layer name for this entity.
`(-2 . <Entity name: 600007A8>)`	Entity name (record index) of the polyline entity to which SEQEND is linked.

`)`

TAPERED POLYARCS

This entry describes two different types of polyline structures: tapered polylines and polyarcs. Figure 2 is a detailed illustration of this polyline structure. The first thing to notice is that, although the illustration shows only two arcs and three vertexes, there are actually four vertex sub-records in this polyline record—the coordinates for the first two vertex records are identical. That's because there are actually three polyarcs, the first of which was forced to have the same starting and ending point.* At the end of this record listing, we'll explain how to extract the arc description information from the bulge factor.

```
(
(-1 . <Entity name: 600009C4>)      Entity name (record index)
(0 . "POLYLINE")                    Entity type.
(8 . "0")                           Layer name for this entity.
(66 . 1)                            Vertex follows flag.
(70 . 0)                            Polyline flag.
(40 . 0.000000)                     Default starting polyline
                                    width.
(41 . 0.000000)                     Default ending polyline
                                    width.
)
(
(-1 . <Entity name: 600009D8>)      Entity name (record index)
(0 . "VERTEX")                      Entity type.
(8 . "0")                           Layer name for this entity.
(10 8.000000 8.000000)              X Y coordinate pair for
                                    this vertex.
(40 . 0.000000)                     Starting polyline width.
(41 . 0.000000)                     Ending polyline width.
(42 . 1.000000)                     Polyline bulge factor.
                                    This is the first polyarc
                                    forced to the same start-
                                    ing and ending point—in
                                    this circumstance, the
                                    bulge factor is always 1.
(70 . 0)                            Vertex flag.
```

---

* You have to use this technique if you're starting a polyline with a polyarc of less than 180 degrees.

`(50 . 0.000000)`	Curve fit tangent direction in radians.
`)`	
`(`	
`(-1 . <Entity name: 600009EC>)`	Entity name (record index)
`(0 . "VERTEX")`	Entity type.
`(8 . "0")`	Layer name for this entity.
`(10 8.000000 8.000000)`	**X Y** coordinate pair for this vertex.
`(40 . 0.000000)`	Starting polyline width.
`(41 . 0.250000)`	Ending polyline width. The first visible polyarc of this structure starts at **0** width, and ends with a width of **.25**.
`(42 . 0.720759)`	Polyline bulge factor. Calculating this bulge factor is explained at the end of this section.
`(70 . 0)`	Vertex flag.
`(50 . 0.000000)`	
`)`	
`(`	
`(-1 . <Entity name: 60000A00>)`	Entity name (record index)
`(0 . "VERTEX")`	Entity type.
`(8 . "0")`	Layer name for this entity.
`(10 5.000000 9.000000)`	**X Y** coordinate pair for this vertex.
`(40 . 0.250000)`	Starting polyline width. This is the same width as the ending polyline width of the previous vertex, but because it's different

	than the *starting width* of the previous vertex, then the starting width has changed which must show up here.*
(41 . 0.500000)	Ending polyline width.
(42 . -0.945986)	Polyline bulge factor. If the bulge factor is a negative number, it means the polyarc was generated clockwise from its starting point.
(70 . 0)	Vertex flag.
(50 . 0.000000)	Curve fit tangent direction in radians.
)	
(	
(-1 . <Entity name: 60000A14>)	Entity name (record index)
(0 . "VERTEX")	Entity type.
(8 . "0")	Layer name for this entity.
(10 2.000000 11.000000)	**X Y** coordinate pair for this vertex.
(40 . 0.500000)	Starting polyline width. This width is, of course, different than the starting width of the last vertex—the starting width of the *next* polyline segment (if there were one).
(41 . 0.500000)	Ending polyline width.

---

* The starting and ending width fields *always* remain at **0** *unless* there's a change in width from the previous vertex record.

```
(42 . -0.571428)
```
Polyline bulge factor. This is the bulge factor of a proposed polyarc of the same radius as the last polyarc and if it were continued until it intersected with the right angle of a right triangle constructed so that the hypotenuse was congruent with the chord of the last polyarc (see Figure 2).

```
(70 . 0)
```
Vertex flag.

```
(50 . 0.000000)
```
Curve fit tangent direction in radians.

```
)

(

(-1 . <Entity name: 60000A28>)
```
Entity name (record index)

```
(0 . "SEQEND")
```
Entity type.

```
(8 . "0")
```
Layer name for this entity.

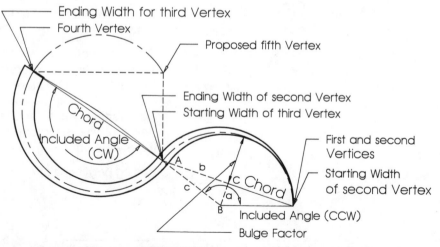

Figure 2: The Bulge factor illustrated.

```
(-2 . <Entity name: 600009C4>)
```
Entity name (record index) of the polyline entity to which SEQEND is linked.

```
)
```

BULGE FACTOR CALCULATIONS

A polyarc isn't constructed from a center point reference like ARCS and CIRCLES. A polyarc is described as having a start point (the current vertex) and end point (the next vertex) and a bulge factor. Sometimes it's important to derive the center point and radius for a polyarc—here is how to do it using the first polyarc in Figure 2 as an example:

First, find the included angle from the bulge factor. The bulge factor is *1/4 the tangent of the included angle of the arc,* so you can apply this AutoLISP form to the second vertex in the preceding listing:

```
(setq incang (* 4 (atan 0.720759)))
```

This returns the included angle of 2.498091 radians.

Now find the length of the chord from the current vertex to the next vertex with this AutoLISP form:

```
(setq chord (distance (list 8 8) (list 5 9)))
```

The chord length is 3.162278.

Next, find the radius of the polyarc by using a little trigonometry. Look at Figure 2. Using half the included angle, and half of the chord length you can find the length of hypotenuse **c** in the right triangle **A B C**—this is the radius of the polyarc. But before you can do that, you have to find angle **A** with this AutoLISP form:

```
(setq anga (- (/ pi 2) (/ incang 2)))
```

Find the radius with this form:

```
(setq rad (/ (/ chord 2) (cos anga)))
```

The radius for this polyarc is 1.666667.

To find the center point, first find the angle of the chord of the polyarc from current vertex to next vertex with this form:

```
(setq chordang (angle (list 8 8) (list 5 9)))
```

Then add angle **A** to **chordang** if the bulge factor is positive, or subtract angle **A** from **chordang** if the bulge factor is negative. The answer is easy, in this case, 0 radians.

Finally, use the **polar** function to find the center point:

```
(setq center (polar <coordinate of current
vertex> <angle from start to center> rad))
```

From this information, it's simple to derive the starting and ending angles for this polyarc.

POLYGONS

POLYGONS are not separate entity types but are simply closed polylines, generated by AutoCAD according to your specifications when you use the POLYGON command. There's no obvious way to set a polyline width when creating a polygon, but you can always give the polygon a line width with the PEDIT command. Below is the association list data record for a hexagon, generated with the POLYGON command:

(	
(-1 . <Entity name: 600004C4>)	Entity name (record index)
(0 . "POLYLINE")	Entity type.
(8 . "0")	Layer name for this entity.
(66 . 1)	Vertex follows flag
(70 . 1)	Vertex flag.
(40 . 0.000000)	Default starting polyline width.
(41 . 0.000000)	Default ending polyline width.
)	
(	
(-1 . <Entity name: 600004D8>)	Entity name (record index)
(0 . "VERTEX")	Entity type.
(8 . "0")	Layer name for this entity.

`(10  8.000000 11.000000)`	**X Y** coordinate pair for this vertex.
`(40  .  0.000000)`	Starting polyline width.
`(41  .  0.000000)`	Ending polyline width.
`(42  .  0.000000)`	Polyline bulge factor.
`(70  .  0)`	Vertex flag.
`(50  .  0.000000)`	Curve fit tangent direction in radians.
`)`	
`(`	
`(-1  .  <Entity name:  600004EC>)`	Entity name (record index)
`(0  .  "VERTEX")`	Entity type.
`(8  .  "0")`	Layer name for this entity.
`(10  8.866025 11.500000)`	**X Y** coordinate pair for this vertex.
`(40  .  0.000000)`	Starting polyline width.
`(41  .  0.000000)`	Ending polyline width.
`(42  .  0.000000)`	Polyline bulge factor.
`(70  .  0)`	Vertex flag.
`(50  .  0.000000)`	Curve fit tangent direction in radians.
`)`	
`(`	
`(-1  .  <Entity name:  60000500>)`	Entity name (record index)
`(0  .  "VERTEX")`	Entity type.
`(8  .  "0")`	Layer name for this entity.
`(10  8.866025 12.500000)`	**X Y** coordinate pair for this vertex.
`(40  .  0.000000)`	Starting polyline width.
`(41  .  0.000000)`	Ending polyline width.

```
(42 . 0.000000)                          Polyline bulge factor.

(70 . 0)                                 Vertex flag.

(50 . 0.000000)                          Curve fit tangent direction
                                         in radians.

)

(

(-1 . <Entity name: 60000514>)           Entity name (record index)

(0 . "VERTEX")                           Entity type.

(8 . "0")                                Layer name for this entity.

(10 8.000000 13.000000)                  X Y coordinate pair for
                                         this vertex.

(40 . 0.000000)                          Starting polyline width.

(41 . 0.000000)                          Ending polyline width.

(42 . 0.000000)                          Polyline bulge factor.

(70 . 0)                                 Vertex flag.

(50 . 0.000000)                          Curve fit tangent direction
                                         in radians.

)

(

(-1 . <Entity name: 60000528>)           Entity name (record index)

(0 . "VERTEX")                           Entity type.

(8 . "0")                                Layer name for this entity.

(10 7.133975 12.500000)                  X Y coordinate pair for
                                         this vertex.

(40 . 0.000000)                          Starting polyline width.

(41 . 0.000000)                          Ending polyline width.

(42 . 0.000000)                          Polyline bulge factor.

(70 . 0)                                 Vertex flag.

(50 . 0.000000)                          Curve fit tangent direction
                                         in radians.
```

```
)

(
(-1 . <Entity name: 6000053C>)     Entity name (record index)
(0 . "VERTEX")                     Entity type.
(8 . "0")                          Layer name for this entity.
(10 7.133975 11.500000)            X Y coordinate pair for
                                   this vertex.
(40 . 0.000000)                    Starting polyline width.
(41 . 0.000000)                    Ending polyline width.
(42 . 0.000000)                    Polyline bulge factor.
(70 . 0)                           Vertex flag.
(50 . 0.000000)                    Curve fit tangent direction
                                   in radians.

)

(
(-1 . <Entity name: 60000550>)     Entity name (record index)
(0 . "SEQEND")                     Entity type.
(8 . "0")                          Layer name for this entity.
(-2 . <Entity name: 600004C4>)     Entity   name   (record
                                   index) of the polyline en-
                                   tity to which SEQEND is
                                   linked.

)
```

TRACE

A TRACE looks something like a polyline. But if you examine the data structure, you'll find it similar to a SOLID. Generally, TRACES have been superseded by polylines.

```
(
(-1 . <Entity name: 60000564>)     Entity name (record index)
(0 . "TRACE")                      Entity type.
```

`(8  .  "0")`	Layer name for this entity.
`(10 15.000000 2.100000)`	**X Y** coordinate of the first corner of the starting side.
`(11 15.000000 1.900000)`	**X Y** coordinate of the second corner of the starting side.
`(12 16.900000 2.100000)`	**X Y** coordinate of the first corner of the ending side. This is a mitered corner, and it shares the same coordinate as the first corner of the starting side in the next TRACE.
`(13 17.100000 1.900000)`	**X Y** coordinate of the second corner of the ending side. This is a mitered corner, and it shares the same coordinate as the second corner of the starting side in the next TRACE.
`)`	
`(`	
`(-1 . <Entity name: 60000578>)`	Entity name (record index)
`(0  .  "TRACE")`	Entity type.
`(8  .  "0")`	Layer name for this entity.
`(10 16.900000 2.100000)`	**X Y** coordinate of the first corner of the starting side. This is a mitered corner, and it shares the same coordinate as the first corner of the ending side in the previous TRACE.

(11 17.100000 1.900000)	**X Y** coordinate of the second corner of the starting side. This is a mitered corner, and it shares the same coordinate as the second corner of the ending side in the previous TRACE.
(12 16.900000 4.000000)	**X Y** coordinate of the first corner of the ending side.
(13 17.100000 4.000000)	**X Y** coordinate of the second corner of the ending side.

)

AUTOCAD 2.6 ENTITIES

The following three entity types have been added to AutoCAD Version 2.6: 3DFACE, 3DLINE and an ASSOCIATIVE DIMENSION. Figure 3 illustrates the database listing that appears below.

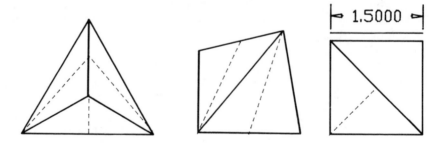

Figure 3: The 2.6 Entity types.

3DFACE

The 3DFACE entity is similar to a SOLID entity in structure. Unlike the SOLID entity, however, the 3DFACE is constructed by picking the corners in a circular fashion, rather than by describing two points for the base and either one or two points for the top of the surface. The 3DFACE always has three coordinates given for each corner and can have either three or four vertexes or corners. When you use the HIDE command, the 3DFACE will appear opaque when the view has its hidden lines removed.

3DFACEs do not make up a true 3D solid. You are actually describing a 3D figure by assembling a bunch of 2D surfaces* together in a 3D environment. If you were to reproduce the tetrahedron (a completely closed solid) in Figure 3 in the "real world," you would cut four triangles out of a piece of paper (2D) and glue or tape them together to form the tetrahedron (3D).

In order to have a proper 3D surface,** each adjacent pair of corners must have one coordinate (either **X, Y** or **Z**) in common.*** For example, Figure 3 features several 3D views of the same tetrahedron described in the data listing below. The first 3DFACE listing describes a triangle where the second corner shares the same **Z** coordinate as the first corner; the third corner shares the same **Y** coordinate as the second corner; and the third corner also shares the same **X** coordinate as the first corner. Since this is a triangle, the fourth corner is identical to the first corner. If this isn't true, then a warped surface will exist and the HIDE command won't operate properly.

To create a 3D solid from 3DFACEs, the appropriate edges of adjacent 3DFACEs must be *congruent.**** The data listing below describes the tetrahedron. You can see that the edge formed by the first and second corners of the first 3DFACE is identical to the edge formed by the third and fourth corners of the second 3DFACE.

```
(

(-1 . <Entity name: 60000014>)    Entity name (record index)

(0 . "3DFACE")                    Entity type.

(8 . "0")                         Layer name for this entity.

(10 -6.668690 4.306549 3.000000)  X Y Z coordinates of the
                                  starting corner.
```

---

* In computer graphics, these 2D surfaces are called *patches.*
** i.e., a *flat* surface.
***In other words, each edge of a 3D surface must lie on the same plane.
****What constitutes an appropriate edge will vary depending on the solid.

```
(11 -8.168690 5.806549 3.000000)
```
X Y Z coordinates of the second corner.

```
(12 -6.668690 5.806549 1.500000)
```
X Y Z coordinates of the third corner.

```
(13 -6.668690 4.306549 3.000000)
```
X Y Z coordinates of the last corner. If this face is triangular, then these coordinates will be the same as the first corner.

```
)

(

(-1 . <Entity name: 60000028>)
```
Entity name (record index)

```
(0 . "3DFACE")
```
Entity type.

```
(8 . "0")
```
Layer name for this entity.

```
(10 -8.168690 5.806549 3.000000)
```
X Y Z coordinates of the starting corner.

```
(11 -8.168690 4.306549 1.500000)
```
X Y Z coordinates of the second corner.

```
(12 -6.668690 4.306549 3.000000)
```
X Y Z coordinates of the third corner.

```
(13 -8.168690 5.806549 3.000000)
```
X Y Z coordinates of the last corner. If this face is triangular, then those coordinates will be the same as the first corner.

```
)

(

(-1 . <Entity name: 6000003C>)
```
Entity name (record index)

```
(0 . "3DFACE")
```
Entity type.

```
(8 . "0")
```
Layer name for this entity.

```
(10 -8.168690 4.306549 1.500000)
```
X Y Z coordinates of the starting corner.

```
    (11 -6.668690 5.806549 1.500000)
```
X Y Z coordinates of the second corner.

```
    (12 -8.168690 5.806549 3.000000)
```
X Y Z coordinates of the third corner.

```
    (13 -8.168690 4.306549 1.500000)
```
X Y Z coordinates of the last corner. If this face is triangular, then these coordinates will be the same as the first corner.

```
    )

    (

    (-1 . <Entity name: 60000050>)
```
Entity name (record index)

```
    (0 . "3DFACE")
```
Entity type.

```
    (8 . "0")
```
Layer name for this entity.

```
    (10 -8.168690 4.306549 1.500000)
```
X Y Z coordinates of the starting corner.

```
    (11 -6.668690 4.306549 3.000000)
```
X Y Z coordinates of the second corner.

```
    (12 -6.668690 5.806549 1.500000)
```
X Y Z coordinates of the third corner.

```
    (13 -8.168690 4.306549 1.500000)
```
X Y Z coordinates of the last corner. If this face is triangular, then these coordinates will be the same as the first corner.

```
    )
```

3DLINE

A 3DLINE entity has the same structure as an ordinary LINE entity except that the coordinate lists (Group Codes **10** and **11**) always contain a **Z** coordinate. The purpose of this entity is to draw lines in 3D space. The **X** and **Y** coordinates are still extracted using the **car** and **cadr** functions. The **Z** coordinate can be extracted using the **caddr** function. The 3DLINE cannot have an ELEVATION nor can it be EXTRUDED, so you'll never find Group Codes **38** or **39** here.[*]

In Figure 3, three 3DLINES are shown on the face of the tetrahedron as dashed lines. The 3DLINE entity *cannot* use different LINETYPES and the dashed lines in the illustration were made with plotter linetypes to give these lines contrast from the 3DFACES on which they're drawn.

The following listing is for only one of the 3DLINEs shown in the illustration.

```
(

(-1  .  <Entity name:  600000A0>)    Entity name (record index)

(0  .  "3DLINE")                     Entity type.

(8  .  "HIDDEN")                     Layer name for this entity.

(10  -6.668690  4.306549  3.000000)  X Y Z coordinates for the
                                     start of this line.

(11  -7.418690  5.056549  1.500000)  X Y Z coordinates for the
                                     end of this line.

)
```

ASSOCIATIVE DIMENSION BLOCK ENTITY

Ordinarily, when you dimension a drawing with the DIM commands, the various parts of the dimension structure such as extension lines, dimension lines and text are made up of LINE and TEXT entities and aren't inherently distinguishable as dimensions in the drawing database.[**]

The ASSOCIATIVE DIMENSION entity represents a unique type of entity. On the one hand, it has many of the properties of a BLOCK entity in that its actual data description is in the Blocks Section and the whole dimension structure of text, extension lines, dimension lines and arrowheads is treated as a single entity in the drawing. On the other hand, when you operate on this entity with the STRETCH, SCALE or

---

[*]   These limitations may change with a future release.

[**] The only unique entity that shows up in this type of dimension is the
      arrowhead which, strictly speaking, is an "anonymous" block.

ROTATE commands, AutoCAD will update the dimension text to reflect its new size or orientation. Every time you add a dimension, AutoCAD creates an unique Block definition for that dimension in the Blocks Section, and then references that Block with a DIMENSION record in the Entities Section.[*] We think it would be wise to use this ASSOCIATIVE DIMENSION sparingly because it seems to take up almost twice the space in the drawing database as an ordinary dimension does, which would tend to create larger drawing files than necessary.

The ASSOCIATIVE DIMENSION entity will be created any time you add a dimension to a drawing when the system variable, **DIMASO**, is set to *ON*. When an ASSOCIATIVE DIMENSION entity is created, a number of special points are inserted into your drawing at strategic locations. Those points are called DEFINING POINTS, and their coordinates are found in Group Codes **10** through **16**. These DEFINING POINTS are always inserted on a special layer AutoCAD creates named DEFPOINTS.

For example, if you were to dimension a line, then DEFPOINTS would be placed at the beginning and end of the line, at the end point of the dimension line and at the center of the dimension text. If, at a later point, you lengthened this line with the STRETCH command, the DEFPOINT for the endpoint of the line would have a new coordinate location and AutoCAD would recalculate the dimension[**] and display that new dimension as the dimension text.

Below is a database listing for a simple horizontal dimension, as shown in Figure 3.[***]

```
(
(-1 . <Entity name: 60000154>)    Entity name (record index)
(0 . "DIMENSION")                 Entity type.
(8 . "0")                         Layer name for this entity.
```

---

[*] If you delete a DIMENSION Entity in your drawing, the Block reference for that Entity will remain in the Blocks Section.

[**] And possibly the dimension text location to keep the dimension text centered.

[***] Also see the Block definition listing for this entity in Appendix B.

`(2 . "*D3")`	Block name. The asterisk at the beginning of the Block name indicates that it's an "anonymous" block created by AutoCAD. **D** indicates that this is an ASSOCIATIVE DIMENSION Block and the **3** indicates the unique block number for this particular dimension entity.
`(10 -6.663841 6.206479)`	The dimension line DEFINING POINT. This point is the actual end point of the dimension line. The distance between this DEFPOINT and the Group Code **13** DEFPOINT below determines the distance between the dimensioned object and the dimension line (and also the length of the extension line).
`(11 -7.413841 6.206479)`	Middle of text DEFINING POINT, usually a point midpoint along the dimension line. This point is recalculated to remain at the midpoint of the dimension line if any of the other DEFPOINTS are moved.
`(12 0.000000 0.000000)`	Insertion points for CLONES of a dimension. This would be the insertion point (Group Code **10**) of the *next* ASSOCIATIVE DIMENSION entity

if you use the BASELINE or CONTINUE options to do a string of dimensions in one direction.

(70 . 0)

Dimension type flag. This is a bit coded flag with the first (**1**), second (**2**) and third (**4**) bit capable of being set. If no bits are set (**0**) then this dimension is a *horizontal, vertical* or *rotated* dimension. Other flag codes: **1**=*aligned*, **2**=*angular*, **3**=*diameter* and **4**=*radius*.

(1 . "")

Explicit dimension text string. When you create a dimension, you're prompted for the dimension text. You have the option of pressing **<RETURN>** to accept the actual measured dimension, or you can type in your own text for the dimension. If you type in your own text for this dimension, then that text will show up here, and it *will not be updated* if you stretch this dimension at a later time. The null string (two quotation marks) in this case means the dimension text will be updated. The actual dimension is calculated from the distance between the coordinates in Group Codes **13** and **14**.

```
(13 -8.163841 5.935429)
```

Extension DEFINING POINT for the starting point of the Dimension entity. This point also corresponds with the starting point of the line being dimensioned in this example.

```
(14 -6.663841 5.935429)
```

Extension DEFINING POINT for the ending point of the Dimension entity. This point also corresponds with the ending point of the line being dimensioned in this example.

```
(15 0.000000 0.000000)
```

Extension DEFINING POINT for diameter, radius and angular dimensions. If this dimension isn't a diameter, radius or angular dimension, then these coordinates will be **0,0**.

```
(16 0.000000 0.000000)
```

Extension DEFINING POINT for the dimension arc in angular dimensions. This would be analogous to Group Code **10** for other dimension types. If this dimension isn't an angular dimension, then these coordinates will be **0,0**.

```
(40 . 0.000000)
```

Leader length for radius and diameter dimensions.

(50 . 0.000000)   Angle of rotation for linear
                                     dimensions.   Specifically:
                                     HORIZONTAL,   VERTI-
                                     CAL or ROTATED dimen-
                                     sions.

)

appendix B DXF DATABASE: COMMENTED LISTING

While there's some overlap of information in Appendix A and this Appendix, we feel that it's valuable to present both the association list and the **DXF** formats of the AutoCAD databases. There are two reasons why we've chosen to comment on both of these formats—their similarity and their differences. These data formats are similar because they carry, for the most part, identical information. The way in which that information is presented, however, is quite different as can be seen by simply comparing the two listings. Deciphering what each Group Code means, many of them previously undocumented, is difficult at best; but having to deal with two very dissimilar looking data formats besides, adds just another hurdle to the task.

These Appendices are meant to be both an overall map of the database structure and a detailed explanation of how every Group Code works within the AutoCAD database.

UNDOCUMENTED DRAWING VARIABLES

We haven't included a listing of the Header Section of the **DXF** file because there is an adequate explanation of the header variables in Appendix C of the *AutoCAD Reference Manual*. There are, however, ten valuable user definable drawing variables not mentioned in the *AutoCAD Reference Manual.*[*] They are: $USERI1, $USERI2,

$USERI3, $USERI4, $USERI5, $USERR1, $USERR2, $USERR3, $USERR4 and **$USERR5**. These are "user variables." That is, they can be set by the user to be any value the user chooses ($USERI1 through $USERI5 must be signed 8 bit integers and $USERR1 through $USERR5 must be real numbers), and these variables will stay set until they are changed by the user.* These variables can be set by either using the **setvar** command in AutoCAD or the **setvar** function in AutoLISP. In AutoCAD these variables are called without the leading $ (that is, $USERI1 in the **DXF** file header is called USERI1 in **setvar**).

COMPARING DXF AND ASSOCIATION LIST FORMATS

There are more similarities than differences between the **DXF** (Data eXchange Format) file database and the association list database format. Most Group Codes are the same in the two data formats, they're just organized differently. Below are some of the differences:

- The **DXF** format has separate Group Codes for both the **X** and **Y**** coordinates of an entity. If you add **10** to the Group Code for the **X** coordinate, you'll get the Group Code for the **Y** coordinate, and if you add **10** to the Group Code for the **Y** coordinate, you'll get the Group Code for the **Z** coordinate (if there is any).

- If a Group Code for an entity isn't applicable or isn't used for that given entity, then it won't appear in the **DXF** listing for that entity. Two examples: If no attributes are linked to a Block insertion, then Group Code **66** (the attributes follow flag) will not appear in the INSERT listing.*** If a 3DLINE entity is listed, but the **Z** coordinate is **0** then the Group Codes (**30** and **31**) for the **Z** coordinates won't appear in the database listing.****

- Entities in a **DXF** file don't have entity names associated with them. Entity names are used within a random access database framework inside of AutoCAD so that you can access any given entity quickly if you know its entity name.

---

* Unlike AutoLISP variables that lose their value when you exit the drawing.

** And the **Z** coordinate if applicable.

***In the Association List format the Group Code **66** will appear but it will be set to **0**.

***It's difficult to comment on fields that don't appear in the database record, so we've added a list of all of the possible Group Codes that could appear in an entity description at the end of that particular entity listing.

· The Group Code **0** appears quite frequently in the **DXF** file. This Group Code acts as a flag to indicate that some change will start with the next line. The exact meaning of Group Code **0** varies depending upon what's on the following line. Group Code **0** could mean the start of a new section, the start of a new entity or the end of a section. It all depends on what's on the next line.

BIT CODED FLAGS

Any Group Code between **70** and **78** is usually (but not always) a *bit coded flag*. An explanation of what a bit coded flag is will probably clear up some of the mystery of how these Group Codes are used in the **DXF** file.

In a bit coded flag, an 8 bit binary code is used. As you may know, a binary number has only two different numbers: 0 and 1. The number 46 (decimal) would be equal to 00101110 in binary format. The right-most digit of a binary number is the 1 digit, the next digit (moving left) is the 2 digit followed by the 4 digit then the 8 then the 16 digit and so on. The place value of an 8 bit binary number can be represented by the following table:

```
128    64    32    16    8    4    2    1
1      1     1     1     1    1    1    1  =255 decimal
0      1     1     1     1    1    1    1  =127 decimal
```

An easy way to convert a binary number to a decimal number is to add the place values of each digit of a binary number that is a 1 (ignoring the digits that are 0). For example:

```
00000111 is, starting from the right digit, 1+2+4=7.
00000101 is 1+4=5
00010101 is 1+4+16=21
01000010 is 2+64=66
01000001 is 1+64=65
01000100 is 4+64=68
```
When an eight bit binary number is used as a flag it is sometimes referred to as a bit field, and the way certain bits are set (set to be either **0** or **1**) determines what that flag means. One advantage of using a bit coded field for setting flags is that you can have as many

as eight different flags set in one byte (eight bits) of memory—that is, one number can hold as many as eight different pieces of information *at one time*.

For example, if the Group Code **70** has a value of **1**, then it means that the first bit (or flag) is set to **1** (or true) and the other seven flags (or bits) are set to **0** (or false). If the value of the Group Code is **65** then the first bit and the seventh bit have been set to true (or **1**). This means that when AutoCAD looks at Group Code **70** in a layer definition, for instance, and sees that the value is **65** then it knows that both the seventh bit flag and the first bit flag have been set to true. The bit field looks like this for several different possibilities:

```
00000001 binary=1 decimal = first bit true.
00000010 binary=2 decimal = second bit true.
00000100 binary=4 decimal = third bit true.
01000001 binary=64+1=65 decimal = first and seventh bit true.
01000010 binary=64+2=66 decimal=second and seventh bit true.
01000100 binary=64+4=68 decimal = third and seventh bit true.
```

See the various listings below for specific information on how these bit coded flags are set in various contexts.

DXF LISTING STRUCTURE

This **DXF** listing was generated from the same drawing as the database listing in Appendix A (Figure 1). The specific format of the **DXF** file is one item per line; the first line carries the Group Code and the next line carries the value for that Group. In most cases we have broken up the **DXF** file into pairs to emphasize that structure. Each Group Code and Group value pair in the following listing will look like this:

```
10              (This is the Group Code.)

10.1            (This is the value for the Group Code above.
                This is also the line where the comments will
                be found.)

20              (The next Group Code.)
```

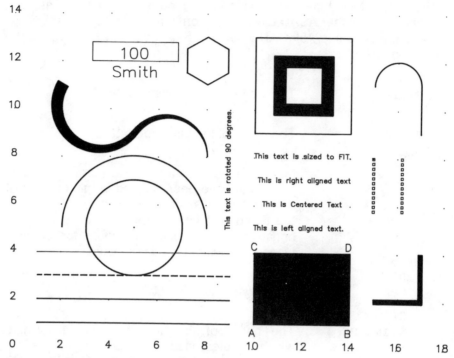

Figure 1: Plot of sample database.

TABLES SECTION

    0
    SECTION   The start of the Tables Section.

    2
    TABLES   The name of the Table Section.

LINE TYPE TABLE

The Line type table contains the definitions of all Line types used (or have been defined by the **LAYER Ltype** command) in a given drawing. Any Line type assigned to a layer in the layer table or to an entity in the Entity Section must first be defined in this table.

The actual Line type definition originally comes from the Line type definition file (either ACAD.LIN or a custom Line type file with a .LIN extension) loaded into AutoCAD when you request a new Line type in the drawing editor.*

0 TABLE		The start of the Line type table.
2 LTYPE		The name of the Line type table.
70	2	Maximum item count. The number of Line types that have been defined in this table must appear here. This number may be larger than the number of Line types defined in the table because it represents the count for all Line types ever defined in this drawing.**
0 LTYPE		A Line type definition starts here.
2 CONTINUOUS		The name of the Line type being defined, which is referenced when Line types are assigned to layers and entities. CONTINUOUS is the default Line type and will appear in the Line type table, even if no Line types have been assigned.
70	64	Line type flag. This is a bit coded flag and only the seventh bit (64) is set. If the seventh bit is set (64), that means that this Line type is used by an entity or has been assigned to a layer in the Layer table. If the PURGE command sees the seventh bit set to 0, then it will remove this Line type definition from the draw-

---

* See Section B.3 in the Appendix of the *AutoCAD Reference Manual* for more information on how Line types are defined.

** If a Line type definition has been PURGED from the drawing, that definition won't be written to the **DXF** file.

ing file unless the Line type is CONTINUOUS.[*]
If this Line type is not referenced anywhere in
the drawing file then the seventh bit of this flag
is set to **0**. See the introduction to this Appendix for more information about bit coded flags.

3
Solid line   This is a "prose description" for this Line type.

72
  65   Alignment code. **65** is the ASCII code for the
letter **A**. This is the only alignment code sup-
ported by AutoCAD[**].

73
0   The number of dash length items. This is the
number of different dashes (including blanks
between dashes) that would be in this Line
type. Because this is a solid continuous line,
there are no dashes.

40
0.0   Total pattern length.

0
LTYPE   A Line type definition starts here.

2
HIDDEN   The name of the Line type being defined.

70
  64   Line type flag. This is a bit coded flag. and
only the seventh bit (**64**) is set. If the seventh
bit is set (**64**), that means that this Line type is
used by an entity or has been assigned to a
layer in the Layer table. If the PURGE command sees the seventh bit set to **0**, then it will
remove this Line type definition from the drawing file.

---

[*] The PURGE command will never remove the CONTINUOUS Line type
since it is the *default* Line type.
[**] See Section B.3 in the *AutoCAD Reference Manual* for more information.

3

– –

> This is a "prose description" for this Line type. In this particular example, this is just a dash and space description of the Line type being defined, taken directly from the .**LIN** Line type file. This is an optional description in the .**LIN** file, so this Group may be blank in certain cases.

72
   65

> Alignment code. **65** is the ASCII code for the letter **A**. This is the only alignment code supported by AutoCAD.

73
2

> The number of dash length items. This is the number of different dashes (including blanks between dashes) that would be in this Line type. Because this is a HIDDEN Line with one dash and one space, the number of dash length items is **2**.

40
0.375

> Total pattern length for this Line type. This is the total length of the dots and/or dashes and the spaces between them in this pattern. If you add all the values in all of the Group **49**s below, this number would be the result.

49
0.25

> Dash length. This is the length of an individual dash, dot or space (a negative number represents a space) in a Line type pattern. Group **49** will appear once in a Line type definition for each individual dash, dot or space. The number of times that Group **49** appears in a Line type definition must agree with the value of Group **73**.

```
    49
-0.125
```
Dash length. Because this number is negative, it indicates that this is the length of the space between the dashes.

```
     0
ENDTAB
```
End of the LINE TYPE Table.

LAYER TABLE

The layer table contains the descriptions of all of the layers that have been defined in a particular AutoCAD drawing. Any entity or Block assigned to a specific layer must have that layer defined here first. The layers in this layer table have been defined using the **LAYER New** command in AutoCAD.

```
     0
TABLE
     2
LAYER
```
Start of layer table.

```
    70
        2
```
Layer table maximum item count. This is the total number of layers that have ever been defined in this table. This number may not agree with the number of layers in the table. See Group **70** in the Line type table for more information.

```
     0
LAYER
```
A layer definition starts here.

```
     2
0
```
Name of the layer to be defined. Layer **0** is the default layer, and will appear in the layer table even if no layers have been assigned to the drawing.

```
    70
       64
```
Layer Flag. This is a bit coded flag where both the first and seventh bits can be set. If the first bit is set (**1**), that means this layer is currently frozen. If the seventh bit is set (**64**), that means this layer is used by an entity in either the Entity Section or in the Block Section. If

the PURGE command sees the seventh bit set to **0** then it will remove this layer definition from the drawing file unless it is layer "**0**".[*] If this layer is not referenced anywhere in the drawing file then the seventh bit is set to **0**. The possible bit combinations for this flag are **0** layer not referenced and not frozen, **1** layer not referenced and frozen, **64** layer referenced and not frozen and **65** layer referenced and frozen. See the beginning of this Appendix for more information on bit coded flags.

62
7

Color number assigned to this layer (**7** is white). If this is a negative number, then that means that this layer is currently turned **OFF**.

6
CONTINUOUS

The Line type assigned to this layer. The CONTINUOUS Line type is automatically assigned to any new layer when it is defined by the LAYER command.

0
LAYER

A layer definition starts here.

2
1

Name of the layer to be defined. The name of this layer is "**1**", a text string, not a number.

70
0

Layer flag. This is a bit coded flag where both the first and seventh bits can be set. If the first bit is set (**1**), that means this layer is currently frozen. If the seventh bit is set (**64**), that means this layer is used by an entity in either the Entity Section or in the Block Section. If the PURGE command sees the seventh bit set to **0**, then it will remove this layer definition

---

[*] The PURGE command will never remove layer "0" since it is the *default* layer.

from the drawing file. This layer is not referenced by an entity since none of the bit flags have been set.

62
7

Color number assigned to this layer (**7** is white). If this is a negative number, then that means this layer is currently turned **OFF**.

6
HIDDEN

The Line type assigned to this layer.

0
ENDTAB

End of the layer table.

TEXT STYLE TABLE

The Text style table contains the definitions of all the Text styles that have been defined with the STYLE command. If any SHAPEs are used in the drawing, the SHAPE file is also defined in this table.

0
TABLE
2
STYLE

Start of the Text style table.

70
3

Text style table maximum item count. The total number of Text styles that have been defined in this table. See Group **70** in the Line type table section for more information.

0
STYLE

A Text style definition starts here.

2
STANDARD

The name of this Text style definition. STANDARD is the default Text style that is assigned to all text in the drawing unless another Text style is defined as the current Text style with the **TEXT S** command.

70

0   Text style group flag. This is a bit coded flag with the first bit **(1)**, the third bit **(4)** and the seventh bit **(64)** capable of being set. If the first flag bit is set **(1)**, that means this definition refers to a Shape file rather than a Font file. If the third flag bit is set **(4)**, then a vertically oriented Text style has been defined.* If the seventh bit has been set **(64)** then this Text style has been used in either a text string or an attribute in this drawing. If the seventh bit flag is set to **0** (false) then the PURGE command will remove the Text style. The possible bit codes for this Group are: **0, 1, 4, 64, 65** and **68**. See the beginning of this Appendix for more information about bit coded flags.

40

0.0   Fixed text height. If you had specified a text height in the STYLE command when you were defining a Text style, then that height would show up here.

41

1.0   **X** scale factor for this Text style.

50

0.0   Obliquing angle for this Text style.

71

0   Text generation flag. This is a bit coded flag with the second **(2)** and third **(4)** bits capable of being set. If both bits are **0** then text will appear normal. If the second bit is set **(2)**, then the text will appear mirrored in the **X** axis (left to right). If the third bit **(4)** is set, then the text will appear upside down. Only one bit will be set at a time. See the beginning of this Appendix for more information about bit coded flags.

---

* If you answered *yes* to Vertical when you defined this style with the STYLE command.

42
0.2   The last text height used for this style in this
                             drawing. Unlike Group **40** (fixed height), this
                             just sets a default height for this style when it
                             is used.

3
txt   Font file name. The name of the font file that
                             contains the actual vector information that
                             AutoCAD uses to construct the text characters
                             used in *this* Text style definition. This file must
                             be in the same sub-directory as AutoCAD
                             when you load a drawing that uses this font in
                             a Text style definition. If you had LOADed a
                             SHAPE file into your drawing the name of that
                             Shape file would appear in this Group.

4
                             If the font used in this style definition was a
                             "bigfont"[*] then the name of that font would ap-
                             pear in this Group. Otherwise, this field
                             remains blank.

0
STYLE   A Text style definition starts here.

2
NORMAL   The name of this Text style definition. NOR-
                             MAL is the name of the Text style that we
                             defined and used in this drawing file.

70
        64   Text style group flag. This is a bit coded flag.
                             See the previous Style listing for more informa-
                             tion.

40
0.0   Fixed text height size.

41
1.0   **X** scale factor for this Text style.

---

[*] See Appendix B.5.4 in the *AutoCAD Reference Manual* for information
     about big fonts.

```
    50
    0.0                        Obliquing angle for this Text style.

    71
          0                    Text generation flag.  See the previous listing
                               for more information.

    42
    0.2                        The last text height used for this style in this
                               drawing.

     3
simplex                        Font file name used in this Text style.

     4
                               "Bigfont" file name, if any.
```

SHAPE FILE LOAD REQUEST

If a Shape file is LOADed into the drawing, that fact will show up in the Style table as a Style definition. This is not a true style definition, however, and only three Groups in this definition are meaningful for Shapes. All of the other Groups are outputted by AutoCAD, but they seem to carry values from other style definitions. These other Groups can be ignored, but they must be present in the definition.

```
     0
STYLE                          A style definition starts here.  (IMPORTANT)

    ·2
                               The name of this style definition.  Because this
                               is a Shape load,  this field is blank.  (IGNORE)

    70
          65                   Text style group flag.  This is a bit coded flag
                               and it is set to 65, which indicates that this is a
                               Shape load request and is referenced by a
                               Shape  insertion  in  this  drawing  file  (the
                               seventh bit (64) and the first bit (1) is set to 1).
                               (IMPORTANT)

    40
    0.0                        Fixed text height size.  (IGNORE)

    41
    1.0                        X scale factor for this Text style.  (IGNORE)
```

```
   50
  0.0                        Obliquing angle for this Text style.  (IGNORE)

   71
        0                    Text generation flag.  (IGNORE)

   42
  9.0                        The last text height used.  (IGNORE)

    3
PC                           The name of the Shape file LOADed.  (IMPOR-
                             TANT)

    4

    0
ENDTAB                       End of the Text style table.
```

VIEW TABLE

The View table holds the coordinates of all the Views that were saved with the VIEW SAVE or VIEW WINDOW commands. This table contains one view window of the Room tag on the sample drawing.

```
    0
TABLE
    2
VIEW                         The View table starts here.

   70
        1                    Maximum number of Views in this table.  See
                             Group 70 in the Line type table for more infor-
                             mation.

    0
VIEW                         A View definition starts here.

    2
ROOM                         The name of the View.

   70
        0                    View flag—not used.  This is a bit coded flag.

   40
2.609776                     View height.
```

```
    10
4.973454            X coordinate of the View center point.

    20
11.713717           Y coordinate of the View center point.

    41
4.109143            View width.

    11
0.0                 X coordinate of the View direction from origin.
                    This is set with the 3D VPOINT command.
                    This value is the default for the "plan" view.

    21
0.0                 Y coordinate of the View direction from origin.
                    This is set with the 3D VPOINT command.
                    This value is the default for the "plan" view.

    31
1.0                 Z coordinate of the View direction from origin.
                    This is set with the 3D VPOINT command.
                    This value is the default for the "plan" view.

    0
ENDTAB              End of the View table.

    0
ENDSEC              End of the Tables Section.
```

BLOCKS SECTION

The Blocks Section contains all of the entity information about every Block in the drawing. Each block definition in this Section is structured exactly like the Entity Section in this file. When you create a block with AutoCAD, the records of all the drawing entities you've chosen to include in the block are copied from the Entities Section to the Blocks Section and the chosen entities are then deleted from the Entities Section.

When you write a block out to disk as a separate drawing with the WBLOCK command, the entity information for the desired block is written to a new file. Other information that is written to this new file includes the Header Section and any Line type, layer and text definitions that are referenced by entities in the block definition.

BLOCK DEFINITION

```
        0
   SECTION
        2
   BLOCKS
```
The beginning of the Blocks Section.

```
        0
   BLOCK
```
A Block listing starts here. This block definition consists of four LINE entities and one ATTDEF entity*. The block definition for the block IN-SERT entity you'll see later in this file. The Header Section for this block contains information about the overall properties of this block.

```
        8
   0
```
Layer name for this block.

```
        2
   ROOMTAG
```
The name of this block definition that INSERT uses to reference this block description.

```
       70
             66
```
Block type flag. This is a bit coded flag where the first (1), second (2) or seventh (64) bits are capable of being set. If the second bit (2) is set, it means that this BLOCK definition has ATTDEFs or attributes. If the first bit (1) is set, this block is an "anonymous" (or pseudo) block. If the seventh (64) bit is set, then this block is referenced by an INSERT record in the Entities Section of this drawing. If the seventh bit is set to 0 (false), then the PURGE command will remove this Block definition. The possible bit codes for this field are 0, 1, 2, 64, 65 and 66.

```
       10
   116.5
```
X coordinate of the base point for this block.

```
       20
   88.0
```
Y coordinate of the base point for this block.

---

* There really should be two ATTDEFs, but we took one out for brevity.

Now the Entities List begins for this Block.

```
   0
 LINE                    A Line definition starts here.

   8
 0                       Layer name for this entity.

  10
 81.0                    Start X coordinate.

  20
 104.0                   Start Y coordinate.

  11
 81.0                    End X coordinate.

  21
 88.0                    End Y coordinate.

   0
 LINE                    A Line definition starts here.

   8
 0                       Layer name for this entity.

  10
 152.0                   Start X coordinate.

  20
 104.0                   Start Y coordinate.

  11
 81.0                    End X coordinate.

  21
 104.0                   End Y coordinate.

   0
 LINE                    A Line definition starts here.

   8
 0                       Layer name for this entity.

  10
 152.0                   Start X coordinate.

  20
 88.0                    Start Y coordinate.
```

```
    11
  152.0                    End X coordinate.

    21
  104.0                    End Y coordinate.

    0
  LINE                     A Line definition starts here.

    8
  0                        Layer name for this entity.

   10
  81.0                     Start X coordinate.

   20
  88.0                     Start Y coordinate.

   11
  152.0                    End X coordinate.

   21
  88.0                     End Y coordinate.
```

ATTRIBUTE DEFINITION (ATTDEF)

The Attribute Definition or ATTDEF entity is always found inside a block definition. This is created with the ATTDEF command in AutoCAD and then saved (along with other entities) as a block with the BLOCK command to make up the block with attributes structure.

```
    0
  ATTDEF                   Start of the ATTDEF entity.

    8
  0                        Layer name for this entity.

   10
  84.928571                X coordinate starting point for attribute text.

   20
  74.571429                Y coordinate starting point for attribute text.

   40
  9.0                      Text height for this attribute definition.
```

```
    1
Vacant
```
Default attribute value for this attribute definition.

```
    3
Employee's Name
```
Prompt for attribute value that appears whenever this block is inserted.

```
    2
EMPNAME
```
The attribute tag, the key searched for when attributes are extracted using the ATTEXT command. The attribute tag remains the same for
all instances of this attribute, while each instance of this attribute can have different
values linked to this attribute tag. Think of the
attribute tag as a FIELD NAME and the attribute value as the value contained in that field
in a database record.

```
   70
      0
```
The attribute flag. It is a bit coded flag with the
first (**1**), second (**2**) and third (**4**) bits capable of
being set. If no bits are set in this Group (**0**),
then this attribute will be visible. If the first (**1**)
bit is set, it means that this attribute will be invisible. If the second (**2**) bit is set, then the attribute value will be a constant. If the third (**4**)
bit is set, then verification will be required on
input of any value for this attribute. Only one
bit will be set at a time in this field. See the
beginning of this Appendix for more information about bit coded flags.

```
    7
NORMAL
```
Text style for this attribute entity.

```
   72
      1
```
Alignment point flag. This is *not* a bit coded
flag. The value of this number determines how
the text is justified. **0** means that the text will
be Left justified and this Group Code will not
appear. Other values: **1**=*baseline centered*

text; **2**=*right justified* text; **3**=*aligned* text; **4**=*"middle" or fully centered* text; and **5**=*"fit"* text.

11
116.0

The actual **centered X** coordinate base of this attribute text string. This, along with Group **21** below, is the point that was picked for inserting the attribute text after the CENTER option was picked in the ATTDEF command when this attribute was defined. These two Groups are optional Groups, and will only appear in an entity listing if Group 72 is present and non-zero.

21
74.571429

The actual **centered Y** coordinate base of this attribute text string.

0
ENDBLK

End of this block definition.

8
0

Layer name for the preceding block definition.

0
ENDSEC

End of the Blocks Section.

ENTITIES SECTION

The Entities Section is the main part of the **DXF** file. All entities in your drawing are described here—either as complete entity descriptions or incidents of Block Insertions.

START OF THE ENTITIES SECTION

0
SECTION
2
ENTITIES

The name of the Entities Section. Any line following Group Code **2** is the name of something.

LINE

This first Line listing is for a simple Line entity.

```
    0
  LINE                    Entity type.

    8
  0                       Layer name for this entity.

   10
  1.0                     Start X coordinate.

   20
  1.0                     Start Y coordinate.

   11
  9.0                     End X coordinate.

   21
  1.0                     End Y coordinate.
```

EXTRUDED LINE

This Line listing is for a Line that has a **Z** coordinate thickness and elevation assigned to it—Group **38** and **39** respectively. These groups will be in the entity record *only* if their value is non-zero. Otherwise, this listing is the same as for a Line entity.

```
    0
  LINE                    Entity type.

    8
  0                       Layer name for this entity.

   38
  2.0                     If the 38 Group exists in the DXF file, then this
                          entity has a Z elevation that is not zero and the
                          next line is the elevation.

   39
  4.0                     If the 39 Group appears in the DXF file, then
                          this entity has a Z thickness that is greater
                          than zero.  The next line is the thickness.

   10
  1.0                     Start X coordinate.
```

```
   20
2.0                     Start Y coordinate.

   11
9.0                     End X coordinate.

   21
2.0                     End Y coordinate.
```

LINE BY LINETYPE

This next Line listing is for a line that has a linetype different than the one set for the layer on which this entity resides.

```
    0
LINE                    Entity type.

    8
0                       Layer name for this entity.

    6
HIDDEN                  If Group Code 6 appears, that means the
                        linetype for this entity is not the same linetype
                        set for the layer for this entity.  HIDDEN is the
                        linetype assigned to this entity.

   10
1.0                     Start X coordinate.

   20
3.0                     Start Y coordinate.

   11
9.0                     End X coordinate.

   21
3.0                     End Y coordinate.
```

LINE "BYCOLOR"

This last Line listing has a different color than the one assigned to that entity's layer.

```
    0
LINE                    Entity type.

    8
0                       Layer name for this entity.
```

```
    62
  1
```
If Group Code **62** appears, then the color for this entity is different than the entity's layer color. Color number 1 is RED.

```
    10
  1.0
```
Start **X** coordinate.

```
    20
  4.0
```
Start **Y** coordinate.

```
    11
  9.0
```
End **X** coordinate.

```
    21
  4.0
```
End **Y** coordinate.

POINT

The POINT is a very simple entity. It has only one coordinate. The different Point Modes available are set with the variable $PMODE in the Header Section of the data file[*].

```
    0
  POINT
```
Entity type.

```
    8
  0
```
Layer name for this entity.

```
    10
  5.0
```
X coordinate.

```
    20
  5.0
```
Y coordinate.

CIRCLE

The CIRCLE has only two defining measurements: the **X Y** coordinates for the center and the **radius**.

```
    0
  CIRCLE
```
Entity type.

---

[*] See 4.2 in the *AutoCAD Reference Manual* for more information about Points.

```
     8
0                          Layer name for this entity.

    10
5.0                        X coordinate for the center of the circle.

    20
5.0                        Y coordinate for the center of the circle.

    40
2.0                        Radius of circle.
```

ARC

The ARC is described with a center, a radius, a starting angle and an ending angle. The arc is *always drawn counter-clockwise* from the starting angle to the ending angle.

```
     0
ARC                        Entity type.

     8
0                          Layer name for this entity.

    10
5.0                        X coordinate for the center of the arc.

    20
5.0                        Y coordinate for the center of the arc.

    40
3.0                        Arc radius.

    50
0.0                        Starting angle in degrees.

    51
180.0                      Ending angle in degrees.
```

SOLID

A SOLID is a filled three- or four- sided figure that is usually *filled*. A SOLID is uniquely described by two opposing pairs of points rather than by four points around the perimeter, as a normal rectilinear shape would be described.

In Figure 1, the SOLID is properly defined by the first pair of points **A** and **B** (the base) and then by the second pair of points **C** and **D** (the top). If this were a square figure rather than a SOLID, it would be correctly described by the following sequence of points: **A, C, D, B** and **A**. If the SOLID is to be triangular in form, it would be described with the first two points as the base (**10** and **11**), and the third point for the apex (**12**).

0 SOLID	Entity type.
8 0	Layer name for this entity.
10 10.0	First **X** coordinate for the base.
20 1.0	First **Y** coordinate for the base.
11 14.0	Second **X** coordinate for the base.
21 1.0	Second **Y** coordinate for the base.
12 10.0	First **X** coordinate for the top.
22 4.0	First **Y** coordinate for the top.
13 14.0	Second **X** coordinate for the top.
23 4.0	Second **Y** coordinate for the top.

TEXT AND SHAPE

The next several listings will deal with various types of TEXT and SHAPE entities.

There's only one TEXT entity, but a number of variations are based on how the text has been formatted in the drawing editor. Those formatting variations of the TEXT entity can be very confusing, so we'll illustrate most of them explicitly by example listings.

In all TEXT entity listings below, the text is the same height and the same style, only the way that the text has been formatted is different (i.e. CENTER, RIGHT, FIT, etc.).

For more information on TEXT and SHAPE entities, see the Text Section in Appendix A.

LEFT TEXT

This first listing is for standard left justified text, or the kind of text that you get when you just pick a starting point in response to the TEXT command.

0 TEXT	Entity type.
8 0	Layer name for this entity.
10 10.0	Insertion point **X** coordinate for this line of text. This coordinate, and the **Y** coordinate that follows, is the actual starting point of the line of text. This point is always at the *beginning* of the text string.
20 5.0	Insertion point **X** coordinate for this line of text.
40 0.2	The body height of the upper case letters for this line of text. This Group will not appear in the **DXF** listing if the Text style has been defined with a *Height* in the Tables Section.

1
`This is left`
`aligned text.`
	The actual text string for this entity. These are the characters that will appear on your screen. This text string can have a maximum length of 255 characters. Because everything stored in disk files is stored as strings, this text string doesn't have to be explicitly quoted as it does in the association list format.

7 `NORMAL`	The name assigned to the style definition for this text style. In this example, the text style is named NORMAL. This is *not* the name of the font file, which appears in the Style Table in the Tables Section of the drawing database, where the complete definition for the NORMAL text style is found (the font file for NORMAL is SIMPLEX).

CENTERED TEXT

The only difference between this TEXT entity listing and the preceding one is that this text is **centered** on an **alignment point** (Groups **11** and **21**). Text always has a base point at the *beginning* of the TEXT entity (in this example, just before the **T** in "This"). If you specify **Center** alignment when you insert your line of text into the drawing, AutoCAD will calculate a point to the left of the center point half the length of your text string. This point is the actual insertion point for the TEXT entity.

0 `TEXT`	Entity type.
8 `0`	Layer name for this entity.
10 `10.357143`	Insertion point **X** coordinate for this line of text. This, combined with Group **20** below, is the actual starting point of the line of text.
20 `6.0`	Insertion point **Y** coordinate for this line of text.

```
   40
   0.2
```
The body height of the upper case letters for this line of text.

```
    1
This is
Centered Text
```
The actual text string for this entity.

```
    7
NORMAL
```
Text style for this entity.

```
   72
       1
```
Text justification type flag. The value of this number determines how the text is justified. In this example, **1** means that the text will be CENTERED. This is an optional Group.

```
   11
   12.0
```
The actual **centered** insertion **X** coordinate of this text string. This Group, and Group **21** that follows, is the point picked for inserting the text after the Center option was picked in the TEXT command. This is an optional Group, and will only appear if Group **72** is in the data description and is non-zero.

```
   21
   6.0
```
The actual **centered** Insertion **Y** coordinate of this text string. This is an optional Group.

RIGHT ALIGNED TEXT

If **r**ight **a**ligned text were specified, then the actual TEXT entity insertion point will be a point to the left of the alignment point *equal in distance to the total width* of the TEXT entity.

```
    0
TEXT
```
Entity type.

```
    8
0
```
Layer name for this entity.

```
   10
10.161905
```
Insertion point **X** coordinate for this line of text. This, combined with Group **20** below, is the actual starting point of the line of text.

```
  20
 7.0
```
Insertion point **Y** coordinate for this line of text.

```
  40
 0.2
```
The body height of the upper case letters for this line of text.

```
   1
This is right
aligned text
```
The actual text string for this entity.

```
   7
NORMAL
```
The name of the text style for this text.

```
  72
     2
```
Text justification type flag. The value of this number determines how the text is justified. In this example, **2** means that the text will be RIGHT ALIGNED.

```
  11
14.0
```
The actual **right aligned** Insertion **X** coordinate of this text string. This Group, and Group **21** that follows, is the point picked for inserting the text after the Right option was picked in the TEXT command. This is an optional Group, and will only appear if Group **72** is in the data description and is non-zero.

```
  21
 7.0
```
The actual **right aligned** insertion **Y** coordinate of this text string. This is an optional Group.

TEXT TO "FIT"

The difference between this TEXT entity listing and standard TEXT entity is that this text is fitted between a starting and ending point. After you pick a starting and an ending point, AutoCAD will adjust the **Relative X Scale Factor** (Group **41**) for this TEXT entity so that it will fit between the specified starting and ending points. An **alignment point** (Groups **11** and **21**), halfway between the starting and ending points, is also calculated. Again, text always has a base point at the *beginning* of the TEXT entity (in this example, just before the **T** in "This"), or at the starting point for **Fitted Text**. This point is the actual insertion point for the TEXT entity.

```
    0
  TEXT
```
Entity type.

```
    8
  0
```
Layer name for this entity.

```
   10
  10.0
```
Insertion point **X** coordinate for this line of text. This, combined with Group **20** below, is the actual starting point of the line of text.

```
   20
  8.0
```
Insertion point **Y** coordinate for this line of text.

```
   40
  0.2
```
The body height of the upper case letters for this line of text.

```
    1
This text is
sized to FIT.
```
The actual text string for this entity.

```
   41
  1.042184
```
Relative **X** scale, or width factor. This is the factor that changes when a TEXT entity is "stretched" or "squeezed" to fit between two points. In this example, the text had to be stretched slightly to fit, because the factor is slightly greater than **1**.

```
    7
NORMAL
```
Text style for this entity.

```
   72
       5
```
Text justification type flag. The value of this number determines how the text is justified. In this example, **5** means the text will be sized to FIT.

```
   11
  14.0
```
The actual **centered** insertion **X** coordinate of this text string. This Group, and Group **21** that follows, is the point calculated by AutoCAD to be halfway between the starting and ending points picked for inserting the text after the FIT option was picked in the TEXT command.

This is an optional Group, and will only appear if Group **72** is in the data description and is non-zero.

```
21
8.0
```
The actual **centered** Insertion **Y** coordinate of this text string. This is an optional Group.

ROTATED TEXT

This example is simply left justified text, rotated **90** degrees counter-clockwise. It illustrates Group **50**.

```
0
TEXT
```
Entity type.

```
8
0
```
Layer name for this entity.

```
10
9.0
```
Insertion point **X** coordinate for this line of text. This, combined with Group **20** below, is the actual starting point of the line of text.

```
20
5.0
```
Insertion point **Y** coordinate for this line of text.

```
40
0.2
```
The body height of the upper case letters for this line of text.

```
1
This text is
rotated 90
degrees.
```
The actual text string for this entity.

```
50
90.0
```
The rotation angle for this line of text in degrees.

```
7
NORMAL
```
Text style for this entity.

SHAPES

A shape file is identical in structure to a text file and almost all information presented about text files and TEXT entities is also true for shapes. The following is the listing for a shape insertion. Notice how close it is in structure to a text insertion.

0	
SHAPE	Entity type.
8	
0	Layer name for this entity.
10	
15.0	Insertion point **X** coordinate for this shape. This, combined with Group **20** below, is the insertion point for this shape.
20	
8.0	Insertion point **Y** coordinate for this shape.
40	
2.0	The size, or relative scale factor for this shape. This shape was inserted at 2x scale. This is an optional Group.
2	
DIP24	The name of this shape (the name is contained in the shape file referenced in the Style Table in the Table Section of this **DXF** file).

OPTIONAL GROUP CODES FOR TEXT AND SHAPES

The following Group Codes will *only appear* in a **DXF** file TEXT entity listing if the value for the Group Code in question is *non-zero*. The order in which these "Optional" Group Codes may appear is not fixed and may vary.

50   The rotation angle for the line of text in degrees. The pivot point for this angle is always at the insertion point (Group Codes **10** and **20**), which may be different from the starting point of the text (dependent on the type of text formatting).

41   Relative **X** scale, or width factor. If, when you defined your text style with the STYLE command, you used a width factor of other than **1**, then this Group Code will show up in the DXF file with the width factor (other than 1) that had been specified for the Text style.

51   The Obliquing Angle of the text in degrees. If you had defined a text style to have slanting letters, the angle of that slant would be in this Group Code and it would appear in the DXF file entry for TEXT.

71   Text generation flag. This is a bit coded flag with the second (**2**) and third (**4**) bits capable of being set. If both bits are **0**, then text will appear normal. If the second bit is set (**2**), then the text will appear mirrored in the **X** axis (left to right). If the third bit (**4**) is set, then the text will appear upside down. Only one bit will be set at a time. See the beginning of Appendix B for more information about bit coded flags.

---

* In the association list format all Group Codes, with a few exceptions, will appear in the entity record regardless of their value.

** See Section 4.10.1 of the *AutoCAD Reference Manual.*

72	Text justification type flag. This is *not* a bit coded flag. The value of this number determines how the text is justified. **0** means that the text will be left justified and this Group Code will not appear. Other values: **1**=*baseline centered* text; **2**=*right justified* text; **3**=*aligned* text; **4**="*middle*" or *fully centered* text; and **5**="*fit*" text.
11 21	Alignment point. These two Group Codes represent the **X Y** coordinate point where the text was inserted. These Groups will only appear in a record description if Group **72** appears. See the comments for the different types of TEXT entities for examples of how these two Groups are used.

OTHER TEXT ENTITY TYPES

Two remaining Text justification types that we haven't illustrated are **ALIGNED** and **MIDDLE**.

ALIGNED is similar to FIT except the text height (Group **40**) is adjusted to fit instead of the relative **X** scale factor (Group **41**). The text justification type (Group **72**) for ALIGNED is **3**.

MIDDLE is similar to CENTER except the text is centered with the alignment point (Groups **11** and **21**) in both the **X** and the **Y** axis. The text justification type (Group **72**) for MIDDLE is **4**.

BLOCK INSERTION, ATTRIBUTE AND SEQEND

The following four **DXF** entity listings represent a BLOCK insertion of a block that contains two attributes. The only difference between this Block Insertion record and that of a Block that doesn't contain attributes is that in the latter, Group **66**, doesn't appear.

The actual list of entities that makes up any given block or attribute can be found in the Block Section of this **DXF** file.

A large number of "optional" Groups for Block insertions and Attributes don't appear in the following DXF listings. These Groups will be listed and commented on at the end of this section.

BLOCK INSERTION

0 INSERT	Entity type.
8 0	Layer name for this entity.
66 1	"Attributes Follow" flag. If this Group appears in the DXF listing for a Block insertion, then all records that follow this record will be attributes attached to this block until a SEQEND entity type is reached. This is an optional Group and will only appear if attribute entities are linked with the Block.
2 ROOMTAG	The name of this block. If an INSERT record is found that has a block name that starts with an asterisk (*), then that BLOCK is an "anonymous" Block, created by an internal AutoCAD operation. Hatch patterns and arrowheads are examples of anonymous blocks.
10 5.0	The **X** coordinate of the insertion point for this instance of the Block.

```
  20
12.0
```
The **Y** coordinate of the insertion point for this instance of the Block.

```
  41
0.05
```
The **X** scale for this insertion of this block. This is an optional Group—if the **X** scale of this Block insertion were **1**, this Group would not appear in this record.

```
  42
0.05
```
The **Y** scale for this insertion of this block. This is an optional Group—if the **Y** scale of this Block insertion were **1**, this Group would not appear in this record.

```
  43
0.05
```
The **Z** scale for this insertion of this block. This is an optional Group—if the **Z** scale of this Block insertion were **1**, this Group would not appear in this record.

ATTRIBUTES

The next two listings are for the two attributes linked to the Block insertion above. Notice the similarity to the TEXT entity listings. Because the attribute entity primarily carries textual data, it could be considered a specialized type of TEXT entity. All text formatting features available with the TEXT command are available with Attributes. The actual attribute prompts that appear when this block is inserted are stored in the Block Section of this DXF file in an entity called ATTDEF.

A number of optional Groups for the ATTRIBUTE entity will not appear in this example. These Groups carry text formatting information and are identical to the optional Groups for the TEXT entity.[*]

```
   0
ATTRIB
```
Entity type.

```
   8
0
```
Layer name for this entity.

---

[*] See the TEXT Section of this Appendix for more information about these Groups.

```
10
4.085714
```
Insertion point **X** coordinate for this attribute. This, combined with Group **20** below, is the actual starting point of the text of this attribute.

```
20
11.328571
```
Insertion point **Y** coordinate for this Attribute.

```
40
0.45
```
The body height of the upper case letters for this attribute. The original height of this text when this attribute was defined was 9". When we inserted the block that this attribute was attached to into the drawing, we scaled the block to .05X scale. AutoCAD automatically recalculated all sizes of the attributes associated with that block to be the same relative size.

```
1
Smith
```
The attribute value we gave to this particular insertion of this attribute, linked to the attribute tag "EMPNAME".

```
2
EMPNAME
```
The attribute tag, the key searched for when attributes are extracted using the ATTEXT command. The attribute tag remains the same for all instances of this attribute, while each instance of this attribute can have different values linked to this attribute tag. Think of the attribute tag as a FIELD NAME and the attribute value as the value contained in that field in a database record.

```
70
    0
```
The attribute flag. It is a bit coded flag with the first (**1**), second (**2**) and third (**4**) bits capable of being set. If no bits are set in this Group (**0**), then this attribute will be visible. If the first (**1**) bit is set, it means that this attribute will be invisible. If the second (**2**) bit is set, then the attribute value will be a Constant. If the third (**4**) bit is set, then verification will be required on input of any value for this attribute. Only one

bit will be set at a time in this field. See the beginning of this Appendix for more information about bit coded flags.

```
    7
NORMAL
```
Text style for this attribute entity.

```
   72
        1
```
Text justification type flag. The attribute text in this example is centered. This Group has the same values as the TEXT entity Group **72**. This is an optional Group.

```
   11
4.975
```
The actual **centered** insertion **X** coordinate of this attribute text string. This, along with Group **21** below, is the point picked for inserting the attribute text after the Center option was picked in the ATTDEF command when this attribute was defined. These two Groups are optional Groups, and will only appear in an entity listing if Group **72** is present and non-zero.

```
   21
11.328571
```
The actual **centered** insertion **Y** coordinate of this attribute text string.

The following ATTRIB listing is almost identical to the one above. We wanted to show you an example of how two (or more) attributes can be linked with the same Block INSERT record. We'll only comment on those fields that are different from the preceding ATTRIB record.

```
    0
ATTRIB
    8
0
   10
4.439286
       20
12.1
   40
0.45
```

```
     1
  100
```
The attribute value for the attribute tag ROOM-NO.

```
     2
  ROOMNO
```
The attribute tag that the value 100 is linked.

```
     70
      0
      7
  STAND
     72
      1
     11
  4.975
     21
  12.1
```

The next entity, SEQEND, only appears at the end of a series of attribute records (or, as we'll see later, at the end of a series of POLYLINE vertices). SEQEND marks the end of a series of attributes that are linked to a Block insertion.

```
     0
  SEQEND
```
Entity type.

```
     8
  0
```
Layer name for this entity.

OPTIONAL GROUP CODES FOR BLOCKS AND ATTRIBS

Several optional Group Codes did not appear in these sample listings and will only appear in a DXF record if their value is other than the standard default value (usually **0**) for that Group Code. They are as follows:

```
  50
```
The rotation angle of the Block insertion in degrees. Will only appear if the angle is *not* **0** degrees.

```
  70
```
Column count for MINSERT. If this or any of the next three Groups have a value other than **0**, then these Group Codes will appear in the INSERT record of the DXF file and indicate that the INSERT was done with the MINSERT

	command, and the record represents multiple occurrences of the referenced block in the drawing file.*
71	Row count for MINSERT.
44	Column spacing for MINSERT.
45	Row spacing for MINSERT.

The following optional Group Codes may be found in ATTRIB records and are identical in meaning to the same codes found in text entities. See the end of the Text Entities Section in this Appendix for a complete explanation of these Group Codes:

50	Rotation angle for the attribute text in degrees. Will only appear if the angle is not **0**.
41	Relative **X** scale, or width factor of the attribute text. This Group Code will only show up in an attribute record if this value is *not* **1**.
51	The obliquing angle of the attribute text in degrees. This is only used if this value is *not* **0**.
71	Text generation flag. See Group Code **71** in the Text Section for explanation of the codes.

---

* See Section 9.1.6 in the *AUTOCAD Reference Manual* for more information about MINSERT

POLYLINES

The polyline data format consists of three parts. The first part is the header record entity called polyline. The POLYLINE record signals the start of the polyline data structure and contains some general information about the polyline. The structure of this record is quite similar to the INSERT record followed by ATTRIB. The second part of the polyline data structure is a series of entity records called VERTEX. The VERTEX record contains the coordinates and other information about each vertex or point in the polyline. Finally the SEQEND entity appears as the last record in the polyline data structure to signal the end of that structure.*

There are several optional Group Codes for polyline and vertex records that will only appear in the DXF file for those records if their value is not zero. These will be listed at the end of the first polyline listing.

POLYLINE HEADER

```
    0
POLYLINE
```
Entity type.

```
    8
0
```
Layer name for this entity.

```
   66
        1
```
VERTEX follows flag. Because the polyline header record cannot exist unless there are at least two VERTEX entities following it, this flag would seem to be redundant. It does, however, follow a consistent data structure.

```
   70
        1
```
Polyline flag. This is a bit coded flag. Currently only the first bit (**1**) is capable of being set. If the bit is not set (**0**) then that means this is an open polyline; and if the bit is set (**1**) (as in this example) this is a closed polyline. When a polyline is defined as **Closed**, it will appear on

---

* See the section on polylines in Appendix A for more information about polylines.

the screen with a line connecting the last VER-
TEX in the polyline with the first VERTEX. A
polyline is closed by using the C option in the
PLINE command. If this flag were set to **0**,
then this polyline would be U-shaped instead
of a square and this Group Code would not appear in this record since it's an optional Group
Code.

VERTEXES

The following four VERTEX records describe a polyline square with the
polylines having zero width.

0	
VERTEX	Entity type.
8	
0	Layer name for this entity.
10	
10.0	**X** coordinate for this VERTEX.
20	
13.0	**Y** coordinate for this VERTEX.
0	
VERTEX	Entity type.
8	
0	Layer name for this entity. Theoretically, you could place each VERTEX of a polyline on a separate layer, but this doesn't seem to have any practical consequence.
10	
14.0	**X** coordinate for this VERTEX.
20	
13.0	**Y** coordinate for this VERTEX.
0	
VERTEX	Entity type.
8	
0	Layer name for this entity.

```
   10
14.0                      X coordinate for this VERTEX.

   20
9.0                       Y coordinate for this VERTEX.

    0
VERTEX                    Entity type.

    8
0                         Layer name for this entity.

   10
10.0                      X coordinate for this VERTEX.

   20
9.0                       Y coordinate for this VERTEX.
```

POLYLINE SEQEND

This SEQEND record is exactly the same record found at the end of a list of ATTRIB Records. It marks the end of the list of VERTEX records that define a polyline.

```
    0
SEQEND                    Entity type.

    8
0                         Layer name for this entity.
```

OPTIONAL GROUP CODES FOR POLYLINE AND VERTEX RECORDS

The following optional Group Codes will appear in polyline and/or vertex records if the value of the Group Code is *not* zero.

```
   40                     Starting width. The only time Group 40 is not
                          0 and will appear either in the polyline record
                          or at the specific vertex record is when the
                          starting width is changed. The starting polyline
                          width is assumed to always be the same until
                          it's changed.

   41                     Ending width. The only time Group 41 is not 0
                          and will appear either in the polyline record or
                          at the specific vertex record is where the end-
                          ing width is changed. The ending polyline
```

width is assumed to be always the same until it is changed. The ending width of the current vertex becomes the starting width of the next vertex.

42   Polyline bulge factor. If this Group Code appears in a vertex record, it means the polyline segment between the vertex this Group appears in and the following vertex record will be a Polyarc. This Group Code will only appear in a vertex record. See the Section on Bulge Factor Calculations in Appendix A.

70   Vertex flag. This is a bit coded flag where only the first (1) and second (2) bit is set. If the first bit (1) is set then it means the next vertex record was added by AutoCAD as an extra vertex to create a smoother curve. If the second bit (2) is set, it means that a curve fit tangent has been defined, and that tangent information will appear in Group Code 50 below. This Group Code will only appear in a vertex record and then only if one of the bits is set. Possible bit combinations for this flag are 1, 2 or 3.

50   Curve fit tangent direction in degrees. This Group Code will only appear in a vertex record if "Fit Curve" has been used on this polyline and the second bit (2) flag in Group Code 70 above has been set.*

WIDE POLYLINE

This next polyline record describes a closed polyline box in which the polyline has a width of .5 inch. Note the starting and ending widths of .5" (Groups 40 and 41) only appear in the polyline record and not in any of the subsequent vertex records. The only time these fields would *not* be 0 in a polyline or a vertex record is when the starting or ending widths are changed *in that record*. These values are kept until changed in another record.

---

*   See Section 5.4.1.1 in the *AutoCAD Reference Manual* for more information about Curve Fitting.

```
  0
POLYLINE              Entity type.

  8
0                     Layer name for this entity.

 66
      1               Vertex follows flag.

 70
      1               Polyline flag.

 40
0.5                   Default starting polyline width.  This is where
                      the polyline starting width is defined.  This is
                      an optional Group Code.

 41
0.5                   Default ending polyline width.  This is where
                      the polyline ending width is defined.  This is an
                      optional Group Code.

  0
VERTEX                Entity type.

  8
0                     Layer name for this entity.

 10
11.0                  X coordinate for this VERTEX.

 20
10.0                  Y coordinate for this VERTEX.

  0
VERTEX                Entity type.

  8
0                     Layer name for this entity.

 10
11.0                  X coordinate for this VERTEX.

 20
12.0                  Y coordinate for this VERTEX.

  0
VERTEX                Entity type.
```

```
   8
0                        Layer name for this entity.

  10
13.0                     X coordinate for this VERTEX.

  20
12.0                     Y coordinate for this VERTEX.

   0
VERTEX                   Entity type.

   8
0                        Layer name for this entity.

  10
13.0                     X coordinate for this VERTEX.

  20
10.0                     Y coordinate for this VERTEX.

   0
SEQEND                   Entity type.

   8
0                        Layer name for this entity.
```

SIMPLE POLYLINE WITH POLYARC

This polyline structure is one straight line followed by a semi-circle (180 degree half circle, the largest arc that can be created with a single polyarc). The only difference between the first vertex record and the second vertex record (other then the coordinates) is the second vertex contains a **polyline bulge factor of 1.** The bulge factor is *1/4 of the tangent of the included angle of the arc.* If the bulge factor is **0,** then the polyline segment that extends from that vertex will be straight. If the bulge factor is **1,** as in this case, then the polyline segment will appear as a semicircle. See the section on Bulge Factor Calculations in Appendix A for information on how to derive the arc information from the bulge factor.

```
   0
POLYLINE                 Entity type.

   8
0                        Layer name for this entity.
```

```
 66
      1              Vertex follows flag.

  0
VERTEX               Entity type.

  8
0                    Layer name for this entity.

 10
17.0                 X coordinate for this VERTEX.

 20
9.0                  Y coordinate for this VERTEX.

  0
VERTEX               Entity type.

  8
0                    Layer name for this entity.

 10
17.0                 X coordinate for this VERTEX.

 20
11.0                 Y coordinate for this VERTEX.

 42
1.0                  Polyline  bulge  factor.    A  bulge  factor  of 1
                     means that this polyline segment will be a semi-
                     circle.

  0
VERTEX               Entity type.

  8
0                    Layer name for this entity.

 10
15.0                 X coordinate for this VERTEX.

 20
11.0                 Y coordinate for this VERTEX.

 42
1.0                  Polyline  bulge  factor.    The  bulge  factor if the
                     preceding polyarc were continued back to the
                     starting point of of the polyarc (a full circle).
```

```
   0
SEQEND                    Entity type.

   8
0                         Layer name for this entity.
```

TAPERED POLYARCS

This entry describes two different types of polyline structures: tapered polylines and polyarcs. Figure 2 is a detailed illustration of this polyline structure. The first thing to notice about this polyline is that, although the illustration shows only two arcs and three vertexes, there are actually four vertex sub-records in this polyline record—the coordinates for the first two vertex records are identical. Because there are actually three polyarcs, the first polyarc was forced to have the same starting and ending point[*]. In The Bulge Factor Calculation Section in Appendix A, we'll explain how to extract the arc description information from the bulge factor.

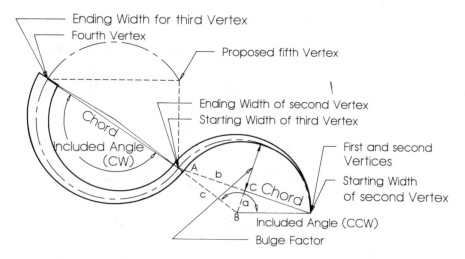

Figure 2: Tapered Polyarc.

---

[*] You have to use this technique if you're starting a polyline with a polyarc and want that arc to be less than 180 degrees.

```
      0
POLYLINE              Entity type.

      8
0                     Layer name for this entity.

     66
          1           Vertex follows flag.

      0
VERTEX                Entity type.

      8                Layer name for this entity.
0
     10
8.0                    X coordinate for this VERTEX.

     20
8.0                    Y coordinate for this VERTEX.

     42
1.0                    Polyline bulge factor.  This is the first polyarc
                       forced to the same starting and ending point—
                       in this circumstance, the bulge factor is always
                       1.

      0
VERTEX                Entity type.

8
0                     Layer name for this entity.

10
8.0                    X coordinate for this VERTEX.

20
8.0                    Y coordinate for this VERTEX.

41
0.25                   Ending polyline width.  The first visible polyarc
                       of this structure starts at 0 width, and ends
                       with a width of .25.

42
0.720759               Polyline bulge factor.

      0
VERTEX                Entity type.
```

8	
0	Layer name for this entity.
10	
5.0	**X** coordinate for this VERTEX.
20	
9.0	**Y** coordinate for this VERTEX.
40	
0.25	Starting polyline width. This is the same width as the ending polyline width of the previous vertex, but since it's different than the *starting width* of the previous vertex, then the starting width has changed which must show up here.˙
41	
0.5	Ending polyline width.
42	
-0.945986	Polyline bulge factor. If the bulge factor is a negative number, it means that the polyarc was generated clockwise from its starting point.
0	
VERTEX	Entity type.
8	
0	Layer name for this entity.
10	
2.0	**X** coordinate for this VERTEX.
20	
11.0	**Y** coordinate for this VERTEX.
40	
0.5	Starting polyline width. This width is, of course, different than the starting width of the last vertex—the starting width of the *next* polyline segment (if there were one).
41	
0.5	Ending polyline width.

---

* The starting and ending width fields *always* remain at **0** *unless* there is a change in width from the previous vertex record.

```
 42
-0.571429
```
Polyline bulge factor. This is the bulge factor of a proposed polyarc of the same radius as the last polyarc and if it were continued until it intersected with the right angle of a right triangle constructed so that the hypotenuse was congruent with the chord of the last polyarc (see figure 2).

```
 0
SEQEND
```
Entity type.

```
 8
0
```
Layer name for this entity.

POLYGONS

POLYGONS are not separate entity types, but are simply closed polylines generated by AutoCAD according to your specifications when you use the POLYGON command. Below is the DXF data record for a hexagon generated with the POLYGON command:

```
 0
POLYLINE
```
Entity type.

```
 8
0
```
Layer name for this entity.

```
 66
    1
```
Vertex follows flag.

```
 70
    1
```
Polyline flag. A polyline generated with the POLYGON command is always properly closed.

```
 0
VERTEX
```
Entity type.

```
 8
0
```
Layer name for this entity.

```
 10
8.0
```
X coordinate for this VERTEX.

```
 20
11.0
```
Y coordinate for this VERTEX.

```
    0
VERTEX                    Entity type.

    8
0                         Layer name for this entity.

   10
8.866025                  X coordinate for this VERTEX.

   20
11.5                      Y coordinate for this VERTEX.

    0
VERTEX                    Entity type.

    8
0                         Layer name for this entity.

   10
8.866025                  X coordinate for this VERTEX.

   20
12.5                      Y coordinate for this VERTEX.

    0
VERTEX                    Entity type.

    8
0                         Layer name for this entity.

   10
8.0                       X coordinate for this VERTEX.

   20
13.0                      Y coordinate for this VERTEX.

    0
VERTEX                    Entity type.

    8
0                         Layer name for this entity.

   10
7.133975                  X coordinate for this VERTEX.

   20
12.5                      Y coordinate for this VERTEX.

    0
VERTEX                    Entity type.
```

```
  8
0                       Layer name for this entity.

 10
7.133975                X coordinate for this VERTEX.

 20
11.5                    Y coordinate for this VERTEX.

  0
SEQEND                  Entity type.

  8
0                       Layer name for this entity.
```

TRACE

A TRACE looks something like a polyline, but if you examine the data structure, you'll find the structure more similar to a SOLID. Generally, TRACES have been superseded by polylines.

```
  0
TRACE                   Entity type.

  8
0                       Layer name for this entity.

 10
15.0                    X coordinate of the first corner of the starting
                        side.

 20
2.1                     Y coordinate of the first corner of the starting
                        side.

 11
15.0                    X coordinate of the second corner of the start-
                        ing side.

 21
1.9                     Y coordinate of the second corner of the start-
                        ing side.
```

```
 12
16.9
```
X coordinate of the first corner of the ending side. This, along with Group Code **22** below, is a mitered corner, and it shares the same coordinate as the first corner of the starting side in the next TRACE.

```
 22
2.1
```
Y coordinate of the first corner of the ending side.

```
 13
17.1
```
X coordinate of the second corner of the ending side. This, along with the Group Code **23** below, is a mitered corner, and it shares the same coordinate as the second corner of the starting side in the next TRACE.

```
 23
1.9
```
Y coordinate of the second corner of the ending side.

```
  0
TRACE
```
Entity type.

```
  8
0
```
Layer name for this entity.

```
 10
16.9
```
X coordinate of the first corner of the starting side. This, along with Group Code **20** below, is a mitered corner, and it shares the same coordinate as the first corner of the ending side in the previous TRACE.

```
 20
2.1
```
Y coordinate of the first corner of the starting side.

```
 11
17.1
```
X coordinate of the second corner of the starting side. This, along with Group Code **21** below, is a mitered corner, and it shares the same coordinate as the second corner of the ending side in the previous TRACE.

21
1.9   **Y** coordinate of the second corner of the start-
                       ing side.

12
16.9   **X** coordinate of the first corner of the ending
                       side.

22
4.0   **Y** coordinate of the first corner of the ending
                       side.

13
17.1   **X** coordinate of the second corner of the end-
                       ing side.

23
4.0   **Y** coordinate of the second corner of the end-
                       ing side.

AUTOCAD 2.6 ENTITIES

The following three entity types have been added to AutoCAD Version 2.6: an Associative DIMENSION, 3DFACE and 3DLINE. Figure 3 illustrates the database listing that appears below.

ASSOCIATIVE DIMENSION BLOCK

Ordinarily, when you dimension a drawing with the DIM Commands, the various parts of the dimension structure such as extension lines, dimension lines and text are made up of LINE and TEXT entities and are not inherently distinguishable as dimensions in the drawing database.*

The Associative Dimension entity represents a unique type of entity. On the one hand, it has many of the properties of a BLOCK entity in that the actual data description for this entity is in the Blocks Section and the whole dimension structure of text, extension lines, dimension lines and arrowheads is treated as a single entity in the drawing. On the other hand, when you operate on this entity with the STRETCH, SCALE or ROTATE commands, AutoCAD will update the dimension text to reflect its new size or orientation. When you stretch or move the Associative Dimensioning DIMENSION Entity, not only do all defining point coordinates in the entity record change to reflect the new position of the entity, the Block definition in the Blocks Section is also changed to reflect the new coordinates of all points in the drawing. Every time that you add a dimension, AutoCAD creates an unique Block definition for that dimension in the Blocks Section, then references that Block with a DIMENSION record in the Entities Section**.

---

*   The only unique entity that shows up in this type of dimension is the arrowhead which, strictly speaking, is an "anonymous" block.

** If you delete a DIMENSION Entity in your drawing, the Block reference for that Entity will remain in the Blocks Section.

We think that it would be wise to use this Associative Dimension sparingly because it seems to take up much more space in the drawing database than an ordinary dimension and would tend to create larger drawing files than necessary*.

The Associative Dimension entity will be created any time that you add a dimension to a drawing when the system variable **DIMASO** is set to **ON**. When a Associative Dimension entity is created, a number of special points are inserted into your drawing at strategic locations. These points are called *Definition Points*, and their coordinates are found in Group Codes **10** through **16** and **20** through **26**. These Definition Points are always inserted on a special layer that AutoCAD creates, named DEFPOINTS. For example, if you were to dimension a line, then definition points would be placed at the beginning and end of the line, at the end point of the dimension line and at the center of the dimension text. If, at a later point, you lengthened this line with the STRETCH command, the **defining point** for the endpoint of the line would have a new coordinate location and AutoCAD will recalculate the dimension** and display it as the dimension text.

Below is a Block Section and an Entities Section listing for a simple horizontal dimension as shown in Figure 3. Compare the coordinates for the different entities (such as LINE, POINT and SOLID) in the Block Section with the Defining Points in the DIMENSION entity in the Entities Section.

ASSOCIATIVE DIMENSION BLOCK DEFINITION

First is the Block definition for the Associative DIMENSION entity described in the Entities Section following. Rather than give a Group by Group comment of each entity, which would get redundant, we will only identify and comment on how each entity record refers to the DIMENSION entity in the Entities Section.

---

* The Associative Dimension in this example uses 13 records. If this dimension was created using the regular Dimensioning command, it would only take seven records to describe it. In addition, if this Associative Dimension were erased from the drawing, the twelve records in the Blocks Section would still exist.

** And possibly the dimension text location to keep the dimension text centered.

```
    0
SECTION
```
Start of section.

```
    2
BLOCKS
```
Start of Blocks Section.

```
    0
BLOCK
```
Start of Block definition.

```
    8
0
```
Layer name for this block.

```
    2
*D3
```
The name of this block. The leading asterisk indicates that this is a "pseudo" block created by AutoCAD and the **D** indicates it's a DIMEN-SION block.

```
   70
        1
```
Block type flag. This is a bit coded flag where the first (**1**), second (**2**) or seventh (**64**) bits are capable of being set. If the second bit (**2**) is set, it means that this BLOCK definition has ATTDEFs or attributes. If the first bit (**1**) is set, this block is an "anonymous" (or pseudo) block. If the seventh (**64**) bit is set, this block is referenced by an INSERT record in the En-tities Section of this drawing. If the seventh bit is set to **0** (false), then the PURGE command will remove this Block definition. The possible bit codes for this field are **0, 1, 2, 64, 65** and **66**.

```
   10
0.0
```
X coordinate of the base point for this block. Since this is a "pseudo" block, there is no base point.

```
   20
0.0
```
Y coordinate of the base point for this block.

This LINE is the Left extension line of the Dimension entity.

0	
LINE	Entity type.
8	
0	Layer name for this entity.
6	
BYBLOCK	This indicates a floating linetype.
62	
0	Color number **0** is a floating color.
10	
-8.163841	Start **X** coordinate.
20	
5.997929	Start **Y** coordinate.
11	
-8.163841	End **X** coordinate.
21	
6.386479	End **Y** coordinate.

This LINE is the Right extension line of the Dimension entity.

0	
LINE	Entity type.
8	
0	Layer name for this entity.
6	
BYBLOCK	This indicates a floating linetype.
62	
0	Color number **0** is a floating color.
10	
-6.663841	Start **X** coordinate.
20	
5.997929	Start **Y** coordinate.
11	
-6.663841	End **X** coordinate.

```
   21
6.386479               End Y coordinate.
```

This LINE is the Left Dimension line of the Dimension entity.

```
    0
LINE                   Entity type.

    8
0                      Layer name for this entity.

    6
BYBLOCK                This indicates a floating linetype.

   62
       0               Color number 0 is a floating color.

   10
-7.983841              Start X coordinate.

   20
6.206479               Start Y coordinate.

   11
-7.968841              End X coordinate.

   21
6.206479               End Y coordinate.
```

This LINE is the Right Dimension line of the Dimension entity.

```
    0
LINE                   Entity type.

    8
0                      Layer name for this entity.

    6
BYBLOCK                This indicates a floating linetype.

   62
       0               Color number 0 is a floating color.

   10
-6.843841              Start X coordinate.

   20
6.206479               Start Y coordinate.
```

```
   11
-6.858841
```
       End **X** coordinate.

```
   21
6.206479
```
       End **Y** coordinate.

This SOLID is the Left Arrowhead in the Dimension entity.

```
    0
SOLID
```
       Entity type.

```
    8
0
```
       Layer name for this entity.

```
    6
BYBLOCK
```
       This indicates a floating linetype.

```
   62
        0
```
       Color number **0** is a floating color.

```
   10
-7.983841
```
       First corner **X** coordinate.

```
   20
6.176479
```
       First corner **Y** coordinate.

```
   11
-7.983841
```
       Second corner **X** coordinate.

```
   21
6.236479
```
       Second corner **Y** coordinate.

```
   12
-8.163841
```
       Third corner **X** coordinate.

```
   22
6.206479
```
       Third corner **Y** coordinate.

```
   13
-8.163841
```
       Fourth corner **X** coordinate.

```
   23
6.206479
```
       Fourth corner **Y** coordinate.

This SOLID is the Right Arrowhead in the Dimension entity.

```
    0
SOLID
```
       Entity type.

```
    8
0                           Layer name for this entity.

    6
BYBLOCK                     This indicates a floating linetype.

   62
        0                   Color number 0 is a floating color.

   10
-6.843841                   First corner X coordinate.

   20
6.176479                    First corner Y coordinate.

   11
-6.843841                   Second corner X coordinate.

   21
6.236479                    Second corner Y coordinate.

   12
-6.663841                   Third corner X coordinate.

   22
6.206479                    Third corner Y coordinate.

   13
-6.663841                   Fourth corner X coordinate.

   23
6.206479                    Fourth corner Y coordinate.
```

This is the current Dimension text for the Dimension entity—the actual dimension between the two extension defining points formatted in the current UNITS format. This Dimension text *will not* appear in the dimension if an "explicit" dimension has been typed in when the user was prompted for the "Dimension text" when this dimension was created.

```
    0
TEXT                        Entity type.

    8
0                           Layer name for this entity.

    6
BYBLOCK                     This indicates a floating linetype.
```

```
  62
      0
```
Color number **0** is a floating color.

```
  10
-7.788841
```
Text insertion point **X** coordinate.

```
  20
6.116479
```
Text insertion point **Y** coordinate.

```
  40
0.18
```
Dimension text height.

```
   1
1.5000
```
The dimension text string.

This POINT defines the extension defining point for the starting point of the Dimension entity. This corresponds to Group Codes **13** and **23**.

```
   0
POINT
```
Entity type.

```
   8
DEFPOINTS
```
Layer name for this entity.

```
   0
BYBLOCK
```
This indicates a floating linetype.

```
  62
      0
```
Color number **0** is a floating color.

```
  10
-8.163841
```
X coordinate.

```
  20
5.935429
```
Y coordinate.

This POINT defines the extension defining point for the ending point of the Dimension entity. This corresponds to Group Codes **14** and **24**.

```
   0
POINT
```
Entity type.

```
   8
DEFPOINTS
```
Layer name for this entity.

```
   6
BYBLOCK
  62
```
Color number **0** is a floating color.

```
      0
   10
-6.663841              X coordinate.

   20
5.935429               Y coordinate.
```

This POINT defines the dimension line defining point for the Dimension entity. This corresponds to Group Codes **10** and **20**.

```
      0
POINT                  Entity type.

      8
DEFPOINTS              Layer name for this entity.

      6
BYBLOCK                This indicates a floating linetype.

   62
      0                Color number 0 is a floating color.

   10
-6.663841              X coordinate.

   20
6.206479               Y coordinate.

      0
ENDBLK                 End of Associative Dimension Block definition.

      8
0                      Layer name for this block

      0
ENDSEC                 End of the Blocks Section.
```

```
     0
SECTION
     2
ENTITIES
```
Start of the Entities Section.

ASSOCIATIVE DIMENSION INSERT

This is the INSERT entity for the Associative dimension block listed above.

```
     0
DIMENSION
```
Entity type.

```
     8
     0
```
Layer name for this entity

```
     2
  *D3
```
Block name. The asterisk at the beginning of the Block name indicates that it's an "anonymous" block created by AutoCAD. **D** indicates that this is an Associative Dimension Block and the **3** indicates the unique block number for this particular dimension entity.

```
    10
-6.663841
```
The **X** coordinate of the dimension line *defining point*. This, along with Group Code **20** below, is the actual end point of the dimension line. The distance between this *defining point* and the Group Codes **13** and **23** *defining point* below determines the distance between the dimensioned object and the dimension line (and also the length of the extension line).

```
    20
6.206479
```
The **Y** coordinate of the dimension line *defining point*.

```
    11
-7.413841
```
The **X** coordinate of the middle of text *defining point*. This, along with Group **21** below, is usually a point midpoint along the dimension line. This point is recalculated to remain at the midpoint of the dimension line if any of the

other *defining points* are moved. There is no point for this defining point listed in the block definition.

21
6.206479

Y coordinate of the middle of text *defining point.*

13
-8.163841

X coordinate of the extension *defining point* for the starting point of the Dimension entity. This point also corresponds with the starting point of the line being dimensioned in this example.

23
5.935429

Y coordinate of the extension *defining point* for the starting point of the Dimension entity.

14
-6.663841

X coordinate of the extension *defining point* for the ending point of the Dimension entity. This point also corresponds with the ending point of the line being dimensioned in this example.

24
5.935429

Y coordinate of the extension *defining point* for the ending point of the Dimension entity.

OPTIONAL GROUP CODES FOR THE DIMENSION ENTITY

Several optional Group Codes may appear in the DIMENSION entity if their value is *not* zero:

12
24

Insertion points for CLONES of a dimension. This would be the insertion point (Group Codes **10** and **20**) of the *next* Associative Dimension entity if you use the BASELINE or CONTINUE options to do a string of dimensions in one direction.

| 70 | Dimension type flag. This is a bit coded flag with the first (**1**), second (**2**) and third (**4**) bit capable of being set. If no bits are set (**0**), then this dimension is a *horizontal, vertical* or *rotated* dimension. Other flag codes: **1**=*aligned*, **2**=*angular*, **3**=*diameter* and **4**=*radius*. |

| 1 | Explicit dimension text string. When you create a dimension, you're prompted for the dimension text. You have the option of pressing <RETURN> to accept the actual measured dimension or you can type in your own text for the dimension. If you type in your own text for this dimension, then that text will show up here, and it *will not be updated* if you stretch this dimension at a later time. The null string (two quotation marks), in this case means that the dimension text will be updated. The actual dimension is calculated from the distance between the coordinates in Group Codes **13** and **23** and **14** and **24**. |

| 15 25 | Extension *defining point* for diameter, radius and angular dimensions. If this dimension is not a diameter, radius or angular dimension, then this Group Code will not appear in the DXF file record. |

| 16 26 | Extension *defining point* for the dimension arc in angular dimensions. This would be analogous to Group Codes **10** and **20** for other dimension types. |

| 40 | Leader length for radius and diameter dimensions. |

| 50 | Angle of rotation for linear dimensions. Specifically: HORIZONTAL, VERTICAL or ROTATED dimensions. |

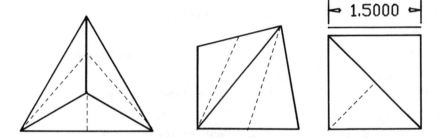

Figure 3: 2.6 Entity types.

3DFACE

The 3DFACE entity is similar to a SOLID entity in structure. Unlike the SOLID entity, however, the 3DFACE is constructed by picking the corners in a circular fashion rather than by describing two points for the base and either one or two points for the top of the surface. The 3DFACE will always have three coordinates given for each corner. The 3DFACE can have either three or four vertexes or corners. When you use the HIDE command, the 3DFACE will appear opaque when the view has its hidden lines removed.

The following listing is for four triangular 3DFACEs that make up the tetrahedron shown in Figure 3. Each 3DFACE is an equilateral triangle with an edge length of 1.5 inches. For more information on 3DFACE, see the same section in Appendix A.

```
    0
    3DFACE              Entity type.

    8
0                       Layer name for this entity.

   10                   X coordinate of the starting corner.

 -6.66869
   20
 4.306549               Y coordinate of the starting corner.
```

```
   30
 3.0                          Z coordinate of the starting corner.

   11
 -8.16869                     X coordinate of the second corner.

   21
 5.806549                     Y coordinate of the second corner.

   31
 3.0                          Z coordinate of the second corner.

   12
 -6.66869                     X coordinate of the third corner.

   22
 5.806549                     Y coordinate of the third corner.

   32
 1.5                          Z coordinate of the third corner.

   13
 -6.66869                     X coordinate of the last corner.  If this face is
                              triangular, then this coordinate will be the same
                              as the first corner.

   23
 4.306549                     Y coordinate of the last corner.  If this face is
                              triangular, then this coordinate will be the same
                              as the first corner.

   33
 3.0                          Z coordinate of the last corner.  If this face is
                              triangular, then this coordinate will be the same
                              as the first corner.

   0
 3DFACE                       Entity type.

   8
 0                            Layer name for this entity.

   10
 -8.16869                     X coordinate of the starting corner.

   20
 5.806549                     Y coordinate of the starting corner.
```

```
  30
3.0                     Z coordinate of the starting corner.

  11
-8.16869                X coordinate of the second corner.

  21
4.306549                Y coordinate of the second corner.

  31
1.5                     Z coordinate of the second corner.

  12
-6.66869                X coordinate of the third corner.

  22
4.306549                Y coordinate of the third corner.

  32
3.0                     Z coordinate of the third corner.

  13
-8.16869                X coordinate of the last corner.

  23
5.806549                Y coordinate of the last corner.

  33
3.0                     Z coordinate of the last corner.

   0
3DFACE                  Entity type.

   8
0                       Layer name for this entity.

  10
-8.16869                X coordinate of the starting corner.

  20
4.306549                Y coordinate of the starting corner.

  30
1.5                     Z coordinate of the starting corner.

  11
-6.66869                X coordinate of the second corner.

  21
5.806549                Y coordinate of the second corner.
```

```
  31
1.5                     Z coordinate of the second corner.

  12
-8.16869                X coordinate of the third corner.

  22
5.806549                Y coordinate of the third corner.

  32
3.0                     Z coordinate of the third corner.

  13
-8.16869                X coordinate of the last corner.

  23
4.306549                Y coordinate of the last corner.

  33
1.5                     Z coordinate of the last corner.

   0
3DFACE                  Entity type.

   8
0                       Layer name for this entity.

  10
-8.16869                X coordinate of the starting corner.

  20
4.306549                Y coordinate of the starting corner.

  30
1.5                     Z coordinate of the starting corner.

  11
-8.16869                X coordinate of the second corner.

  21
5.806549                Y coordinate of the second corner.

  31
3.0                     Z coordinate of the second corner.

  12
-6.66869                X coordinate of the third corner.

  22
5.806549                Y coordinate of the third corner.
```

```
32
1.5                           Z coordinate of the third corner.

13
-6.66869                      X coordinate of the last corner.

23
5.806549                      Y coordinate of the last corner.

33
1.5                           Z coordinate of the last corner.
```

3DLINE

A 3DLINE entity has the same structure as an ordinary LINE entity except that the coordinate lists (Group Codes **10** and **11**) always contain a **Z** coordinate. The purpose of this entity is to draw lines in 3D space. The 3DLINE cannot have an ELEVATION nor can it be EXTRUDED, so you'll never find Group Codes **38** or **39** here.*

In Figure 3, three 3DLINES are shown on the face of the tetrahedron as dashed lines. The 3DLINE entity *cannot* use different LINETYPES and the dashed lines in the illustration were made with plotter linetypes to give these lines contrast from the 3DFACES on which they were drawn.

```
0
3DLINE                        Entity type.

8
HIDE                          Layer name for this entity.

10
-6.66869                      Start X coordinate.

20
4.306549                      Start Y coordinate.

30
3.0                           Start Z coordinate.

11
-7.41869                      End X coordinate.
```

---

* These limitations may change with a future release.

```
 21
5.056549          End Y coordinate.

 31
1.5               End Z coordinate.
```

HOW TO CREATE YOUR OWN SWD FILES

appendix C

An **.SWD** file is simply a list of the character widths of each character in the font file along with their ASCII codes. The BASIC text formatting program at the end of Chapter 9 uses this file to determine how many characters should be placed in each line of text. An **.SWD** file *must* have the same name as the font file it's used for with an **.SWD** file extension attached to it. See the **SIMPLEX.SWD** listing in the next section as an example of what the file should look like.

SWD FILE STRUCTURE

There are two numbers on each line separated by a comma. The first number is the ASCII code for the character and the second number is the *total width for that character, in Vectors,* including any space before and/or after that character. The first line of the **.SWD** file is **0**, followed by the total height in vectors of an upper case character (the first number on the second line of the **.SHP** file).

The second line is **10**, followed by the line feed (ASCII code **10**) length in vectors (the number after the minus on the fifth line of the **.SHP** file). *

If your **.SHP** file starts out looking like this:

```
*0,4,[Name of a font]
35,9,0,0
*1,2,sot
5,0
*10,5,1f
2,8,(0,-50),0
```

then your **.SWD** file should start out like this:

```
0,35
10,50
32,(width of space in vectors)
33,(etc,etc)
. . . .
228,50 (last entry in file-vector width the same as the
                second entry.)
```

If there are some ASCII numbers that haven't been coded in your **.SHP** file, simply skip those numbers in the **.SWD** file.

HOW TO DETERMINE THE VECTOR WIDTH OF YOUR FONT

Using the above .SHP file fragment as an example, go into your drawing editor. Set the style of your font and in the text command set the text height for 3.5 inches (35 vectors high). Set snap to .1 inch and type in several letters. Every time that you hit the right cursor key, you will be moving the screen crosshair one vector width across the character. Be sure to include any leading or trailing space as part of that character's width.

---

* See Appendix B in the *AutoCAD Reference Manual* for more information on how fonts are constructed.

THE SIMPLEX.SWD FILE

Below is the complete listing of the **SIMPLEX.SWD** file that is used with the text formatting program that appears at the end of Chapter 9. This file contains all of the ASCII character codes, followed by the vector width of each character in the **SIMPLEX.SHX** font file that comes with AutoCAD. To use this file, type in each pair of numbers (including the comma) in the listing below into your text editor and save it under the file name **SIMPLEX.SWD**. The listing below has been formatted into three columns to save space.

0,21	60,20	90,20
10,36	61,26	91,15
32,19	62,20	92,22
33,13	63,18	93,12
34,15	64,24	94,20
35,19	65,22	95,24
36,20	66,21	96,9
37,30	67,21	97,19
38,23	68,21	98,19
39,9	69,19	99,18
40,14	70,18	100,19
41,14	71,21	101,18
42,16	72,22	102,12
43,26	73,8	103,19
44,10	74,16	104,19
45,26	75,21	105,8
46,10	76,17	106,10
47,22	77,24	107,17
48,20	78,22	108,8
49,16	79,22	109,30
50,20	80,21	110,19
51,20	81,22	111,19
52,20	82,21	112,19
53,20	83,20	113,19
54,20	84,18	114,13
55,20	85,22	115,17
56,20	86,20	116,14
57,20	87,24	117,19
58,15	88,20	118,16
59,14	89,20	119,22

120,17	124,7	128,26
121,16	125,11	129,19
122,17	126,26	228,36
123,12	127,8	

appendix D USING A TEXT EDITOR INSIDE AUTOCAD

First, find a small text editor or word processor that you would like to use. It must be smaller than 50k in size, and it must not use any overlays or separate HELP files. We've been using PC-WRITE Version 1.05* and find it to be quite adequate. PC-WRITE is a SHAREWARE product and can be obtained from numerous sources for $10 or less. When you've decided on a suitable text editor, find out how large it is by listing the file in DOS with **DIR**. Take the file size for your text editor and add 17,000 to it for necessary DOS functions and then add 30,000 or 40,000 to that number for file buffer. The example below could be the memory requirements for a typical text editor:

	SIZE
TEXT EDITOR	50,000
DOS	17,000
TEXT FILE AREA	40,000
TOTAL MEMORY REQUIRED	107,000

---

* The later versions with more features are too large.

Using your text editor, load the **ACAD.PGP** file that came with your copy of AutoCAD. Add the following line to the end of this file using the file name of the text editor that you've chosen and the total memory required number based on the size of the text editor chosen:

```
EDIT,[your text editor], [memory required],,0
```

For example, the entry on our ACAD.PGP file is:

```
EDIT,PC-WRITE,80000,,0
```

Save the modified **ACAD.PGP** file and copy the chosen text editor program to your AutoCAD subdirectory on your hard disk.

Now, whenever you want to create a text file from inside the AutoCAD drawing editor, simply type **EDIT** at the **Command** line and you'll enter your text editor. When you exit your text editor, you'll be back in the AutoCAD drawing editor exactly where you left. You may find some "garbage" on your drawing screen when you leave the text editor, but issuing a **REDRAW** command should eliminate the problem.

FOR FURTHER READING:

- Bradlee, R. C., *Programming AutoCAD Volume I*, ADSI, Naperville IL.

- Green, Adam B., *Advanced dBASE II User's Guide*, Prentice-Hall, Englewood Cliffs NJ.
ISBN 0-13-011271-2.

- Jones, Frederic H., *Computer Aided Architecture and Design*, William Kauffman, Los Altos CA.
ISBN 0-86576-102-7.

- Schaefer, A. Ted and Brittain, James L., *The AutoCAD Productivity Book*, Ventana Press, Chapel Hill, NC.
ISBN 0-940087-00-6.

- Schilling, Terrence G. and Particia M., *Intelligent Drawings*, McGraw-Hill, New York NY.
ISBN 0-07-055317-3.

- Winston, Henry Partick and Horn, Berthold Klaus Paul, *LISP Second Edition*, Addison-Wesley, Reading MA.
ISBN 0-201-88732-8

Index

Function 85, 87
Function Call 81
Function, Bodily 87
Function, Concept 80
Functions, List Manipulating 91

G

Group Code 14, 104 - 105, 120,
   162

H

Header Section 161, 164 - 166

I

Infix Notation 88
Insert
    See Entity Type
Instance Attribute 18

K

Key 100
Key to INSBASE 165

L

last
    See AutoLISP Functions
Layer Name Translation 154
line
    See AutoCAD Commands
Line, Concept 118
LISP 75 - 77
LISP Primitives 81
list
    See AutoLISP Functions
List Evaluater 84, 89, 91, 125
List, Concept 79, 86

Logistics 3
LOGO 77
Lotus 1-2-3 11, 38

M

Mailing List 12
Math Functions 88
Memory Size 159
Multiplication, AutoLISP 90

N

New Services 4
Nil 79, 85, 87, 96
Notation
    See also Conventions and
Notations

P

Pascal 47, 122
Postfix Notation 89
Prefix Notation 89
Printer Echo 122
Procedures 80
Producing Reports 131
Productivity 4
Programming Convention 82
Property List 135, 146

Q

Quantity Count 131
Quoted List 78

R

RBASE 11
Record 13, 40, 119
Recursion 115

HATE TO TYPE?

The AutoCAD Database Diskette runs on any 360K IBM-standard format computer and can save hours of tedious, error-prone typing. All programs, functions and routines listed in the book appear on the diskette, including:

- The bill of materials program from Chapter Four (provided in dBASE or compiled so it can be run without dBASE).

- An AutoLISP program that allows you to update any chosen attribute in an AutoCAD drawing from an outside database.

- A program that automatically writes all blocks in a drawing to a disk file.

- The text program from Chapter Nine that allows you to format text within a drawing, including text size, type size, line length, proportional spacing and multiple columns. A compiled version is also included that will run five times as fast.

Bonus! *The AutoCAD Database Diskette* includes a Wordstar-style text editor designed specifically for AutoLISP. Includes an automatic indent feature; also "error-checks" for pairs of parentheses.

- -

_____ Yes, please send _____ copies of *The AutoCAD Database Diskette*, at $29.95 per diskette. No charge for normal shipment. Add $3.00/diskette for UPS "two-day air." North Carolina residents add 5% sales tax. Immediate shipment guaranteed.

Name_____

Address (no P.O. Box)_____

City_____State_____ Zip_____

Telephone_____

_____ Payment enclosed (check or money order; no cash please)

_____ Charge my: VISA Acc't #_____ Exp. Date_____

MC Acc't #_____ Exp.Date_____ Interbank #_____

Signature_____

MAIL TO: Ventana Press, P.O. Box 2468, Chapel Hill, NC 27515. Or, if you'd like it even sooner, call 919/490-0062.

TEAR HERE

BUSINESS REPLY MAIL

FIRST CLASS MAIL   PERMIT #495   CHAPEL HILL, NC

POSTAGE WILL BE PAID BY ADDRESSEE

Ventana Press

P.O. Box 2468

Chapel Hill, NC 27515

HATE TO TYPE?

The AutoCAD Database Diskette runs on any 360K IBM-standard format computer and can save hours of tedious, error-prone typing. All programs, functions and routines listed in the book appear on the diskette, including:

- The bill of materials program from Chapter Four (provided in dBASE or compiled so it can be run without dBASE).

- An AutoLISP program that allows you to update any chosen attribute in an AutoCAD drawing from an outside database.

- A program that automatically writes all blocks in a drawing to a disk file.

- The text program from Chapter Nine that allows you to format text within a drawing, including text size, type size, line length, proportional spacing and multiple columns. A compiled version is also included that will run five times as fast.

Bonus! *The AutoCAD Database Diskette* includes a Wordstar-style text editor designed specifically for AutoLISP. Includes an automatic indent feature; also "error-checks" for pairs of parentheses.

Note: If order form is missing, please see previous page, or write Ventana Press, P.O. Box 2468, Chapel Hill, NC 27515, 919/490-0062.

_____ Yes, please send _____ copies of *The AutoCAD Database Diskette*, at $29.95 per diskette. No charge for normal shipment. Add $3.00/diskette for UPS "two-day air." North Carolina residents add 5% sales tax. Immediate shipment guaranteed.

Name_____

Address (no P.O. Box)_____

City_____State_____ Zip_____

Telephone_____

_____ Payment enclosed (check or money order; no cash please)

_____ Charge my: VISA Acc't #_____ Exp. Date_____

MC Acc't #_____ Exp.Date_____ Interbank #_____

Signature_____

MAIL TO: Ventana Press, P.O. Box 2468, Chapel Hill, NC 27515. Or, if you'd like it even sooner, call 919/490-0062.

TEAR HERE

NO POSTAGE
NECESSARY
IF MAILED
IN THE
UNITED STATES

BUSINESS REPLY MAIL

FIRST CLASS MAIL   PERMIT #495   CHAPEL HILL, NC

POSTAGE WILL BE PAID BY ADDRESSEE

Ventana Press

P.O. Box 2468

Chapel Hill, NC 27515

TEAR HERE